ABE LINCOLN'S AMERICA

A. Lincoln by Homer S. Sewell III

Abe Lincoln's America
Homer S. Sewell, III

Copyright 1994
Homer S. Sewell, III

ISBN 0-932281-12-5

Manufactured in the United States of America by
Quill Publications
Columbus, GA 31908

This book will entertain you with stories...from Homer's adoption at ten weeks old to his search and reunion after 49 years with his biological family...from his years at the White House to his various business ventures...from reading the Gettysburg Address in the sixth grade to reciting it a thousand times across the country. It includes helpful hints for day-to-day survival and moral-value lessons.

The book weaves Homer's true-life experiences with his script about ABE LINCOLN'S life.

A MUST READ FOR ALL AGES!

HOMER AT OLD CABIN IN BIG CANOE RESORT, GEORGIA

Photo by Gwen Knight

Table of Contents

A Very Special Thank You to These People

For editing and editorial assistance:

Gwen Knight
Jacque Blackstone Waller
Sally Ann Smith
Jim Smith

*For helping convert files from
Apple IIGS to IBM compatible:*

Jim Smith
Rhoda Warren

Dedication

This book is dedicated to GOD who has given me the strength to never give up...and to a lot of very special people in my life. There have been so many people who have meant so much to me these past 51 years.

To my three children—Homer IV (Chip) 26, Jason Leon and his twin sister, Kimberly Irene, 17.

To my mother and father who raised me—Homer, Jr. and Dorothy.

To my newly-found birth-mother and father—Millie Levitz Ferency Franklin and Alex Ferency.

To my brother and sister with whom I grew up—Michael and Dottie Ann (D.A.) and to my three newly found brothers—Barry, Stuart and Gershon; and to all my nieces, nephews and cousins scattered around the world from Massachusetts to Florida, California, Washington and all the way to Israel.

To a very special lady who always believed I could make it and never gave up trying to help me get there—Gwen Knight.

To my friend—Jacque B. Waller, in Atlanta who needlepointed my favorite motto.

To my favorite people all over the world...my teachers, principals, librarians, nurses, counselors, custodians, cafeteria workers and all the others who work so hard (for so little money!) in our schools...who see that our next generation of leaders is properly trained in reading, writing and arithmetic. Thank you for all you do for students everywhere! I know GOD has a very special place waiting for you.

To Senior citizens everywhere!

To all the people who took me into their lives and their homes and fed me great meals, visited with me and gave me warm places to sleep as I traveled all over this great, big beautiful country I so lovingly call—ABE LINCOLN'S AMERICA.

And last, but certainly not least, my Masonic friends all over the world. Masons throughout the world do so much good to help children and all mankind. I am very proud to be a small part of this great fraternity.

Preface

I feel there needs to be some explanation about the title of this book in order to give the reader an understanding of how one man's life has become consumed by his interest in, and resemblance to, this country's greatest President...Abraham Lincoln.

This book is titled "ABE LINCOLN'S AMERICA" because that is the name of the show I perform at locations all over the country. The show is a look into the life of ABE LINCOLN from the log cabin to the White House. Excerpts from the show will be woven into the story of my life.

What this book will try to do for you, the reader, is take you on a journey through the life and times of the man who, since 1975, has been portraying ABE in front of over one million people in more than half of our states and at hundreds of locations. And, how, in his pursuit of ABE LINCOLN'S AMERICA, he has discovered "HOMER S. SEWELL III'S AMERICA". It is a story about never giving up in the pursuit of your goals; how one man's dream of being a full-time ABE LINCOLN has finally materialized; and, of the many lessons in life I have learned through trial and error.

This book is also about a man who was raised by an adoptive family and after 49 years finally found his birth parents. The author tells the story of his search for his birth parents and gives you suggestions and help in case you, too, might be looking for long-lost loved ones. It is the story about a man who was raised in Protestant churches and found out in 1992 he was born Jewish, has a Rabbi for a step-brother and 17 generations of Rabbis in the family.

Even though I will address many of my messages to students in this book, it is indeed a book written for people of ALL ages! We ALL need to be inspired to do greater things with our lives!

This book is a story of love, caring about others and of teaching our youth (The students who ARE the future of our great country!) to stay off drugs, do what they can to stop youth violence in America, read lots of good books and have more respect for parents, teachers and everyone they come in contact with each day.

If the author accomplishes what he wants to with this book, YOU will have more self-esteem, will want to continue to read more good books and will learn what it means to be...

"A DREAMER, A STARGAZER, A RAINBOW CHASER
AND TO SOAR WITH THE EAGLES!"

I believe that in our society today, our children are innocent victims of senseless violence and IF WE HAD MORE HUGGING...THERE WOULD BE LESS MUGGING! Give someone a hug today!

Thank you for your interest and may GOD continue to bless you, your family and our country.

HOMER S. SEWELL III aka
ABRAHAM LINCOLN

Foreword

Once upon a time...near Mickey Mouse town... in Altamonte Springs, Florida (about 25 miles from Walt Disney World, Orlando)...there lived a man by the name of Homer S. Sewell III.

No this is not a real fairy tale but the story about how one man became "ABE"...as in LINCOLN!!

One day in 1975 as I was driving along I-4 in Orlando, I heard a public service announcement from the local school district. They were looking for volunteers to talk to students about any subject of interest. I wondered how many students had ever had the opportunity to talk to and visit with someone who had actually worked in the White House? I called and volunteered to speak to the students about my experiences during the Johnson Administration.

At that same time I had started growing a beard and local people started telling me how much I looked like "ABE". That suggestion made me think perhaps I should study and do more research into the life and times of our 16th President.

The first few schools I visited, I delivered the Gettysburg Address and spent the other 50 minutes of my program talking to the students about my activities at the White House and on the road with the President and First Family. We will go into a lot more details about these past 19 years of being ABE but let me say it has been a rewarding experience to see the looks on students' faces when ABE walks into their schools. I will show you copies of letters from students, teachers and principals about how I have, as ABE, touched their lives...for the better.

...AND NOW...THE REST IS HISTORY!!!

For those of you who have not had the opportunity to witness first-hand this one-hour program, I will at least give you SOME of the wording of what we do in the show. *(The italic words in the beginning of each chapter are from my show.)*

You may want to get in touch with ABE to have an in-person visit to your school, church, synagogue, temple, Masonic Lodge, civic group, sales meeting or whatever. Please call the number listed in this book to arrange for a visit with ABE.

Chapter 1

The Birth of this Abe and Early Years

I was born on Sunday morning, February 12, 1809 in Hardin County, Kentucky in a dirt-floored log cabin with no running water and only one window. My sister, Sarah, was already two years old when I came bouncing into this world...just exactly like all of you did...crying!

I was born on Wednesday, August 4, 1943 at 8:20 AM, in a doctor's office in Hinesville, Georgia. My dad, Alex Ferency, 21, was in the Army stationed at Ft. Stewart, near Savannah. My mom, Millie Levitz Ferency, was only 19 years old. The thought of raising a baby during the war, and with a husband away in the Army, was more than she could handle.

They decided to give me up for adoption and went in search of a good family who might be interested in adopting a baby boy. My mother somehow ended up in a dress shop run by Madeline Simpson. She indicated that her sister-in-law, Dorothy Sewell, might be interested in adopting. She was and the adoption took place in an attorney's office in Hinesville on October 13, 1943, when I was 10 weeks old.

I was fortunate enough to be adopted by a very loving couple who had been married for six years and had not been able to have any children. My new mom, Dorothy Simpson Sewell, was a legal secretary and my new dad, Homer S. Sewell, Jr., was a salesman.

...of the United States of America, and to the republic for which it stands; one Nation indivisible, with Liberty and Justice for all!"

*Not bad for an **American Citizen**, who just Arrived August 4, 1943*
Who weighs only 12½ lbs. now
And whose name is
Homer Simmons Sewell III

Adopted by Dot and H.S on October 13, 1943

Adoption announcement sent out by my adoptive parents

Pvt. Alexander Ferency 35534659
5th POIC Ordnance School Barracks No 1
Aberdeen Proving Ground,
Aberdeen, Md.
Darling – Hope to see you Thursday Everything turned out grand. Ronnie adopted by grand family. Will explain when I see you – Love
Milly

I was born Ronald E. Ferency and this is a copy of the contents of a telegram sent from my birth mother to my birth father in Maryland.

State of Georgia
Department of Public Health

T. F. ABERCROMBIE, M. D., DIRECTOR
ATLANTA

October 19, 1945

Mr. S. F. Memory
Attorney at Law
Blackshear, Georgia

Dear Mr. Memory:

We acknowledge receipt of your letter of September 15 regarding the birth certificate for a child born August 4, 1943 in Hinesville, Georgia, and adopted by Mr. and Mrs. Homer Simmons Sewell, Jr.

We are very sorry to state that we have been unable to locate the original certificate of birth from the information given and enclose a certificate to be filled in and signed by one of the foster parents. The child's name in item one should be shown as Homer Simmons Sewell, III and the foster parents should be listed as though they were the real parents. We still have not received a certified copy of the adoption papers and suggest that you have a copy sent to us so that the certificate may be placed on file when it is completed.

If the parents wish a certified photostatic copy of the certificate when it is filed the statutory fee is one dollar payable in advance by money order.

Yours very truly,

RICHARD BREWER, DIRECTOR
DIVISION OF INFORMATION AND STATISTICS

Martha Pattillo

(Miss) Martha Pattillo

Enclosures

MP:et

S. F. MEMORY
S. F. MEMORY, JR.

November 15, 1945.

Mrs. Dorothy S. Sewell,
Belle Glade, Florida.

Dear Dorothy:

I have at last obtained certificate of birth for
Homer Simmons Sewell, III, and enclose it herewith.

I also enclose copy of letter that I wrote to th
director, Hon. Richard Brewer, which explains itself.

With best wishes, I remain,

Sincerely yours,

S. F. Memory

RONALD BEING HELD BY BIRTH MOTHER, MILLIE FERENCY

HOMER IN STROLLER WITH ADOPTIVE MOM,
DOROTHY SEWELL

I have a few memories from my early childhood, growing up in South Florida.

I attended my first year of school in Belle Glade. I really enjoyed going to school and learning how to read and write.

Once when I was very little, maybe about six or so, I was playing below a porch in a large, empty refrigerator box. Mike and I were building a playhouse in that big box. I asked Mike for a hammer and he tossed it down to me. I was hit in the head. Mother had to rush me to the hospital for stitches. I still have a scar on my head from that blow.

One scary time was during a bad hurricane. Dad was downtown at Royal's Department Store boarding up windows and the water was already waist-deep from the lake overflowing. The whole town of Belle Glade was under about three or four feet of water for several days and there was a lot of damage everywhere.

Mom and Dad both worked hard to support us. We were very fortunate and I don't ever remember our family having any shortage of food to eat or a place to live. There were several times as I was growing up in Belle Glade that men stopped by the house looking for something to eat. My mother always had the makings for an extra sandwich and something cold to drink for those less fortunate people.

Most people think Florida is all beaches and sand but some of the richest, most fertile land anywhere is found in the Belle Glade area of South Florida. There are a lot of vegetables grown there, which are shipped all over the country. Consequently, a lot of migrant workers live in the area.

The plight of these folks is still the same as it was in my youth, and even in the 1990's these people are sometimes treated like the slaves were in ABE's time. Those of us who care about people need to investigate migrant workers' camps all over this great, big, beautiful country of ours and do whatever we can to improve their conditions.

MOM AND DAD HOLDING SISTER, DOTTIE ANN, AND HOMER

I learned at an early age that there were people in our world who didn't have a roof over their heads or a meal to eat. I also learned that those of us who did have the basic essentials of life should share with others.

LESSON TO BE LEARNED HERE IS: When GOD blesses us enough to have a little extra, share it with those in need! Our world will become a better place to live when we all care more about each other.

MY FIRST GRADE CLASS. CAN YOU FIND ME?
(I'M THE CUTE ONE...TO THE RIGHT OF THE TEACHER.)

Chapter 2

Early Years Continued

When I was seven years old, Dad heard the land was better in Indiana so we packed up our belongings and moved. Two years later my mom died. A year later Pa went back down to Kentucky and married a widow-lady by the name of Sarah Bush Johnston. She had three children from her previous marriage: John, Elizabeth and Matilda.

We moved to Savannah and I attended second and half of third grade there. We then moved to Central Florida and lived in Altamonte Springs. My grandfather, Homer S. Sewell,Sr. had moved into the area back in 1929 and there are still streets named after him.

When I was in third grade our family attended the Methodist Church on Hwy 17-92 in Casselberry. The pastor, Rev. Darwin Shea, was a pilot and told the young people that if we would come to Sunday School for six months without missing a Sunday, he would take us for a ride in his airplane. I attended at least six months without missing a single Sunday and couldn't wait for my first airplane ride.

The date for the big flight was finally arranged and we flew out of a small grass-strip landing field called Slade Field. This is where the Woodlands Subdivision on Highway 436 in Longwood is now located. That first airplane ride was a thrill for me and is probably when I got the notion that someday I wanted to be able to fly my own airplane. There is nothing to compare to the feeling of flying in a small airplane.

My dad sold ladies' shoes at a large department store in Orlando and when I was in sixth grade, he was asked to transfer to a store in Ocala, Florida.

While living in Ocala, we took a class trip to St. Augustine, the oldest city in the United States, and visited Fort Castillo de San Marcos. That was a wonderful trip back into history and may have been one of the first things that got me started on my interest in history.

That same school year, I was asked to deliver the Gettysburg Address on a radio talk show in Ocala. I know I didn't have a beard then but perhaps I was already tall and skinny and someone thought I looked enough like ABE that I should be the one to do his most famous speech. A BIT OF HISTORY CROSSES MY PATH! After six months we moved back to Altamonte Springs.

One day when I was only 11 or 12 years old, my brother and I got into a fight about something. When Mom came home from work she found out about the fight we had and proceeded to give me a well-deserved spanking. When she finished punishing me I turned to her and said, "You're just picking on me because I'm not really your child!" Well, I want to tell you the next statement that came out of her mouth, I will never forget! Mom said to me, "Son, we picked you out! Your brother and sister just came along!" Boy, did that straighten out my thinking about being adopted. Those of you who are adopted, please be sure to let your adoptive parents know how much you really do appreciate what they did for you.

I've known I was adopted for as long as I can remember. My parents told me as soon as I was old enough to know what it meant. For you parents who either already have or are considering adopting, please ALWAYS let your adoptive children know they are adopted and that you love them and respect them just as much as your biological children.

One morning in 1955 I woke up to find out the old Altamonte Hotel had burned down during the night. It was at the intersection of Hwy 436 and Maitland Avenue and less than a mile from our house. A lot of famous people had stayed in the hotel and it was sad to see it burned to the ground. One of those who had stayed there was Ulysses S. Grant, Commander of the Union Forces during the Civil War and our 18th President. ANOTHER BIT OF HISTORY CROSSES MY PATH!

I loved school and during my 12 years there I didn't miss very many days. I always wanted to be there to learn and to be with my friends.

I remember those days in the "Friendly City" of Ocala. I made a lot of friends and still have the autograph book I started at that school. I have included some of the more interesting poems, etc. from that book.

These things were written in my autograph book during the years I was in sixth through twelfth grades:

Just to be naughty. Just to be nice. I'll be naughty and write my name twice. EARL CLARKSON EARL CLARKSON

Best of luck this summer in your job. It has been my pleasure knowing you all these years. God bless you. CHRISTENA RITCHISON

Remember the girl from the country, Remember the girl from the town, Remember the girl who ruined your book, By writing her name upside down! ꓱꟽꓵH ꓥINI⅁ꓤIꓥ

May you have the best of luck and may the girl you like (whoever it is) like you. Love, PAT MORGAN

There may be Golden Ships or Silver Ships but there is no ship like FRIENDSHIP. Yours truly, MIKKIE DELANEY

If you see a monkey up in a tree, don't throw a stick. It might be me. Your pal, PAT DELANEY

When you get married and live in the south, Remember me and my big mouth. PRISCILLA NIXON

The higher the mountain, the cooler the breeze, The younger the couple, the tighter they squeeze.
JUDY HARDWICKE

Make it a rule as long as you live, no matter who's wrong, you always forgive. Your's 'till Alaska drinks Canada Dry. Your friend always, JOYCE

The best of luck to a swell guy. Yours truly,
ALICE ANN HULL

If you get to heaven before I do, Pinch a little hole and pull me through. A friend, SHIRLEY LARGENT

I wish you the best of everything in anything you do. Keep up the good work. EILEEN MARSH

To a sweet boy. Success will come your way. Let me know where you'll be a chef and I'll come and try it. Love & best wishes, JANET ELGIN

When you get married and live in a tree, send me a coconut C.O.D. KAYE CLARK

When you get married and think you are sweet, pull off your shoes and smell your feet. A very nice, well behaved young man. Sincerely, CHI-CHI HALLETT

Roses are red, violets are blue, I have found a friend in you. Lots of luck & happiness in the future. Love ya, FRAN

Fall in a barrel, fall in a tub, But whatever you fall in, don't fall in love! Lots of luck and best wishes, PAT MCNEIL

You are a nice boy and I like you (as a friend) very much. I wish you the best of luck in the years ahead. 2-young 2-go 4-girls. 2-sweet 2-be 4-gotten Your friend, DIANE WHARTON

To a guy who will go places in this world. Lots of luck in the future with a special girl. PAUL MAE LEMONS

Any time you need any help just remind me that I owe you a couple of favors. You're a swell pal. Thanks a lot and good luck. ADRIAN WAHLBERG

You're one of the nicest boys I've ever known. Please stay that way and I know you'll go far if you do. I'll always remember your jokes. Keep telling them. Best wishes. CAMILLA KIRKLAND

To a very sweet & cute boy who asked me to the Prom & made me very, very happy. May you always find success in everything you do. Thank you for the very pretty flowers & I'll always remember you. When the sun has set its' last & the earth no longer stands, may the good Lord bless & keep you 'till you reach the promised land. Thank you again. Good luck always, PATRICIA MORENE

Roses are red, violets are blue, I've never seen such a cute boy as you. 2-good 2-be 4-gotten U.R.A.Q.T. FOR GET ME NOT. Love, JOAN

Remember Grant, remember Lee, the heck with them, remember me. Your friend, LYNDA LEARY (Isn't it strange Lynda wrote this in my book about 15 years before I started portraying ABE?)

I've enjoyed knowing you this year and last year too. Love ya always, LANA EVERSOLE

May you have the best of luck through your years at L.H.S. & may God richly bless you through all the days of your life. Love, SHIRLEY STAMPER (Shorty)

TEACHER'S CORNER...
My best wishes, Homer, for a happy summer and my commendation for you as a pupil and a person.
MARTHA E. THOMPSON (My typing teacher)

When you enter an empty room, make it instantly a shrine, for thoughts clothe an empty room with more certainty than wallpaper.THOMAS R. DIXON,JR (My Biology teacher for two years) GREAT QUOTE!!

It has been a pleasure having you in class. I hope for you the best of everything. A great success in life.
RALPH BREWER, JR. (My History teacher)

GOOD LUCK & BEST WISHES. SAS=SAS CHRISTY M. HARP, SR. (My math teacher, who had a heart attack at our 20th class reunion. My ex-wife, Kathy, was able to give him CPR and saved his life. HE WAS A GREAT TEACHER AND WE ALL LOVED HIM!)

The very best of everything. Sincerely, J.G. PAYNE (My Science teacher and coach)

It is a joy to teach one who is so conscientious in his work. I know that you will be successful in all that you undertake. Sincerely, ALDIA MILWEE (My English teacher grades 9-12. If it weren't for her, this book would not be written! ANOTHER REALLY GREAT TEACHER!)

That is the end of my little autograph book. Do any of those sound familiar to you older folks? Remember how much fun it was signing all those annuals and autograph books for your friends?

LESSON TO BE LEARNED HERE IS:
FOR STUDENTS: Have fun in school. Whether you know it or not, these are the best years of your life. You will never again have as much fun as you are having in school. You will also never learn as much in any other 12 or 16-year period as you will while still in school. Please pay attention to your teachers and let your minds become a sponge to soak up knowledge. Make sure you hug (for those older students, a handshake will suffice.) a teacher every day and tell them how much you appreciate them.

LESSON TO BE LEARNED HERE IS:
FOR ADULTS: Take time to remember the good times you had while you were in school: the fads, music, movies, etc. As you deal with our youth of today, remember the times when you were young. Were the fads from YOUR days any stranger to YOUR parents than the fads of today are to YOU?? Take time to stop and smell the roses.

Chapter 3

Growing Up and the Diary of a Sixteen-Year-Old

I remember chopping down a lot of trees while growing up in Indiana. I was always helping my pa building fences, barns, cabins and working in the garden.

THE DIARY OF 1959....

This is the only year I ever kept a diary and I thought it might be interesting for you to see what we teenagers did back then. This is also the year I turned 16.

Looking back while I write this book, I don't know why I chose to keep a diary in 1959. But, 16 is a good age with lots of exciting things happening all around us and within our bodies. For those of you guys and gals who aren't already doing so, you might want to consider keeping a diary or journal of what you do each day. It will make interesting reading later in life.

I have deleted the more boring days.

Were those of us who are now "OVER 50" so different than today's teens??

JANUARY
THURSDAY, 1-1-59: We ate New Year's dinner at my grandmother's house.

MONDAY, 1-5: Started first day of school after Christmas

vacation. I started the first day of a church study course.

TUESDAY: I went to second day of study course and then went to Boy Scout meeting.

SATURDAY: Boy Scout Troop 38 went on a hike to Sweetwater Hills from 10 AM to 5:30 PM.

WEDNESDAY: I got exempted from World History and English semester tests. I ran the 220-yard-dash in 36.

FRIDAY: Frank Loeser and I took a bouquet of flowers to Janet Elgin.

MONDAY, 1-19: I cut some oak logs for the fireplace. A man gave me a dollar for taking his boat to him.

TUESDAY: Boy Scout meeting. I cut some firewood and then went to Allen's house.

WEDNESDAY: I mopped and waxed the kitchen and bathroom floors.

SATURDAY: Mike and I left at 1:00 PM to go camping at Bear Island on the south side of Orlando.

MONDAY, 1-26: We went to see the movie, "THE LIGHT IN THE FOREST". My uncle, Bob Anderson, was in it.

WEDNESDAY: Barry brought me a pound of plaster-of-paris so I could take castings of animal tracks. I went to Paul's house and then rode my bike to church.

THURSDAY: I raked the front yard and then went skating with the church choir.

FRIDAY: Barry brought me another pound of plaster-of-paris. Harry, Barry, Greg, Allen, Teddy and I spent the night at the clay pit and went frog-gigging.

SATURDAY: Barry and I came home and we cooked the frog legs along with toast, coffee and spuds. Mom didn't like the frog legs jumping all over the pan! I then cleaned the kitchen and around the back door for grandmother. Pop Sewell (my grandfather) took Barry and me into Winter Park and later we went frogging.

FEBRUARY

MONDAY, 2-2: Mother had to work tonight. I called Elizabeth Banks about going to the Sweetheart Banquet with me.

THURSDAY: Allie gave me a quarter. I now have a total of $1.71.

FRIDAY: I vacuumed the living room for Mother. Allen, Barry, Mike and I camped out at the clay pit.

SUNDAY: Mr. Bradford gave me an usher's job at church. Mom cut my hair and talked to Mrs. Banks about the banquet.

MONDAY, 2-9: I did some work for Mrs. Jackie Douglas. She paid me $1.50.

TUESDAY: Barry didn't come to Scouts so I took over. Elizabeth called.

THURSDAY: I went back to work for Mrs. Douglas. She paid me $2.00. I called Elizabeth.

FRIDAY: I mopped the kitchen and the bathroom. We went to get Dad in Orlando and ate at Morrison's Cafeteria. Mike, Allen, Gregory and Teddy went camping. I had a patrol meeting. I washed Mrs. Spain's Cadillac for a dollar.

SATURDAY: I took Elizabeth to the Sweetheart Banquet and to the school dance. (I didn't know how to dance and would only attempt the slow stuff!) Her first date! What a ball!

TUESDAY: I got a letter from Margy Ryder (I met her last summer while she was visiting her grandparents, the Watsons, that live in Altamonte Springs) from Massachusetts. We had a Board of Revue meeting at Scouts. I received my Second Class rank. We started track today at school. I ran the 30-yard dash in 3.2 and the 50-yard dash in 6.8.

FRIDAY: I went to Orlando to get Dad and put a roll of film in a drug store to get developed.

MONDAY, 2-23: We went to the Prairie Lake Drive-in Theater to see "HOUSEBOAT". I vacuumed the living room rug. Mr. Dixon gave me a C+ for my fourth six-weeks Biology notebook.

TUESDAY: I went to Scouts. Dad brought my pictures and all 12 were good. I pulled some more moss down. I ran the 440 in 1:13 and the 50 in 6.8.

WEDNESDAY: Mom cut my hair. Allen and I got some crawfish for Biology class. I got a "C" on my English notebook. I took three pictures of Victor and Smoky, our dog and cat.

FRIDAY: I didn't have a patrol meeting. There was a tornado warning. No tornado!

MARCH
SUNDAY: I went to church and then I put up a fence for Mother. I took a negative to get duplicated and enlarged at Keyser's Drug Store.

MONDAY, 3-2: I went to Barry's house for a Patrol Leader's Council. I cut some kindling for Pop Sewell.

TUESDAY: Mike and I walked to Scouts. I mopped the floor for Mother.

THURSDAY: Elizabeth called me. Mike, D.A. and I went to Martha Wahlberg's birthday party.

SATURDAY: Mr. Kopp brought the hut out to the cow pasture. I did some work for Mrs. Douglas and she paid me $1.25 for the one hour I worked. Mike, Allen and I went skating at the Coliseum in Orlando.

MONDAY, 3-9: I worked two hours mowing part of Mr. Hoberg's back yard. He gave me a $1.50. I dissected a frog for Biology. Barry and I caught him in the cow pasture and operated on him at Barry's house. I went to my first night of typing class at school. I don't feel so good. Mr. Payne gave me some formaldehyde for the frog but I didn't use it. He didn't tell me that the stuff could kill me. I feel like it is going to.

TUESDAY: Dad had me up at 6:30 this morning planting azaleas. I walked with Barry to Scouts.

SATURDAY: I got a new pair of shoes in Orlando. Mother

took me to Elizabeth's house to give her some pictures. Mike, Allen and I slept in the hut.

SUNDAY: Mike, Allen and I cooked pancakes for breakfast at the hut. We had our first Scout Court of Honor at the church. It was candlelight service. I finished a roll of film tonight.

MONDAY, 3-16: I went to typing class again. I have a bad cold. I gave my roll of film to Dad this morning to get developed.

TUESDAY: It is still raining. I went to Scout meeting. Mike slammed the car door on three fingers of my right hand. Dad brought home my pictures and all 12 were good.

WEDNESDAY: Barry and I went down to the cow pasture. It is overflowing again. I called Elizabeth. We planted some castor bean seeds in the back yard.

THURSDAY: The cow pasture is a lake again like it was last year.

FRIDAY: We didn't have to go to school because of a teachers' convention. I mopped the kitchen. Barry and I went frogging in the boat but we didn't get any.

MONDAY, 3-23: I went to typing class at school. Barry, Teddy and I went down to the cow pasture and set out a trout line. Mike caught 8 bass in the lake.

SATURDAY: I helped Mr. Kopp take the dirt from around his orange trees. Mother, grandmother, D.A. & I went out to Colonial Plaza and got a banana split for 37 cents.

SUNDAY: I got up at 5:30 to go direct traffic for the Easter sunrise service. It rained so we had the service in the church. I just finished writing a 361-word essay on mental health for English. All I had to write was 250 words. I went to 6 hours of church today.

MONDAY, 3-30: I ate supper at the hut. Then I went to typing class. I rode home with Connie. I wrote a 4-page essay on political parties for English.

TUESDAY: There was a baseball game at school during 5th and 6th periods. I didn't go. We went to Prairie Lake Drive-in Theater to see "TOM SAWYER" and "GULLIVER'S TRAVELS".

APRIL

THURSDAY: There was a tornado in Orlando. Mr. Dixon gave me a C+ on my biology notebook.

SATURDAY: I mopped the front porch. I cut Mrs. Spain's lawn for a dollar an hour. I earned $2.25. I cleaned the rug on the front porch. Dicky Moore came over and he, Mike and I went swimming in the lake.

SUNDAY: We caught 31 catfish on the troutline. We started building a 3-story hut and look-out tower in the clay pit.

SATURDAY: I left about 7:30 AM to go with the Bradfords to Sanibel Island. We went to Thomas Edison's home in Fort Myers and ate at the Edison Cafeteria. We spent the night at the Hurricane House on the island. We gathered lots of sea shells.

SUNDAY: We left Sanibel Island and stopped at the Shell Factory and a wildlife farm.

MONDAY, 4-13: I mowed the Hoberg's yard for $3.00. I went to typing class. Mrs. Douglas told me to mow her yard in about a week and a half.

TUESDAY: I went to typing class. I pulled some weeds at Mrs. Douglas' sister's house on Forest Avenue. It took me about 30 minutes and she gave me 75 cents.

THURSDAY: I mowed Mrs. Spain's yard for 1-1/2 hours for $1.65. I went to Scouts. I have $9.56 towards a scooter in my savings account.

FRIDAY: We got out of school at noon to go to a Boy Scout camporee.

SATURDAY: I camped with Greg, Jerry and Allen in Greg's tent. We had campsite number 25. About 4:30 PM the camporee was called off because of rain. Our troop decided to stay but about 10:00 PM the rain was so bad we had to leave too.

SUNDAY: I helped Mother and Dad paint the living room.

MONDAY, 4-20: I put on the second coat of paint in the living room. I went to typing class. It is raining, thundering and lightening like mad. Mom mailed a letter for me for some Write-Right Presidential coins.

TUESDAY: It is raining hard again. I went to typing class and a PTA meeting. Mr. Metts made me do 50 pushups for talking in study hall.

WEDNESDAY: I mopped and waxed the kitchen floor. I played the chimes at the church.

THURSDAY: I went to Scouts. I worked two hours from 3:45 to 5:45 at Mrs. Spains' today. She is going to pay me Saturday. I still ache all over from doing those pushups.

FRIDAY: I put $10 in my savings account.

SATURDAY: I worked at Mrs. Douglass' house from about 9 to 10. She is going to pay me when she gets home tomorrow. I've got a steady job at the Halls, Hobergs, Douglas' and Spains. I bought a can of oil and some gas. I mowed Mrs. Spain's yard. She gave me $3.25. I mowed our yard.

MONDAY, 4-27: I went to typing class. I can type 16 C.W.P.M. I have $16.02 in my savings account. I mowed Mr. Hall's yard. He gave me $1.50. It took me one hour. Mrs. Douglas paid me $1.60.

TUESDAY: I washed Mr. Hoberg's car for a dollar. I went to Barry's house. I went to typing class but the lights wouldn't work so we came home at 8:00 PM. I now have $17.02.

MAY

SUNDAY: I got up this morning and made a coffee cake. I served Mother and Dad breakfast in bed: eggs, bacon, toast, coffee, juice and coffee cake. Mother cut my hair. I got my

Presidential coins.

THURSDAY: I went to Scouts but Jabo didn't come so we played games. I made a flower garden for Mother outside of our window. I worked from 4:30 to 5:30 for Mrs. Spain hauling some leaves and mowing her back yard. She paid me a dollar. I made a 7-layer casserole for supper.

FRIDAY: I got the ground inside the fence by the back door ready to plant some beans.

SATURDAY: I mowed the Douglas' and Bryant's lake front. They didn't pay me yet. We went to Orlando and I mailed some more coupons for Presidential coins.

SUNDAY: I got up at 7 AM, baked a coffee cake and served Mother and Dad breakfast in bed. Dad, Mike and I have been hauling some bricks all day. Mother saw an ad in the paper for 1,000 free bricks at the Sweeney's house so we made four trips to the south side of Orlando.

TUESDAY: I typed some biology and world history homework. I went to typing class and can type 22 WPM.

WEDNESDAY: It rained all afternoon. I have $10 in the bank and $14.75 here. I went swimming.

THURSDAY: I went swimming. I stayed at Robby Bradford's house from 6:30 to 10:00 PM while his mother and father went to a Garden Club meeting. Mrs. Bradford gave me $2 and I now have $16.77.

FRIDAY: I went swimming. I got five more Presidential coins.

SATURDAY: I raked the Stewart's yard from 8:30 to 10:30 and got paid $3. I bought a new spark plug for the lawn mower at a cost of $1.06. I went to Barry's house from 7:30 to 11:00 PM. We played four games of Parchessi. We each won two games.

MONDAY, 5-18: I mowed Mrs. Spain's yard from 3:30 to 5:15 and got paid $2. I now have $29.50. I went to typing class but the lights didn't work again so I came home at 8 PM. I sent off for five more Presidential coins.

THURSDAY: I started mowing the Hoberg's yard and got about half way through when the starter rope broke on the mower. Mr. Hoberg gave me a dollar and I went to Scouts.

FRIDAY: Mother put $20 in the bank for me. I got five more Presidential coins.

SATURDAY: I worked two and one-half hours at Mrs. Hall's for $3. I mowed Pop Sewell's yard. It took me three hours and I earned $3.65. Barry and I went camping in the hut. I started mowing our yard.

JUNE

MONDAY, 6-1: D.A. and I cleaned up the house. I got up at 6:30 this morning and baked a coffee cake. Mr. Harp called and told me he got some information for me about the C.I.A. (CULINARY INSTITUTE OF AMERICA). It has rained all afternoon.

WEDNESDAY: I worked three and one-half hours mowing a yard for Pop Sewell. I went swimming. I went to Scouts at the firehouse. I went to school to see Mr. Harp about the C.I.A. info.

THURSDAY: I worked three and one-half hours mowing a yard for Pop Sewell. He still hasn't paid me.

FRIDAY: I went to school again. Pop Sewell gave me a check for $7. D.A. and I spent all afternoon in Orlando. We went to the Beecham Theater and saw the "SHAGGY DOG".

SATURDAY: I got up at 6 AM and went swimming with Bob and his brother. Then I finished mowing our yard. I am getting ready to go on a Boy Scout camp to Wilderness.

TUESDAY: I started working in Pop Sewell's real estate office. I worked from 8:30 to noon and from 2:00 to 6 PM. We got a female hamster.

THURSDAY: We got a canary. I worked for Pop Sewell from 8:30 to 1:15 and from 2:00 to 7 PM.

FRIDAY: I worked from 9:45 to 12:30 and from 2 to 7 PM. Barry, Mike and I went camping. I mailed a story to

Reader's Digest.

SATURDAY: I worked from 8:30 to 12:30. Bob, Bill and I went swimming. Pop Sewell gave me a check for $15 for working for him this week. I went over to Barry's house. We played Monopoly and I won.

WEDNESDAY: I called Elizabeth.

THURSDAY: Bob, Mike, D.A. and I went swimming this morning at 7 AM. I then worked for eight hours. I went to Barry's and won two games of Monopoly. Bob left with his family to go back to Pennsylvania.

FRIDAY: I worked a total of 40 hours this week. I went camping with Mike, Allen, Harry, Barry, Doug and Jerry.

SATURDAY: I worked from 8:45 to noon. Pop Sewell paid me $15. I mowed our yard.

JULY

FRIDAY: I worked 40 hours this week for Pop Sewell.

MONDAY, 7-6: The canaries now have five eggs. I worked eight hours and then went to typing class. Allen and I went swimming tonight. Pop Sewell finally paid me $12.50 from last week.

FRIDAY: I worked 38 hours this week.

SATURDAY: I worked for three and one-half hours. Mike and I went swimming. Allen came over tonight.

SUNDAY: I went to church this morning. Dad and I mowed the yard. Mom cut my hair. It has rained all afternoon. I bought some pants, belt and socks for $5.68.

MONDAY, 7-13: I worked for eight hours and then went to typing. Dad bought me some shoes that cost me $10.

FRIDAY: I worked 40 hours again this week. Mom, grandmother and I went to get Dad in town. We went to J.P. Morgan's Army Store. I spent $2 on a belt and a flashlight.

SATURDAY: I worked three and one-half hours. I spent $6.50 for food for camping.

PICTURE OF MY GRANDFATHER, "POP SEWELL" AT HIS REAL
ESTATE OFFICE WHERE I SPENT A LOT OF HOURS

SUNDAY: Dad and I went swimming this afternoon. I bought some hair wax at Keyser's Drug Store.

MONDAY, 7-20: I worked eight hours and then went to typing. We went down to Allen's tonight.

TUESDAY: I worked eight hours and then went to typing. We are leaving tomorrow to go on a camping trip.

WEDNESDAY: Pop Sewell gave me $5 for Monday and Tuesday's work. We left at 10:00 AM to go camping.

THURSDAY, FRIDAY & SATURDAY: Camping at Bear Island.

MONDAY, 7-27: I mowed our yard and Mike and I went swimming.

TUESDAY: I worked with Harry Brown on Mrs. Spain's yard for five hours. She gave me $5.25.

WEDNESDAY: Harry and I worked five hours at Mrs. Knudsen's house and each earned $6.25. Mother cut my hair and Dad made me shave. I went to a DeMolay meeting in Winter Park.

THURSDAY: We got a new 1959 green Brookwood Chevrolet. I got a card from Bob Sands.

FRIDAY: I worked two hours mowing Mrs. Kain's yard.

AUGUST

SATURDAY: I mopped and waxed the bathroom. Mrs. Kain gave me $2.50. A woman gave me a dollar for changing a flat tire for her.

SUNDAY: We went to Cypress Gardens. I took 11 pictures. We stopped at Gatorland.

MONDAY, 8-3: Allen, Nancy Blackmer and I went to the cow pasture and rowed around in a boat. I went to the Highway Patrol station in Orlando and passed the test for my restricted driving license. I went to typing. I got a swimming mask, watch, shirt, pencils, stapler and memo pad for my birthday. I still have a bad earache.

TUESDAY: Today is my birthday! Big 16! Allie and Pop Sewell gave me $5. Allen, Steve Gillespie and I went to the cow pasture and then went swimming. I went to typing. Marilyn Baker called me twice.

WEDNESDAY: Allen and I worked two hours mowing Mrs. Harris' yard. We each made $2.50. Allen, Steve and I went swimming. I walked to Scouts.

MONDAY, 8-10: It has rained all day. I went to typing. I did 30 C.W.P.M.

TUESDAY: D.A. and I were in Orlando all afternoon. I paid $5 on a $8.22 pair of pants. I went to typing. I went frogging with Harry and Barry. We slept in the hut. Mom cut my hair.

WEDNESDAY: I finished mowing the yard. I mopped and waxed the kitchen. I was initiated into DeMolay tonight.

TUESDAY: I went swimming this afternoon. Teddy, Harry, Greg, Allen, Steve and I went to the Prairie Lake Drive-in to see "THE GIRL IN THE BIKINI" and "BRAVADO".

WEDNESDAY: I worked for three hours at Mrs. Spain's. She paid me $3.25. I mowed our yard.

THURSDAY: I worked for Pop Sewell for two hours. I went swimming at Allen's beach. Mowed the Douglas' yard. Took me 45 minutes and I got paid $1.75.

FRIDAY: I worked at Mrs. Spain's for three hours. Got a check for $3. I worked for Pop Sewell for one and one-half hours. The Woodcocks (our rich relatives from Gainesville, Georgia) sent Mike, D.A. and I each a box of candy.

SATURDAY: We went to Sanford. I bought a hasp and lock for $1.50. Then we went to Winter Park and I bought four shirts for a dollar each, a notebook for a dollar, a painting for $2 and ice cream for a dollar. Greg and I went swimming.

SUNDAY: We went to New Smyrna Beach. Uncle John, Aunt Faye and Cousin Harriet Woodcock came down from Georgia. I went to church.

MONDAY, 8-24: We went to school to get registered. I went swimming. We went to Prairie Lake Drive-in to see the "TEN COMMANDMENTS".

THURSDAY: Allen and I worked for two hours at the Harris' and then we went on a 20-mile hike to Sweetwater and other places.

SATURDAY: I went to a Troop and District Boy Scout swim meet in Orlando. I swam 175 yards.

SUNDAY: Mike and I went to work with Dad from 7:30 to 12:15 PM. His boss, Mr. Holbrook, gave us each a dollar. Mother cut my hair.

MONDAY, 8-31: We started school. I have Physical Science-1st; Health-2nd; English-3rd; American History-4th; Algebra II-5th and Study Hall-7th. I went to typing class.

SEPTEMBER

TUESDAY: I fixed spaghetti supper. I built a badminton court across the street and went to typing class.

WEDNESDAY: I mowed the yard and went to Scouts.

MONDAY, 9-7: We went to the fort in St. Augustine.

TUESDAY: Allen and I built a bicycle for two.

WEDNESDAY: We rode the bicycle to school. I went to DeMolay and received my Second Degree.

THURSDAY: Mother had to work late so I fixed supper.

SATURDAY: DeMolay meeting at Dad Lehman's house.

MONDAY, 9-14: I went to typing class.

FRIDAY: I mowed the yard in one and one-half hours. We left to go to the beach. The Moons let us use their beach house.

MONDAY, 9-21: Allen and I worked on the hut and I went to typing class.

WEDNESDAY: I went to a DeMolay meeting.

SATURDAY: I mowed Mrs. Spain's yard from 4:00 to 5:45 and she paid me $2.25. Allen, Mike and I went skating.

MONDAY. 9-28: I went down to Allen's and to typing.

TUESDAY: Allen and I cut wood and I went to typing.

WEDNESDAY: I worked in the yard and went to Scouts.

OCTOBER

FRIDAY: Allen and I cut down a tree in Pop Sewell's yard. He paid us $2.50 each. Mike, Allen and I went camping.

SATURDAY: I worked at Mrs. Spain's. She gave me $2. I bought a pair of pants and a belt.

TUESDAY: I baked a cherry pie.

WEDNESDAY: I mowed Mrs. Douglas' yard for $2.

THURSDAY: I baked three nut cakes.

SATURDAY: Mike and I mopped and waxed the front porch. I bought myself a radio-phonograph.

SUNDAY: I went with the DeMolay to the Winter Park Methodist Church. I baked another cherry pie.

MONDAY, 10-12: I went to typing class. I came in second in the cherry pie baking contest.

WEDNESDAY: I fixed supper. DeMolay meeting.

THURSDAY: I mowed Mrs. Spain's yard for $2.25.

FRIDAY: I mopped and waxed the kitchen and bathroom.

THURSDAY: I sold some magazine subscriptions.

FRIDAY: I earned $1.75 at Mrs. Douglas'.

SATURDAY: At 9 AM I took a S.A.T. at school. It lasted until 12 noon. I babysat for the Gerhardts from 7:30 to 12:15 and earned $3.

MONDAY, 10-26: Allen and I worked at Mrs. Douglas' house. She gave us 75 cents each.

TUESDAY: I sold $37 worth of magazine subscriptions.

WEDNESDAY: I mowed the yard with Allen's mower. I went to a DeMolay meeting.

THURSDAY: I babysat for Mrs. Gerhardt from 7:30 to 12:00 midnight.

FRIDAY: I have sold $42.29 worth of subscriptions. I drove a car during half-time at the homecoming game.

NOVEMBER

SUNDAY: Allen and I went fishing in the cow pasture. I have now sold $65.07 in subscriptions.

MONDAY, 11-2: I got $1.25 from Mrs. Gerhardt. I have sold $73.37.

TUESDAY: Got another silver dollar. I have sold $103.

WEDNESDAY: I mopped and waxed the kitchen.

THURSDAY: I have sold $113.96.

FRIDAY: I came in second in the magazine sales contest. I won a stuffed dog.

WEDNESDAY: I went to DeMolay. I mopped and waxed the bathroom.

THURSDAY: I have been hauling leaves all afternoon. I got five more silver dollars for magazines. I loaned one to Bill Franklin.

SATURDAY: I hauled leaves this afternoon. Pop Sewell gave us a check for $50.

SUNDAY: I got up at 7:30. Dad took me to a DeMolay practice. I came home and went to church. At 1:00 we (DeMolay) left for Sanford. We did some initiation work. I was a guard. We ate supper at S&S Cafeteria & I spoke to the manager about a job. He told me to come back in two weeks. I went to church.

TUESDAY: I baked a cherry pie. I gave Mother a hair dryer for her birthday tomorrow.

WEDNESDAY: We took a cake to Allie and Pop Sewell for their 52nd anniversary. I am studying for two tests.

THURSDAY: I have $112 in the bank.

MONDAY, 11-23: Mike and I worked in the yard. I went to Barry's. Bill Franklin paid me the dollar he owed.

SUNDAY: Dad and I helped take inventory at his shoe store in Orlando from 8:30 to 1:30 and from 2:30 to 5:45. I got paid $2.

MONDAY, 11-30: I went to DeMolay. We are going to

have a dinner December 9 and a hayride on December 19.

DECEMBER

THURSDAY: I went to see a play at school. I mopped and waxed the kitchen.

THURSDAY: I made three 100's on tests at school.

FRIDAY: I made an 86 on a health test. We got out of school for Christmas holidays.

MONDAY, 12-21: We went to town and I bought the rest of my Christmas presents. I took $32 out of the bank.

TUESDAY: Mike and I raked the yard.

FRIDAY: I got a .22 rifle, shirts, clock, socks and clothes for Christmas.

MONDAY, 12-28: I cut some kindling for Pop Sewell.

WEDNESDAY: We caught nine flying squirrels. I did some typing for Mrs. Bradford and went to a party at Sharon Taylor's house.

THURSDAY: I worked for Mrs. Bradford. She gave me five dollars.

That is the end of my one and only DIARY OF 1959. I hope you've enjoyed reading it as much as I enjoyed living it.

Even in my teen years I was already doing whatever I could to help with chores around the house. I didn't expect my parents to give me an allowance for doing what needed to be done. I did it because I appreciated having a house to live in and wanted to do my share. Teenagers of today think their parents should give them an allowance to do things like keeping their rooms picked up, helping with the dishes, taking the garbage out, etc. I say to them, "Do it because you care, not just for the money!"

As you can see from my diary, I started earning my own spending money at an early age. The quickest way for teenagers to learn respect for money is to do some jobs around the neighborhood to earn their own money. Do some babysitting, mow yards, rake leaves or run errands for a neighbor. You will very quickly develop a new understanding of the value of money!

My dad used to tell me all the time, "Son, if it's worth doing at all, do it right the first time!" An important message for all of us...regardless of age.

This would be a good place for me to say something of importance to teenagers. Today's morality is a lot different than it was in my teen years or in the teen years of ABE. You are under a lot of pressure to do drugs, sex, smoke and lots of other things I didn't do at that age.

Please don't let peer pressure cause you to do something you will live to regret. I was under a lot of pressure to do all of the same things you are/will be asked to do. I had made my mind up early that I had too much respect for girls and for myself than to give in to peer pressure. You will always be a lot happier with yourself if you wait to have sex until after you are married and NEVER smoke, drink or do drugs...at any age!!

LESSON TO BE LEARNED HERE IS: Have fun during your teen years but don't let anyone talk you into doing anything you will be sorry for later. Respect your bodies and respect all those you come in contact with...particularly those of the opposite sex.

Chapter 4

Storms in Life

I was asked by James Gentry to build a flatboat and take some goods downriver a 1,000 miles to New Orleans and sell them for him. His son, Alan, and I built that boat. Let me tell you what happened on that trip...

Do you think we were able to get to New Orleans without having any trouble of any kind? No sir're bubba roo, we did not! I am here today to tell you life's NOT going to always deal you a straight, narrow road to walk down! Sometimes in your life, you might have to do a little zig-zagging, just like that old river did for a 1,000 miles, to get where you want to go. But, do you ever give up? NO! Don't you ever give up in the pursuit of whatever you want out of life.

I never gave up and I don't want you to ever give up either. No matter how bad it gets today, just remember tomorrow will always be a better day. Don't ever give up! I want all of you to learn to do something starting today that I learned at an early age. I promise if you do, you will be big successes in your lives.

Starting today, I want you to learn to..."Be dreamers, stargazers, rainbow chasers and to soar with the eagles." You can become whatever you want. Just don't ever give up! And there is one more thing very essential to being able to obtain your goals in life. Someday, someone might come up to you and try to talk you into doing drugs, alcohol or tobacco. When that happens, I want you to look them in the eye and say "NO"!

I want all of you to raise your hands right now and repeat after me..."I promise...I will always...say 'NO' to drugs". And I'll tell you something else. If someone ever does try to talk you into doing drugs and you get real serious, look them in the eye and tell them you promised ABE LINCOLN you would always say 'NO' to drugs, they will think you're already "high" and leave you alone anyway!!!

GOD gave each and every one of you a brain to become something very special and important...and you can't do that if you ever mess it up with drugs. Please, always say "NO" to drugs!!

Even at an early age, I was already being creative, experimenting with electricity and taking on all kinds of projects around the house. I installed a doorbell system and driveway lights for our house and was always tinkering and fixing anything that was broken or needed fixing.

In 1959, when I was in 10th grade, we were studying all about the United States...maps, capitals, locations, etc. I decided there needed to be a fun way to learn all of these things so I designed and built a board game I called "STACAPILMAP" for STATE-CAPITAL-MAP. It was approx. 4' x 3' with a map of the United States, a light, a buzzer and two wires hanging from the middle of the board. If you stuck one of the wires into the hole beside GEORGIA and stuck the other wire either into the map location for GEORGIA or into the hole beside ATLANTA, you would complete a circuit and the buzzer/light would come on.

I had a lot of wire I'd gotten from the phone company's scrap pile so I used it to wire the back of the board. I took it to school and everyone had fun playing the game and learning at the same time.

Certificate
Registration of a Claim to Copyright
In a drawing or plastic work of a scientific or technical character

CLASS	REGISTRATION NO.
I ∪	12787

FORM I

DO NOT WRITE HERE

This Is To Certify that the statements set forth on this certificate have been made
a part of the records of the Copyright Office. In witness whereof the seal of the
Copyright Office is hereto affixed.

Arthur L. Kreishlein

ARTHUR L. KREISHLEIN

Register of Copyrights
United States of America

1. Copyright Claimant(s) and Address(es):

Name   **Homer Simmons Sewell III**

Address   **P. O. Box 484, Altamonte Springs, Florida.**

Name

Address

2 Title: **"DRAWING OF STAOAPLMAP"**
                         (Title of the work)

3. Nature of Work: **Drawing**

4. Optional Deposit:

Basis for claiming option:
[ ] Monetary value (retail value per copy)   [ ] Weight (in pounds)
[ ] Size (give dimensions)
[ ] Fragility (give details)

5. Author:

Name   **Homer Simmons Sewell III**   Citizenship **U. S. A.**
                                             (Name of country)

Domiciled in U. S. A. **Y[X]** No[ ] Address **P. O. Box 484, Altamonte Springs, Florida**

6. (a) Date of Publication:

(b) Place of Publication:

Completed, Manufacture Outside United States copyright the right to secure copyright is not and cannot be restored.

FOR COPYRIGHT OFFICE USE ONLY

Application received
AUG 26 1963

One copy or reproduction received
MAY 28 1962

Two copies received

Photographs or reproductions received

Fee received
15151 AUG26'63

In the middle of February, 1960, Harry Brown, Allen Hardwicke and I were on the Wekiwa River and discovered what we at first thought was a log sticking out of the water. Upon closer investigation, we realized it was the remains of a 14' long Indian dugout canoe estimated to be about 500 years old. We donated it to the Anthropology Department at Rollins College in Winter Park. ANOTHER BIT OF HISTORY CROSSES MY PATH.

I've enjoyed writing stories since I was a teenager and one of the first I wrote was during a hurricane.

HURRICANE DONNA

Today is Saturday, September 10, 1960. Hurricane Donna is almost here!

It all started about a week ago when we heard there was a hurricane forming in the Caribbean Sea. Central Florida has not had a hurricane since about 1950.

Yesterday afternoon radio reports indicated that the hurricane was about 350 miles southeast of Key West and was moving at nine MPH in a northwesterly course. It was then everyone started worrying about it and began to ready themselves for the storm.

This morning when I woke up at about 7:30 AM and turned on the radio, I heard Donna had hit Key West with full force and was moving up the Keys slowly but surely. The hurricane had done tremendous property damage to the Keys but there had been very few casualties. Winds up to 166 MPH were recorded on some Keys!

The radio reported 80% of the 4,000 people on the second largest island in the Keys, Marathon, were evacuated to the mainland. Some of the people who did stay on Marathon went through a night of terror. Water reached a level of three feet in some of the houses. Most of the houses and buildings on this island have been blown down and completely demolished. Small outboard boats and large cabin cruisers have been snatched from their places in the water and thrown onto the land. A UPI reporter gave an eye-witness report from the island that thousands of blue-shelled crabs are covering the roads and dodging automobiles. The main water line from the mainland to the Keys has been broken and communications lines are down everywhere.

At 8:30 this morning our family went to our neighborhood grocery store to do our last-minute shopping. Everyone else had the same idea we did and the store was crammed full of shoppers. The shelves were emptying fast! We did our shopping and running around and came home to prepare ourselves for the storm.

In an 11:00 AM report, the "EYE" of the hurricane was located between Everglades City and Naples and still moving northwesterly at about nine MPH.

The wind has been blowing about 20 MPH with gusts up to 30 MPH. It is expected to get as high as 75 MPH today and tomorrow.

All stores in Orlando were closed by 12:00 noon but some had closed earlier because of the danger of the storm. People are warned to stay at home and stay off the streets in Winter Park because of the many large, old oak trees which might fall. Emergency shelters have been set up all over this area.

Small limbs and moss have been blowing out of the trees all day and a large oak tree has just fallen into our yard from our neighbor's yard.

In a radio report at 3:15 PM the "EYE" of the hurricane was reported to be near Fort Myers in south Florida. The "EYE" is expected to be in the Tampa area tonight by midnight.

It is about 4:00 PM now and the hurricane is about 140 miles from Orlando. The temperature is 76 degrees. The storm is still moving at about nine MPH in a northwesterly direction.

It is 5:00 PM now and I just noticed a very tall pine tree at the edge of our lot looks like it might be blown over because it is top-heavy. I have just heard Hurricane Donna's main intensity will reach this area at about 12:00 midnight tonight. Right now in Orlando it is still 76 degrees with the winds at 20 MPH and gusts up to 30 MPH. The barometric pressure is 29.55 and falling. It has been requested by city police and safety officials that the streets in Orlando be cleared for safety sake.

It is 5:35 PM and the hurricane's forward movement has increased to 11 MPH within the last half hour. It is a few miles north of Fort Myers and is carrying winds up to 125 MPH in a small area. The sky is a foggy-looking gray color and it is beginning to get dark. It is 76 degrees outside and the wind gusts are increasing to 35 MPH.

It is now 7:30 PM and I am writing by candlelight. All electricity in this area went off at exactly 6:30 PM. Fortunately, we were able to prepare our supper before the power went off. We have no portable radio so the only way we can get news of Donna's progress is for one of us to make a run for the car every hour or so and use the car radio. It is extremely dark outside and the wind has died down some for now. It is still raining "moss and limbs" continuously.

It is 8:10 PM. The electricity just came back on. I have no idea how the lines were repaired so fast in this bad weather and I doubt the power will last for long. The latest radio bulletin said the "EYE" of the storm was 95 miles south of Orlando with a forward speed of 10 MPH and by 10:00 PM tonight there would be winds up to 75 MPH. The temperature still stands at 76 degrees with winds from the east at 27 MPH and gusts up to 35 MPH. The barometric pressure is 29.49.

It is 8:55 PM. I tried to take a short catnap but I couldn't sleep because of the weather. In the 8:50 bulletin, the wind had increased to 28 MPH with gusts up to 44 MPH and the barometric pressure had dropped to 29.43 inches.

It is 2:00 AM. The winds must be as high as 100 MPH and are blowing constantly.

It must be between 2:30 and 3:00 AM and the winds which were blowing so hard from the east-northeast have changed to the west-southwest. The "EYE" has just passed us.

It is 3:00 AM Sunday morning. The electricity went off again at about 11:45 PM. I was asleep when it did go off but Mother just told me the power went off just before Miss America was crowned. I think the worst of the storm has already passed but the wind is still blowing considerably. It is too dark outside to investigate for damage but there are probably trees and limbs all over our yard.

It is 3:15 AM and I am going back to bed and try to get some sleep.

The time is 7:15 AM. I ventured outside in the high winds to check for damage. Besides the one oak tree I have already mentioned, no trees have fallen in our yard. Every square inch of ground is covered with either moss, limbs, pine needles or other debris. It is really a big mess! Yesterday morning I looked on top of our house at the large television antenna there. It is now broken in the middle and laying on the ground. In our neighbors' yards whole pine trees are down, palm trees bent double and the top is completely blown out of a large ear tree. In the woods across the street I can see big limbs and trees down everywhere.

It is almost 9:00 AM. I just got back from a trip around town. There are trees all over the roads everywhere in town. One of our friends across Lake Florida from us has eight big pine trees down in his yard and one of them is on his house. There is water across one of the main roads in town and the lake is beyond its banks. It is the worst mess I have ever seen in Altamonte Springs.

On one street in town all the neighbors have gotten together and are trying to move some of the larger debris out of their yards. The wrecker from the Altamonte Garage is helping to move the larger trees out of the streets.

The time is 1:00 PM Sunday afternoon and the weather is getting considerably better all the time. My brother, Mike, and I have been trying to clean up around here and I tried to fix the broken TV antenna.

It is 5:00 PM. We have been cleaning up all afternoon. The streets are finally being cleared for traffic and the wind is dying down. We still don't have electricity and won't have until tomorrow.

One of the bad things that came of the storm is we don't have school tomorrow. I will miss seeing my friends and teachers. I would have it a whole lot easier at school instead of helping with all the cleanup here at home. All of us survived Hurricane Donna and all her fury! It is time to go back to school and I am ready.

In high school I was not the athletic type and didn't go out for many sports. The only sports I was interested in was baseball, track, swimming....AND GIRLS. I do remember running some pretty fast 100-yard-dashes and playing some pretty good baseball.

I was one of the few people at school who knew how to run the old 16-mm projectors so I was always getting out of class to show movies to other classes. That was something I enjoyed being able to do.

Back then boys were not allowed to take Home Ec. I really wanted to, so my parents got special permission from the principal, Mr. E.S. Douglas, who was a personal friend of my grandparents. We affectionately called him "CHROME DOME" because he was bald-headed and the top of his head always shone in the sun.

I wanted to be an executive chef when I graduated so I really needed that Home Ec. training. My plans were to attend the Culinary Institute of America (CIA) in New Haven, Connecticut to learn how to be a great chef.

DRAWING BY ONE OF MY CLASSMATES OF ME AS A CHEF

Florida Power Corporation each year sponsored a cherry pie baking contest for high schools all over the state. In my first year of Home Ec. class, I entered the contest and with my very first cherry pie, I came in second at my school. Darlene Shea, our pastor's daughter, had been winning it for years! I entered the contest again in my senior year and I won at the school level.

My pie had a solid top-crust and I decorated it by using toothpicks dipped in red and green food coloring to make a big cherry with a green stem as the vents.

I then went on to a district contest in Winter Park. When the judging was all over, I went in to pick up my pie plate and saw that only a small piece had been cut out of my pie. The filling was running all over the place! I had either over-cooked or under-cooked the filling. Needless to say, I didn't win anything at district. Just to have been able to win at the school level and go on to district level was an achievement though. The guys were always teasing me after that about baking them a cherry pie.

I was asked to escort the homecoming queen in my senior year. We rode in a nice convertible and I enjoyed being part of the festivities.

I was on the annual staff as the chief photographer and manager for ad sales and had my name printed in a Curtis Publishing book for being one of the top magazine subscription salesmen for my school fund raising event. I was already on my way to becoming a good salesman!

During school years I had several part-time jobs to earn spending money. I pumped gas at Newell's Gas Station and bagged groceries at the Super Value Store on Highway 436. I also did a lot of yard mowing, leaf raking and baby-sitting for neighbors.

One of my neighbors, who lived right behind our house, was Mr. William Wrigley, who had retired from Martha's Vineyard, Massachusetts. I enjoyed visiting with him and listening to stories from his youth. He was always telling me, "Homer, you're a gentleman and a scholar."

One of my best friends was Bob Sands from Pittsburgh, Pennsylvania. He came down each summer to visit his grandparents, Mr. and Mrs. Cliff Sands. Bob and I had some great times running around together all summer. We did a lot of swimming and boating on Lake Florida. Every time I would say, "Dad gum it...such and such", Bob would reply, "Well, mom glue it..."

Those were the good ole days! Nothing to worry about except chasing girls and playing the pinball machines at Sgt. Bilko's Restaurant on Highway 436.

I dated a lot of different girls during my high school days. A few of the girls were not necessarily the most beautiful ones available but we had some great times going to movies or to the beach. I believed then as I do now that "beauty is only skin deep". There were a lot of girls who were very beautiful on the inside but no one was asking them out. Guys, you can't always judge a book by its cover!

As you can see, I had a lot of fun during my school years. I paid attention to my teachers, did whatever homework needed to be done in a timely fashion and helped around the house. I didn't need to be told what chores to do. I just did what I knew needed to be done!

LESSON TO BE LEARNED HERE IS: Work hard! Play hard! Don't ever let the "STORMS" in your life get you down. Good or bad, make the best of everything!

Chapter 5

Moving...Jobs...Love

When I turned 21, my pa decided to move up to the Decatur-Springfield area of Illinois. At 21, a young man is supposed to move out on his own but Pa said times were kinda hard and wanted me to stick around for another year to help support the family. I agreed to do that. A year later it was definitely time for me to move out on my own. I packed up my few belongings and moved about 30 miles out of Springfield to a new little village growing up there on the river...called New Salem.

When I first arrived in New Salem, I stayed at the Rutledge Tavern and Inn. Mr. Rutledge had some rooms to rent. Well, fellows, he also had something else of interest to me. He had a beautiful daughter named Anne, with long brown hair and beautiful green eyes. She was a sight to behold!

My first job after I graduated from Lyman High School in 1961 was in a management training program with a cafeteria in Winter Park, Florida.

I would go in about 3:00 AM and start getting vegetables and meats ready for the cooks. I soon became Storeroom Manager. I could de-bone a 50-pound beef rump roast in 10 minutes and have it standing tall like a Christmas tree...ready for the oven. I learned how to quarter a case of chickens in less than 15 minutes and how to filet a 50-pound box of Spanish mackerel in 20 minutes. If we left the skin on and broiled it, we sold it as

Broiled Spanish Mackerel. But, if we skinned it, pounded it with crackers and almonds and deep-fried it, we sold it as Trout Almondine. Same fish...different name! What a deception that was!

I put in some long hours in the cafeteria business for about 75 cents an hour. I also learned a lot about preparing food for hundreds of people. After I had run the storeroom for a while, I then worked in the bakery. Have you ever made 50 apple or custard pies at a time...from scratch? Lots of fun!

As part of my management training program, I also worked on the serving line. It was a challenge to see how thin I could carve those roast beef slices and to serve food to as many as 100 people an hour.

The cafeteria was a good learning experience and with this first full-time job I started doing something all teenagers still living at home should do. I started paying my mom and dad $25 a week. Any teenager who thinks he/she can live cheaper on their own should go try it after they graduate from high school. I felt it was the least I could do to pay back my parents for all they had done for me over the years.

For those of you still living at home, as soon as you are able to get a job, start giving your parents something each week. They will appreciate it and you will feel better as a person.

I saved my money and bought my first car. A 1951 Pontiac, I believe it was. I only paid $300 for it and then had it painted, installed new Fingerhut seat covers, new tires and had NO PAYMENTS. To newly licensed students...you will have more respect for your first car if you save your own money to buy it instead of having your parents give it to you. DO NOT PUT YOURSELF IN DEBT FOR A CAR WHILE YOU ARE STILL IN SCHOOL! You will become a slave to your car payments!

After a year in the food business I decided it wasn't for me, so I went to work for Florida Gas Company in Orlando. One of my first assignments was to paint 600 gas lights and posts in front of everyone's houses in the Sky Lake Subdivision in south

Orlando. It took me all summer to do it. What an experience!

Later, I went to work in the accounting department in the home office in Winter Park. I processed invoices, worked in the print shop and then became station clerk at the Orlo Vista compressor station. I handled payroll, all shipping and receiving, answered phones, did TWX (teletype) operations and whatever else needed to be done, including being a gopher!

As I have been going through my files and doing research for this book, I have come across a lot of interesting letters, pictures, etc. I will share some of them with you throughout the book. I found the following poem written by my grandfather, Homer Sewell, Sr. for my birthday in 1962. I hope you enjoy it as much as I did.

Nineteen years ago today
Out of the sky like a cosmic ray
A baby boy came hurtling down
And after a while he hit the ground.
His parents were very overjoyed
To know they had a baby boy.
He finally grew up and went to school,
Learned everything by the rule.
Physically active and very mature,
He was to the girls quite allure.
After going to school, early til late,
This fine young man did graduate.
Then he went to work in the Super Value store
To learn all he could of grocery lore.
Now he is working for Florida Gas
And looking for a likely lass
That he can marry and some fine day,
Out of the sky comes a cosmic ray.
Not a cosmic ray but a fine young boy
That will be his parents pride and joy.

My dad was on the town council for Altamonte Springs for several years and we both belonged to the volunteer fire department. Each year the old Prairie Lake Drive-in Theater (Currently the site of a Circuit City Store.) would give all of the councilmen a free annual pass. Dad and Mom didn't care much for movies so Dad would give me the pass. I could have a cheap date with another couple. We could load up a car and all get in free. All we had to pay for was the drinks and popcorn. Mrs. Hansen, the town clerk, was one of the ticket-takers at the drive-in and she was always very friendly as I would come through with another carload of my friends.

In 1963 I sold my '51 Pontiac and bought an old '54 Chevy. I had a small tape recorder rigged up under the seat with a hidden microphone and start/stop switch. When my buddy and I would leave the car to go get drinks and popcorn for the girls, we would secretly turn on the tape recorder so we could tape what the girls had to say while we were gone.

When we came back to the car and the girls would go up to the bathroom, we could then play back the tape. It was interesting to hear what they had to say. Perhaps an early version of Water Gate! THOSE WERE THE NIGHTS...ALRIGHT!!

I had my Chevy all painted up nice and even installed my own seat belts. They were not standard equipment back then like they are now. I was always tinkering around with electricity and building and installing various things around the house or in my car. I decided I would put a warning system into my Chevy which would remind me and my passenger to fasten our seat belts.

PLEASE BE SURE YOU AND EVERYONE WHO RIDES WITH YOU IN ANY VEHICLE ALWAYS FASTENS THEIR BELTS. SEAT BELTS DO SAVE LIVES!

I had an engineer draw up everything for me and had it all ready to send to the U.S. Patent Office in Washington, D.C. Back then a Patent Application cost $300 and I just didn't have it. In 1963 there were NO buzzer/light indicators to remind you to fasten seat belts. In fact, most cars didn't even come with seat belts. If I had been able to get that patent, I would be getting royalties from every car, truck and van that rolls off the assembly line now! So, for the lack of $300, I lost out on the possibility of a lot of money!

President Lincoln is the only President, even today who holds a Patent on anything. Here is a copy of his patent taken from an 1850 book I bought in Gettysburg in January of 1994.

31st Congress, [SENATE.] Ex. Doc
1st Session. No. 15.

REPORT

OF THE

COMMISSIONER OF PATENTS,

FOR

THE YEAR 1849.

PART I.

ARTS AND MANUFACTURES.

CONTENTS.

WASHINGTON:
OFFICE OF PRINTERS TO THE SENATE.

1850.

No. 6469.—*Improved method of lifting Vessels over Shoals.*

What I claim as my invention and desire to secure by letters patent, is the combination of expansible buoyant chambers, placed at the sides of a vessel, with the main shaft or shafts C, by means of the sliding spars or shafts D, which pass down through the buoyant chambers, and are made fast to their bottoms and the series of ropes and pulleys, or their equivalents, in such a manner that by turning the main shaft or shafts in one direction, the buoyant chambers will be forced downwards into the water, and at the same time expanded and filled with air for buoying up the vessel by the displacement of water, and by turning the shaft in an opposite direction, the buoyant chambers will be contracted into a small space, and secured against injury.

A. LINCOLN.

HOMER SIMMONS SEWELL III

UNITED STATES CITIZEN

P.O. BOX 484,

ALTAMONTE SPRINGS,

FLORIDA

CAR SEAT BELT "BUZZER" INDICATOR

C L A I M

When a person gets into his car and starts the motor, if he has not
fastened his seat belts, as he always should do, the buzzer will
BUZZ until he remembers to fasten them. This CAR SEAT BELT "BUZZER"
INDICATOR circuit in a car and/or a truck and/or any other vehicle
with seat belts, will decrease, by a large per cent, the number of
people who have seat belts in their car and either don't remember to
use them or just don't use them. This will, in turn, greatly reduce
the number of accidents and deaths that could have been prevented if
the seat belts had been fastened.

TO THE COMMISSIONER OF PATENTS:

Your petitioner, Homer Simmons Sewell III, a citizen of the
United States and a resident of Altamonte Springs, County of
Seminole, State of Florida, whose postoffice address is P. O. Box
484, prays that letters patent may be granted to him for the
improvement in CAR SEAT BELT "BUZZER" INDICATOR , set forth in the
following five (5) pages of specification.

CAR SEAT BELT "BUZZER" INDICATOR

BRIEF DESCRIPTION

From the ignition switch a wire is picked out and "tapped" to pick up
a hot positive 12 volts only after the ignition key is turned on. This
wire is taken to a toggle switch mounted on the dash. This switch is
for the purpose of turning off the whole alarm system if any reason
should arise to do so. The switch would remain in an ON position
normally. From this switch the positive wire is then taken to one side
of a fuse to prevent any unwanted overloading or shorting out of the
circuit. From the fuse the positive current is split wired and taken
to the lower contact on the relay and to one side of the coil. The
hot positive wire is taken from the other side of the coil to one side
of the seat belt. At the belt buckle it is bolted down; putting current
into the buckle itself. The positive wire is also taken from the other
relay contact point to the positive side of a buzzer. The negative side
of the buzzer is taken to a convenient ground point and this ground is,
in turn, also taken to the other side of the seat belt where it is bolted
to the buckle itself. Thus we have a positive current at the right seat
belt buckle and a negative current at the left seat belt buckle. (This
could just as easily be reversed.) At this point, I should suggest
that the positive side of the seat belt, whichever it may be, should be
insulated (plastic covered or protected the best way) because unless some
care is excerised a small shock could result if both buckles were held
at the same time. This matter could be taken of very easily in manufacturing of the seat belts. Thus if the ignition switch is on and
the toggle switch is on, the normally closed relay allows current to
energize the buzzer and the buzzer will remain on until the seat belts
are fastened together, which completes the circuit, energizes the relay
and coil, opens the contacts, and turns off the buzzer.

54

DETAIL DESCRIPTION

(Key to Drawing)

1.) Dash board

2.) Ignition switch

3.) Any wire that is hot positive current only with ignition switch
     on

4.) Any type toggle switch mounted on dash board and/or anywhere else
     convenient for driver or operator

5.) Insulated single strand of heavy gauge automotive wire and/or
     any other type insulated wire of sufficient gauge

6.) Fuse, 9 amp. in holder. Other amp. fuse could be used or it could
     be taken to the fuse block of the car or truck

7.) Insulated single strand of heavy gauge automotive wire and/or
     any other type insulated wire of sufficient gauge.

8.) Twelve (12) volt D. C. normally closed single pole, single throw
     relay and coil or 6 volt D. C. relay and coil or 8 volt D. C.
     relay and coil of any type pole and throw.

9.) Insulated single strand of heavy gauge automotive wire and/or
     any other type insulated wire of sufficient gauge.

10.) Insulated single strand of heavy gauge automotive wire and/or any
     other type insulated wire of sufficient gauge, sewed to seat belt
     and/or could be made into the belt.

11.) Seat belts

12.) Side view of seat

13.) Positive wire bolted and/or attached by best means to belt buckle

14.) Insulated single strand of heavy gauge automotive wire and/or any
     other type insulated wire of sufficient gauge.

15.) Any type 12 volt or 6 volt or 8 volt D. C. buzzer and/or noise
     device of any kind and/or flashing light and/or any type signal
     indication

55

16.) Insulated single strand of heavy gauge automotive wire and/or any other type insulated wire of sufficient gauge

17.) Ground (could be bolted and/or attached anywhere sufficient to pick up a strong negative current)

18.) Insulated single strand of heavy gauge automotive wire and/or any other type insulated wire of sufficient gauge.

19.) Insulated single strand of heavy gauge automotive wire and/or any other type insulated wire of sufficient gauge sewed to seat belt and/or could be made into the belt

20.) Negative wire bolted and/or attached by best means to belt buckle

21.) Cover box of any type bolted and/or attached under seat and/or anywhere else convenient for manufacture or installation

HOMER SIMMONS SEWELL III, the above-named petitioner, being sworn (or affirmed), deposes and says that he is a citizen of the United States and resident of Altamonte Springs, County of Seminole, State of Florida, that he verily believes himself to be the original, first, and sole inventor of the improvement in CAR SEAT BELT "BUZZER" INDICATOR described and claimed in the foregoing specification; that he does not know and does not believe that the same was ever known or used before his invention thereof, or patented or described in any printed publication in any country before his invention thereof, or more than one year prior to this application, or in public use or on sale in the United States for more than one year prior to this application; that said invention had not been patented in any country foreign to the United States on an application filed by him or his legal representatives or assigns more than twelve months prior to this application; and that no application for patent on said invention has been filed by him or his representatives or assigns in any country foreign to the United States.

_____ III
(Inventor's full signature)

STATE of _FLORIDA_ _ _ _

COUNTY of _SEMINOLE_ _ _   ss:

Sworn to and subscribed before me this _12th_ day of _August_ _ _,

19 _63_.

(SEAL)

_____ III
(Signature of notary or officer)

_____
(Official character)

Notary Public, State of Florida at Large
My Commission Expires Jan. 15, 1966
Bonded By American Fire & Casualty Co

57

Always be on the look-out for a way to improve something that's already been built or to make something which will make life easier or safer for others. When you do, get your invention protected and then find a way to get it marketed.

In 1964 we still had the draft and the Vietnam War was going strong. I was about to be drafted and knew I would not get any choice about my enlistment training. I decided to enlist in the Army instead of waiting to be drafted. I was officially sworn in on May 14, 1964 and was placed in charge of a group of soldiers taken by train from Orlando to Jacksonville for testing and other induction activities.

I ended up in Ft. Gordon, GA for my eight weeks of Basic Training. During one particularly hot summer day a couple of weeks after we had started training, I was called out of the exercises we were doing and told to report to the CO's office...dirty green fatigues and all.

When I arrived in the CO's office, I was introduced to five distinguished-looking men dressed in shirts, ties and coats. They said they were from the White House and that I should take a seat! I did! I wondered aloud what I had done that was so bad it required people from the White House to come looking for me. I was told my "201-file" (my military personnel file) had been selected from a couple of thousand files. Because of my test scores, work experience, etc., I had been chosen for potential assignment to the White House Communications Agency (W.H.C.A.). This is the Agency which takes care of all types of communications requirements for the President and his family, the Vice President and his family in the White House and on the road.

I was told they did not need anyone in computers, which was what I had signed up for, but they did need people to operate the switchboard. If I was interested I would have to waive my enlistment assignment and agree to go to Switchboard School for eight weeks at Ft. Gordon. I would be required to pass a background investigation for a Top Secret Clearance (TSC) and also pass the required training classes in the top 5% of my class.

U S Army Training Center - Infantry
Fort Gordon, Georgia

HOMER AT FORT GORDON, GEORGIA FOR BASIC TRAINING IN 1964

59

Knowing my other options might be going to the front lines in Vietnam, it did not take me long to decide right then and there that this sounded a whole lot better. I signed all of their papers seeking this W.H.C.A. assignment quickly...before they could change their minds!

It was amazing how much easier Basic Training got from that point on...knowing that no matter how bad my day was, I was going to the White House instead of Vietnam. Long, hot marches, gas chamber training and being shot at in the infiltration courses were suddenly a lot easier to deal with.

I finished up Basic and began my 8-weeks of Switchboard Training. It was a breeze! I did graduate in the top 5% of my class and the last day of school, we were given our orders for our next duty stations.

When I got mine and started looking them over... I was shocked!! My orders were for Germany!! Well, the last time I had looked at a map, the White House was still in Washington, DC...not Germany! Wouldn't you know...if anything could go wrong, it would happen to a fellow from Altamonte Springs, Florida!!

I had been given a number to call COLLECT in case I had any problems, so I couldn't wait to get to a phone to make my call. When the Ft. Gordon base operator answered the phone, I said, "I want to make a COLLECT CALL to the White House." When she stopped laughing, she said, "Yeah, sure, soldier, everyone wants to call the White House COLLECT!" I finally convinced her I knew what I was doing and we got the call through.

I told the people in W.H.C.A. I had orders to go to Germany! They assured me the White House had not been moved and they would get the mistake straightened out very soon.

Well, I don't know whether you've ever had to deal with the government in trying to straighten out ANYTHING, but if you have, you know it doesn't happen very fast! So I had my serious doubts! I was pleasantly surprised the next day when I had new orders to report to Washington, DC.

My TSC had not come through yet and I wasn't going to be able to report directly to the White House without it. I spent a couple of days in a small post in Suitland, Maryland... U.S.A.S.E.S.C.S. Don't ask me what it stands for but I remember those were the initials for it! I also remember it had great food cooked by civilian chefs and the best, richest chocolate milk I ever drank!

Shortly thereafter, I moved into the barracks at Ft. Myer, Virginia across the Potomac River from DC. I had my own private room and could see the Arlington National Cemetery, Potomac River, the White House, Pentagon, Lincoln Memorial and Washington Monument from my room.

I was assigned to the headquarters office building of Defense Communications Agency (DCA). I worked there as a Xerox copy machine operator until I received my TSC. They sent me to a special Xerox Training Course to learn to clean and change the photographic drums and other maintenance duties. I was running approximately 5,000 copies a day on two Xerox 914 copiers. A lot of what I was copying was Top Secret material even though I didn't yet have my TSC.

During the time I waited for my TSC to come through, I had two part-time jobs. I worked for a while in a bank sorting checks and I worked at McDonald's cooking hamburgers and fries. You'd be surprised how fast you can cook three dozen hamburgers! (I read somewhere recently that one out of every five adults in America had worked for McDonald's sometime in their lives.) It was a great work experience!

After six months of waiting for my TSC to come through, someone finally called me from WHCA. They were having trouble figuring out why there was a difference on my birth certificate between the date of my birth and the date the certificate was actually recorded ten weeks later.

I told them of my adoption and explained why the birth certificate had been re-issued. I said, "Why did it matter? What did you think I was doing at ten weeks of age? A little diaper espionage!?" I got my TSC the next day.

I was told to report to the security people in the Executive Office Building (E.O.B.) next door to the White House. They took my picture and issued me a photo ID pass to get in and out of the White House each day. I HAD FINALLY ARRIVED!

VIEW OF WHITE HOUSE FROM PENNSYLVANIA AVENUE
Photo by Gwen Knight

It was exciting to report to work in the White House each day and I was in and out of there as easily as you go in and out of your own home, office or school. For a while, I had to show my ID but after I had been there a couple of weeks, the guards got to know me and didn't even ask to see it.

I became good friends with one of the guards and he got me started selling Cutco knives. Ed and I went out demonstrating knives to single ladies and couples all over greater Washington and Virginia. I sold quite a few sets. They are great knives and I still have a set in my home I use every day.

It took the first few days on the White House switchboard to learn the names and code names of all the people for whom I would have to answer the phone. It didn't take long to learn it all and to learn how to operate the board. In addition to running the regular board to handle calls for military staff, etc., we also had to keep up with the Police Board. On that board, the policemen who guarded the White House grounds had to call in to us every 15 minutes to let us know at which post they were stationed and to record their movements.

The communications center where I worked was located under the White House and behind foot-thick bomb-proof doors. These doors were guarded by surveillance cameras and cipher locks. One night while I was on duty, there was a frantic call from the phone at one of the entrances to the Comm. Center. The President was trying to get in to show someone around. The aide who was with him had forgotten the code for that day and could not get the door open. I ran up there to get the door opened quickly and came face-to-face with a very embarrassed President.

In case of an attack on the White House, the President and First Family would be able to seek shelter and safety and have uninterrupted communications lines to the rest of the world. During the time I worked at the White House I discovered the famous RED PHONE to Moscow was NOT a phone at all...but a TWX (teletype) link.

I could call anywhere in the world free. I would call back to Florida and talk to my family and old girlfriends every day or so. I also had a friend in Weisbaden, Germany. She lived for a while at the Amelia Earhart Hotel so when I worked midnights I would call her at about midnight DC time...which would be about 7:00 AM Germany time...and give her a wake up call. I spoke to her for several months. One night while I was on duty, one of the guards called me on the switchboard to say there was someone at the gate asking for me. I went outside and was pleasantly surprised to finally get to meet my friend from Germany. We sat and talked for an hour or so and then she had to catch a flight to somewhere.

Those were adventurous times working at the White House and getting to travel all over the country with the President and the First Family. I was able to go to South America in 1967 when President Johnson went down there for a Peace Conference. I spent two weeks in Paramaribo, Surinam, which was the refueling stop for Air Force One on its way to Punta del Este, Uruguay. It was a beautiful country and I met a lot of nice people while I was there.

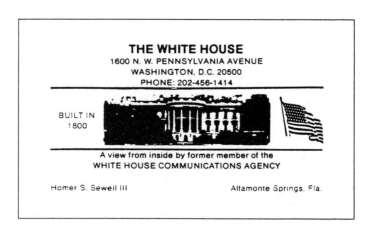

THE WHITE HOUSE
1600 N. W. PENNSYLVANIA AVENUE
WASHINGTON, D.C. 20500
PHONE: 202-456-1414

BUILT IN
1800

A view from inside by former member of the
WHITE HOUSE COMMUNICATIONS AGENCY

Homer S. Sewell III

Altamonte Springs. Fla.

S U R I N A M E   T O R A R I C A   H O T E L - C A S I N O

Ref.:TH/408/P/WG

Paramaribo, April 26th, 1967

Mr. Homer S. Sewell III,
912 N. Daniel Street,
ARLINGTON, VIRGINIA 22201

Dear Homer:

Thank you so very much for your very nice letter to us all. It
really was very much appreciated and we meant it when we said
it was our pleasure having you all here.

It was so kind and thoughtful of you to send us the label strips
and acetate protectors for our switchboard.

The hotel really seems quiet now after all the excitement but
it was nice that the stop over, although short, was successful.
I think Surinam got a lot of very valuable publicity out of the
occasion.

I must thank you and your boys once again most sincerely for the
wonderful opportunity to speak to my family in England. It was a
great priviledge to be permitted to us such important communication
facilities.

We all send you our warmest best wishes, especially from Evelyn,
Beverley and all using the switchboard. Don't be surprised if half of
Surinam suddenly descends upon you in Orlando.

Very Sincerely,
SURINAME TORARICA HOTEL CASINO

BILL PULLEN
GENERAL MANAGER

THE WHITE HOUSE

WASHINGTON

October 27, 1965

Dear Colonel Albright:

I want to say how grateful I am for your efforts on my behalf at
Bethesda.

The medical men took the spotlight, but I am aware and apprecia-
tive of those in the wings whose hard work made my stay so much
easier.

It is always reassuring to know that I can count on your talents
and your loyalty, no matter what the pressure of events.

Well done.

Sincerely,

/s/

LYNDON B. JOHNSON

Colonel Jack A. Albright
Commanding Officer
White House Communications Agency
The White House
Washington, D. C.

WHCA

1 November 1965

MEMORANDUM TO: All Personnel, WHCA

All Personnel, DCSU

SUBJECT: Letter of Appreciation

The attached letter was received from the President of the United States expressing his appreciation for our support during his stay at the Bethesda Naval Medical Center.

I wish to add to the remarks of the President and express my personal thanks for the highly professional and efficient job each of you perform within these organizations to enable us to support the President in this manner.

Letters of thanks such as the attached should give each of you a warm feeling and a greater incentive to continue your efforts to make these units outstanding in their communications support for the President of the United States and the Staff of the White House.

1 Incl

JACK A. ALBRIGHT
Colonel,   USA
Commanding

December 14, 1965

MEMORANDUM TO ALL WHITE HOUSE PERSONNEL:

The President and Mrs. Johnson invite the members of the White House staff for a Christmas Party at 6:30 o'clock on Friday, December 17th.

The enclosed admit card should be signed and presented along with your pass (White House, E. O. B., or military) to the police officers on duty in the mansion. Unfortunately, because of the large number of people invited, we regret that we are unable to include husbands and wives of White House personnel.

We are all looking forward to seeing you on the 17th.

Bess Abell
Social Secretary

Please use East Gate.

January 28, 1966

Dear General Starbird:

I would like to take this opportunity to express
my appreciation to Colonel J. A. Albright and
his fine staff of the White House Communications
Agency for the excellent communications support
furnished to me, my military aides, and my Secret
Service staff during 1965.

Please convey my personal thanks for a job well
done to all concerned, particularly the officers
and men who so ably supported my trip to the
Caribbean this past November.

With best regards.

Sincerely,

/s/

Hubert H. Humphrey

WHITE HOUSE COMMUNICATIONS AGENCY
THE WHITE HOUSE
WASHINGTON, D. C. 20500

WHCA

1 March 1966

SUBJECT: Letter of Appreciation

TO: All Personnel WHCA and DCSU

I am extremely pleased to pass on to all the members of this
Agency the expression of appreciation by the Vice President and Lt
General Starbird.

This recognition is further proof of your devotion and dedication.

It is a privilege to serve the leaders of our country, and a great
honor to be praised by them. Let's keep up the good work.

JACK A. ALBRIGHT
Colonel,   USA
69 Commanding

October 11, 1967

TO WHOM IT MAY CONCERN

This is to commend to you Mr. Homer S. Sewell, III, who
served at the White House from March 1965 to May 1967.

Mr. Sewell consistently demonstrated outstanding professional
ability in an unusually sensitive and, at times, most difficult
job. His tact, willingness to work long hours, and energetic
approach to each task were most exemplary. His cheerful and
willing manner engendered a spirit of friendly cooperation
among those with whom he worked. He constantly evidenced
resourcefulness and initiative in his work and, as a result,
received many commendatory comments from members of the
White House staff.

It is my considered opinion that Mr. Sewell would be a valuable
employee and a credit to any employer.

Haywood R. Smith

HAYWOOD R. SMITH
Lieutenant Colonel, U. S. Marine Corps
Marine Corps Assistant to the
Armed Forces Aide to the President

DCOU-A   11 October 1967

To Whom It May Concern:

Homer S. Sewell III was a member of my command during the period
25 March 1965 to 12 May 1967. During this time he worked in the Communications Branch of my unit. Mr. Sewell always presented a neat
appearance and was a willing, efficient worker. He has an outward
disposition and is able to put people at ease and develop loyalties
easily.

While assigned under my command, Mr. Sewell was required to
travel widely and meet highly-placed military and civilian, communications and embassy personnel. Many times during these situations he
was required to work under extreme pressure. At all times he reacted
calmly and was able to meet these conditions head-on and perform at
maximum efficiency. I have received many favorable plaudits, com-
mending Mr. Sewell for his performance.

I would welcome Mr. Sewell back under my command and without
reservation would endorse him for his future employment.

JAMES E ADAMS
LTC, SigC
Commanding Officer
Defense Communications Operations Unit

Trips were always something to look forward to because we traveled in style with any of the First Family. Wherever they went...we were there too. On at least one trip, I stayed at the Waldorf Astoria Hotel in New York City for only $5 a night! That was the White House rate and I was being reimbursed TDY (Temporary Duty Assignment) pay for all my lodging and meals. I was able to visit parts of the world I wouldn't have otherwise been able to...at the expense of the government.

Even if one of the President's daughters or Mrs. Johnson wanted to go on a shopping trip to New York City, some of us went with them...in case they needed to call back to the White House.

I still have a baby blue Princess telephone one of the New York City telephone people gave me for a souvenir of a trip there with Lady Bird or one of the girls.

One trip I took was to the LBJ Ranch in Texas for two weeks of training on the ranch switchboard. I was disappointed in the size of the ranch house. I had expected the President to have some enormous house but it really wasn't that big. If the Pedernales River in front of the ranch was up very high you couldn't drive over the low-water bridge and would have to take a helicopter across.

I also took several trips to Chicago when President Johnson went there to visit his friend, Mayor Daley. It definitely was a cold, windy city!

I went on a trip to Billings, Montana and after we were there for several days we were told to pack it up and come on back to Washington. The President had changed his mind and cancelled the trip.

Here is a story I wrote while stationed at the White House.

TRIP TO DULLES

One evening I took a drive out to the new Dulles International Airport.

At the time this was one of the world's most modern, technologically advanced airports and I was very impressed with what I saw.

Driving off the nice, big, smooth highway we stopped beside a small entrance gate and took a ticket out of a machine which had automatically printed the date and time on it. It read 2349 hours, January 1, 1965. The gate swung open and we drove into the spacious parking lot. We had no trouble finding a parking place near the front of the huge terminal building.

There was a very light snow falling as my friends from church, Dave, Karyl, Clara and I walked into the terminal building. We walked up a concrete ramp and then rode an escalator up to the main floor. After we stepped off the escalator, I looked up at a large board in front of me. Flight numbers, arrival and departure times were being posted automatically on the board. Every minute there was a "click-click" and the time was changing on a four-position, rectangular, modern clock.

On the runway side of the building there were approximately 30 gates for arrivals and departures of passengers. At each gate was a board overhead showing arrival and departure schedules and over the intercom system a voice was heard clearly stating the same information.

The building was truly ULTRA-MODERN in every respect! There were beautifully designed glass windows everywhere. If one became tired of standing, there were comfortable chairs throughout the building.

We walked into a large area which protruded from the main building out to the control tower. We sat down in comfortable lounge chairs and looked out onto the runways with all their blue and white lights. There was a plane taxiing in on the long jet runway to the ramp area about a half-mile from the control tower. We walked out to the observation deck to watch. There were coin-operated binoculars mounted along the wall ledge for those who were specific curiosity seekers.

As we stood watching the airplane taxi and stop in the distance, I was suddenly aware that this was only the second time in my whole life I had seen snow. As the four of us stood there under the enormous control tower which towered 250 feet above us, I couldn't help but think of how marvelous everything looked. It was cold, but not too cold; there were thousands of sparkling blue lights all along the runways; everything was quiet and peaceful in the black of the night with soft white snow all around us. It was very refreshing! This was in so many ways different from the warm ocean breezes I had known so well in sunny Florida. We just stood there for a few moments admiring this part of GOD'S BEAUTIFUL WORLD!

After about ten minutes, we returned to the inside. As the warm air hit us, we shook off all the remaining snow and turned our thoughts to Gate 8 where a mobile lounge car was just arriving from the plane that had landed a few minutes earlier. About 50 people walked out of the car into the terminal...men and women in Army, Air Force, Navy and Marine uniforms; boys and girls. Businessmen officially visiting DC hurried through with their briefcases at their sides. They had all enjoyed a pleasant trip and their feet had not touched ground since they boarded the plane.

We decided to get a closer look at the mobile lounge (ML) after it had unloaded its passengers. As we stepped into the vehicle, our feet sank into a luxurious bright red carpet. The ML had black leather chairs and had a seating capacity of 72 passengers with room for 19 more to stand, if necessary.

As luck would have it, the driver, wearing his Dulles Airport uniform, asked if we would like to come aboard and look around. We were delighted to be given the opportunity and for the next forty minutes we were conducted on a "first class tour" of this magnificent vehicle. It was a mobile lounge (ML) used to take passengers from the terminal to their planes and vice-versa, no matter what the weather might be, in comfort and ease. The passengers needed only to walk about a hundred feet from the ticket office to the ML and then be transported to their planes.

The agent-driver explained to us that Dulles is the only one of its kind in the world. They had 22 MLs like this one we were exploring and each one cost approximately $225,000. They were powered by two eight-cylinder Chrysler engines...one at the front and one at the rear of the 60 foot vehicle. They travel between 20 and 30 MPH and with a control booth at each end of the car, they don't have to turn around on the runway. The car was even equipped with soft music coming out of the intercom system. The driver could talk to the passengers or to the control tower via a two-way radio. There were even outside speakers. The ML was air conditioned by a large system which would keep it quite comfortable in the summer months.

There were two ramps at the rear of the ML which could be automatically maneuvered up, down or from side to side to perfectly reach the passenger door of any aircraft. All a passenger had to do is step out of the ML directly into a waiting plane or to step from the plane to the ML and relax as he/she is taken to the terminal. There is even a specially designed wheelchair for terminal-to-airplane-seat transportation for anyone needing that service. The ML was a fantastically ultra-modern convenience in all respects. As we left the ML we thanked the driver for his time and interest.

We were quite wide-eyed and thrilled as we took the escalator down to the ground floor and walked to the front door. The cold night air roused us once more and as we were heading for the car I noticed a snowball (that had obviously missed its mark) on the ground. Never having thrown a snowball, the temptation was too great and I hurled it at Dave. War was declared and I headed for the car. I arrived just as a cold, wet snowball found its mark on the back of my head. With much laughter, we managed to get into the car and headed for the exit gate.

Even though it seemed like such a short time, we had been in the airport for one hour and fifteen minutes. The man at the gate charged us fifty cents and away we went.

On the return trip home, our thoughts were still centered around the beautiful Dulles Airport and I couldn't help but say, "If I ever fly home or anywhere, I would surely like to begin the trip at Dulles International Airport".

When I first got to the White House, I started having trouble with my stomach. I went to the doctor's office there in the White House to see what was wrong. I remember sitting down in the reception area next to a very attractive young lady. I started flirting a little with her and then in a few minutes, she got up and went in to see the doctor. When I finally was called in, I asked the doctor why the young lady had been called in ahead of me since I had been waiting the longest. The doctor told me it was Luci Bird Johnson...the President's youngest daughter. I had been flirting with the President's daughter and didn't even recognize her! She was much prettier in person than on the TV. I never did get a date with her!

I was dating a lot of different girls I met either at church or through working at the White House. I was seeing a lady named Marty who worked at the F.B.I. switchboard and then met her sister, Sally.

We started dating in 1965, developed a serious relationship and set a wedding date for August of 1966. We got married in her hometown of New Castle, Pennsylvania.

In January of 1966 my grandfather died at the age of 84. He had been active in real estate in Altamonte Springs for almost 40 years. He was well known for his bright red cars as he sped around town selling homes and lots. One of his favorite stories he used to tell all newcomers in the area was about the man who died and knocked at St. Peter's gate. When the gate was opened, St. Peter asked him where he was from and when the man answered "Altamonte Springs", St. Peter bid him enter but said, "If you're from Altamonte Springs, you won't like it here!"

In May of 1967, when my enlistment was up, I was told there would be no guarantees any of us would be able to stay at the White House. I decided not to re-enlist. I got out of the service and my wife of nine months and I moved to Altamonte Springs, Florida. We bought our first house there on Hermit's Trail.

Florida Gas Company was saving a job for me and I returned to work in their accounting department in the Winter Park headquarters office. After a few months with them I could see I wasn't going anywhere very fast so I started looking for something else.

HOMER IN HIS YOUNGER DAYS WITHOUT A BEARD

W. J. BOWEN
PRESIDENT

June 23, 1967

Dear Homer:

On July 2, 1967, you will attain your fifth anniversary as a Florida Gas employee. Your loyal service has been appreciated, and I want to take this opportunity to offer my personal congratulations.

We are certainly pleased that you elected to return to Florida Gas after recently completing your military obligation, as we feel that your experiences during the last several years will be of value in your company career.

I have always been very proud of the high caliber men and women who represent Florida Gas Company. You have contributed much by your hard work, cooperation and interest in the future of our Company. These are the principal ingredients so necessary for our progress and prosperity.

As our Company grows, we will always have a place for capable and ambitious individuals. Our policy always has been to promote from within, whenever possible, so I urge you to learn as much as possible about our Company operations and the gas industry so that you may be considered for further advancements.

It has been a pleasure working with you.

Sincerely,

W. J. Bowen

Mr. Homer Sewell
Post Office Box 265
Altamonte Springs, Florida

Chapter 6

Jobs...Jobs...Jobs

I was doing a lot of different things there in New Salem...storekeeping, postmaster, surveying and blacksmithing...nothing very successfully.

In 1832 I decided to get into a little politicking in Illinois. I ran for state legislature. I lost! But I still didn't give up. I ran again in '34, '36, '38 and '40...four consecutive terms and I won. And I was a good, "HONEST" politician. Something we need MORE of in Washington these days!

I've had a lot of different types of jobs during my lifetime...the longest I spent at any one place was with Sears Roebuck & Company and with Big Canoe Resort...each for five and one-half years. I thought it might be interesting for you to see the wide and varied types of things I have been involved in. Most of it has been sales or sales management. Some of these have been successful and MANY of them have been failures. But, how would I have known if they would work IF I NEVER TRIED!! I never gave up!

JOBS LISTING FOR 35 YEARS...

Accounting, advertising sales, author

Babysitting, bagging groceries, bakery, board games designing, business card sales, bus sales

Calculator sales, camper sales, car sales, chocolate sales, clerical

Display panel sales/manufacturing

Encyclopedia sales

Fire extinguisher sales, freight company sales

Game room operation

Home sales, household products (MLM-x3)

Insurance sales (MLM, Multi-level marketing)

JSB portable phone sales

Knife sales, Kathy's Kandy & Gifts

Line server in cafeteria, log home sales

Magazine sales, McDonald's hamburgers, microfilm equipment sales, mini-emergency kit sales

Name tag sales/manufacturing

Owner/operator 4-wheeler race track

Phone answering machine sales, pizza operation, portraying ABE, printing shop, pumping gas

Quartz clock sales/mfg

Real estate office management

School desks sales, security systems sales, sewing machine sales, skating rink owner/operator, sorting checks at bank, storeroom manager, storm shutter sales, substitute teacher, systems manager

T-shirt design/sales, Terra Jet sales, theater operator/owner, time share sales, tour bus operator

U.S. Army, White House Communications Agency

Vacuum cleaner sales

Water filter sales (MLM)

Xerox copier operations

Yard work, mowing and raking

Zwieback toast sales, Nabisco

AS YOU CAN SEE, I'VE GONE FROM A TO Z...

If you believe in something strongly enough and think you might be able to make it work...then try it!! Give it 110% to TRY to make it work. If after six months or so, you can't make it work, then go on to something else with the satisfaction of knowing you at least tried your best! Always remember there are lots of people out there who would never have tried at all!!

In September of 1967 I left Florida Gas and went to work in sales for Nabisco. I started my training in the Orlando area. I will never forget the man who helped train me in the Orlando area stores. His name was Pete Blanco. Pete had been with Nabisco for several years and he really knew his way around. We became good friends and I still run into him once and a while. We had some good times together stocking shelves in those Orlando grocery stores. After several months of training, I was given my own territory in Ft. Myers, Florida. I had over 100 stores to sell and stock with cookies and crackers. I had a company car and was making a whopping $12,000 a year. I was really rolling now!

My favorite stores to call on were on Sanibel Island at Bailey's General Store and the Bee Hive and the Little Store on Captiva Island. Every Wednesday the company paid the $3 toll for me to take my little trip to "paradise". We sold a lot of cookies during the winter months but during the summer months my business on the islands died. I enjoyed those trips to the shell gathering capital of the world. If you've never taken a vacation to Sanibel or Captiva Island, you should plan do so. You can fly into the airport at Ft. Myers.

On August 2, 1968 we had our first child, Homer S. Sewell IV. We called him "CHIP" for Chip off the old block or the Chips Ahoy cookies I was selling. My father was still living so there were three Homer Sewells running around.

I recently came across a letter dated September 4, 1968 from my Nabisco District Manager, Harvey Alexander. I won't bore you with the whole letter but he ended it by saying, "Keep up the fine sales job you are doing. P.S. Hope the baby, Homer Simmons, IV, is doing fine. Or, I should say "Chip". We suggest you not let him start putting up stock until he is a little older. Some fathers start this training at about one year, but it is a little hard for them to reach the top shelf. So don't rush it. Ha! Ha!"

I would walk into a big Publix or other large grocery store and there would be my order waiting for me to price, rotate and put on the shelves. You don't realize how many cookies there are in a store until you face a stack 60 feet long and six feet tall!! When I first started, I was pigging-out on cookies. I could sample whatever I wanted to...and I did just that! Pete had told me there would come a time when I wouldn't be able to decide what I wanted to eat. He was right! Within a few weeks of sampling everything Nabisco baked, I couldn't eat any more! I had seen too many cookies!

After a year of being a glorified stock boy, I had enough of cookie selling and shelf-stocking. I went looking for a job with Sears.

SEARS, ROEBUCK AND CO.

HOMER SEWELL, III
Manager
Sewing Machines & Vacuums

Altamonte Mall
POB 20008
Orlando, Fla. 32894
Phone: 830-1616

thank you for shopping at Sears

I started with Sears in the Edison Mall in Ft. Myers selling sewing machines and vacuum cleaners. Within six months I was their Number One Salesman and became the Department

Manager at about $18,000 a year. Our department was consistently in the top three or four in the nation of all the Sears stores of the same size.

I learned a lot about servicing sewing machines and vacuum cleaners so customers with minor problems wouldn't have to leave their equipment in the service department to be repaired. I had a lot of happy customers and my five salespeople and I got along beautifully together. We worked hard, but we had fun, too.

One of my salesmen was a man by the name of Bob Lyons and Bob always kept us in stitches... literally. Ha! Ha! Stitches! Sewing machines! Get it?

Have you ever seen someone do "LIVE MANNEQUIN"? I would stand perfectly still on top of one of our canister vacuum cleaners. Bob and my other salespeople would come over and dust me off once in a while...as if I were a real mannequin. We were trying to get the attention of the customers who were passing by and we did!

One day someone took a picture of me standing on top of a vacuum and sent it to our Atlanta office to Bobby Sullivan, my Regional Manager. His reply was, "Just think what you could do if you moved!" Bobby definitely believed we should be grabbing the customers off the aisles to show them what we had to sell in our department! Bobby was NOT impressed!

One weekend, about 15 young people stood in front of me for 20 minutes or so...just staring at me. I never moved! They all agreed..."Oh! It's just a dummy...a mannequin". As they all headed out into the mall about 30 feet away, one of the girls turned around for one last look. I couldn't stand it any longer so I gave her a big WINK. She about died! "He's alive! He's real!" she screamed.

I want to share a lesson I learned with salespeople everywhere. My store manager, Mr. Richards, came by one time and asked me why we didn't have any customers in the department looking at our sewing machines and vacuum cleaners. I said, "There aren't any buyers in the store! They are all just looking!"

Boy, was that the wrong thing to say to a 30-year Sears Manager! He marched me over to the mall entrance door and had a long talk with me. He said, "Homer, I am going to give you two boxes of buttons. One of these boxes contains buttons that say in big letters...LOOKER and the other box contains buttons that say in big letters...BUYER".

"I want you to stand here at this main entrance and stop everyone who comes into our store. I want you to ACCURATELY pin one of these buttons on them. Then all of the salespeople throughout the store will know which ones might need help and which ones to avoid!" I GOT THE POINT AND IN ALL MY YEARS OF SELLING, I HAVE NEVER FORGOTTEN IT.

LESSON TO BE LEARNED HERE IS: There is no way to judge a book by its cover! We don't ever know whether someone is a buyer or just a looker. Lookers may be converted to buyers if we are friendly enough to them, knowledgeable about our products and can show them how our product/service will benefit them. All people are potential buyers! Don't ever forget this valuable lesson if you want to be a successful salesperson.

Chapter 7

More Jobs

One day, while I was storekeeping, a family stopped by my store. They said they were heading out west and their wagon was so loaded down with goods that there was barely enough room for the family. They told me this one barrel was really in their way and wanted to know if I would give them 50 cents for it and get it off their wagon. I finally agreed to do so.

I stuck the barrel over there in the back of the store because I didn't have time to worry about it right then. I later discovered a complete set of law books, "BLACKSTONE'S COMMENTARIES ON LAW", in the bottom of the barrel. The more I read and studied those books, the more excited I got. This looked like something for me to give some serious thought to.

While I was in management with Sears in Ft. Myers I decided to get into the all-terrain vehicle business. I had seen an ad in a magazine for an all-terrain vehicle that looked like something I could sell in South Florida. In 1972 I bought the franchise for Florida and Georgia for Terra Jet, a four-wheel drive vehicle that would go anywhere...including into the water. I flew up to Drummondville, Quebec, Canada to the factory and I really liked what I saw. I took out a loan at the bank, bought 18 Terra Jets and set up a sales office near the airport.

The Terra Jets were fun to drive. I had approximately $1,200 in them by the time I got them delivered from the Canadian factory and I sold them for $1,800 each.

SEWELL & SON MOTORS & SPORTS

Florida-Georgia Distributor
Terra Jet & MP Camper

P.O. BOX 6426
606 DANLEY DRIVE
FT. MYERS, FLA.
33901

HOMER S. SEWELL III
OWNER-MANAGER
BUS. (813)-939-1365
RES. (813)-936-0314

One evening I was demonstrating the vehicle to a young couple who were interested in buying one. I showed them how easily it climbed in and out of a big drainage ditch near my office. Then I got out to let the husband drive. That was my first mistake! He didn't know you had to be careful not to let water run over the back-end and into the engine compartment. He tried to climb out of this steep water-filled ditch front-end first. When he did, the back-end was left in the water and the engine compartment quickly filled up.

I got the family out of the vehicle and stood there on the edge of the ditch watching my new Terra Jet sink. MY HEART SANK WITH IT! I NEEDED THAT SALE! I went back to the office, got my new Ford pickup truck and a big rope. I hooked the rope to the Terra Jet and pulled it onto dry land. I drained the water, pulled the spark plugs, dried and replaced them and it started right up. Needless to say, I didn't sell that couple a vehicle!

Sports Car Likened to Goat, Mud Turtle or Desert Fox

Terra Jet is like a sure-footed mountain goat, bear, mud turtle, sea lion and desert fox all rolled into one.

Its a new four-wheel drive sports vehicle designed to cross the deepest ponds, gooiest muck, shiftiest and and thicket palmetto patch and Homer Sewell of Grove Avenue is the newly appointed distributor for the vehicle in Florida and Georgia.

Sewell, just 29 but a salesman with several years experience, first saw the Terra Jet at a recreational vehicle show last fall and decided it was a car for Florida sportsmen. He has named his business Sewell & Son Motors and has located offices at 606 Danley Drive in Page Park.

"People are almost as curious of the name as they are the vehicle," he said last week. "Actually my four-year-old son is my partner."

Besides being the owner of the Fort Myers Terra Jet agency, Sewell, as the Florida-Georgia distributor, is establishing agencies in several parts of the two states and so far has set up agencies in Naples for Collier County and in Orlando. In about two weeks the first shipments will begin arriving and already 15 have been sold.

"Its the darndest thing I've ever seen," Sewell said. "One day I drove the demonstrator down a boat ramp at a marina into the Caloosahatchee River. It floats fine and the big cleated wheels will move it forward in the water about three miles an hour and about six miles an hour in reverse."

The upper part of the body is fiberglass but the underneath is steel which completely encloses the drive train, motor and transmission. The engine is a 28 horsepower, air cooled one that get about 45 miles to a gallon of gas. The driver's seat is the middle of three side-by-side bucket seats.

Sewell said he also is offering a camper that matches the Terra Jet and it will go anywhere the car can go. Even if the going gets wet, the camper floats along behind.

"All the driver does is step on the gas and the car goes," Sewell said. "It has an automatic transmission and constant four-wheel drive that'll scoot it along at 45 miles an hour."

Terra Jet has a fault. It won't pass Florida's vehicle inspection because of its plexiglass windshield so it can't be driven on the streets.

"'But that's being corrected. This fall the new models will have a safety glass windshield that meets Florida law and we will have the windshields available to put on the older models," Sewell said.

"In the meantime when someone wants a demonstration ride we go through the canal behind Page Field, jump the railroad tracks and head out in the woods."

Homer Sewell drives his Terra Jet through a drainage canal behind Page Field to a campsite. The camper goes along behind anywhere he decides to take the recreational vehicle. Sewell is the Florida and Georgia distributor for the $1,800 car.

It took me a while to sell those 18 units. I even delivered one with a trailer all the way to Hattiesburg, Mississippi. I finally decided this was not a good part-time business to be in.

Unfortunately, Sally and I were having problems, and in 1973 we were divorced.

I left Ft. Myers and moved back to Altamonte Springs. I was home again. I opened up a new Sears store in the Altamonte Mall, as the sewing machine and vacuum cleaner department manager.

My new store manager was Dan F. Holley and you just don't find a finer man to work for anywhere! It was a pleasure and a privilege to work for a man of such character, integrity and knowledge of the retail business. He was also a man who was very close to his wife, Bess, and their children, Debbie, Danny and David. They are the "Ideal American Family". (As of the time we are going to press, Dan and his sons are running a very successful residential contracting company in Columbus, Georgia. Dan is very active with the Columbus area and Georgia State Home Builders Associations.)

I stayed for another year in the retail business and then decided it was enough for me so I left Sears in search of something different to do.

For a while I tried a lot of different types of selling: phone answering machines, security systems, engraved plates for doors and desks, (I still have my own Scott Engraving Machine), magazine advertising, T-shirts and a MINI EMERGENCY KIT I sold for $1. It had 50 items crammed into a 35-mm film can: things like a safety pin, a dime for a phone call, water purification tablets, hook & line, matches, aspirin and other items you would need in an emergency.

In 1974 I was selling advertising for Sunshine Artists Magazine and as I went around to art shows I noticed the lack of good display systems. I decided there was a market for lightweight, portable and easily assembled display panels. I made some inquiries with aluminum suppliers in the Orlando area and started a business I called A.I.M. FIXTURES. The name stood for Aluminum-Intergrated-Modular and that was just what they were. I started manufacturing and selling them from my home in Forest City, Florida.

In September of 1974, I met a nurse named Kathy as I was going by bus from Orlando to Ft. Myers. Kathy was from New York and was living in Memphis, Tennessee at the time. She was on the way to see her parents who lived in Punta Gorda, Florida. We visited on that bus trip for about three hours and I decided I wanted to get to know her better.

We called and wrote each other constantly. The phone bills were getting bigger and bigger. I even wrote love letters to her with my sewing machines at Sears...monogramming on long pieces of starched demo material. She invited me to spend the upcoming Thanksgiving holidays with her and her family in Memphis. I cooked Thanksgiving dinner for her twin sister, Paula and Paula's husband, Dave and her nieces: Susie and Jennifer. I even went to work with Kathy one midnight shift so we could see each other during the night. We had some great times together!

When she came down to Florida for Christmas, I gave her an engagement ring and we set a wedding date for Valentine's Day, February 14, 1975. We got married in a small, old chapel in Altamonte Springs and bought a house in Forest City just a few miles from Altamonte Springs.

SINGER/FRIDEN
BUSINESS MACHINES

HOMER S. SEWELL III
Sales Representative

SALES AND SERVICE   305-851-2530
1933 PREMIER ROW, ORLANDO, FLORIDA   32809

At the time, I was selling calculators for Singer-Friden all over the Orlando area. It was strictly on a commission basis. The home office was in Tampa. I was calling on stores all over Central Florida trying to sell my calculators. There was a lot of stiff competition and sales were not good. I ended up having to sue the owner to get all of my commissions. That was a bad experience!

In October of 1975, I was driving down I-4 in Orlando when I heard a Public Service Announcement asking for volunteers to talk to school students about any subject of interest. I called to ask if they had anyone talking to students about the White House. I was told they did not but would like me to do so. My intention was to talk to students about my personal experiences working the switchboard for the Johnson Administration. About that time, I started growing a beard and the students started calling me ABE. So began a 19-year portrayal of our country's greatest president, as I took ABE part-time to school children all over Central Florida.

At the same time I was selling calculators and display equipment, I was getting into designing T-shirts. Since Kathy is a nurse, we designed one for nurses..."LOVE A NURSE, PRN". We sold over 12,000 of them from 1975 to 1977 through stores all over the country. For a long time we were buying the shirts and working day and night, with two presses we had bought, pressing transfers onto them. Then I found a company in Alabama that could sell us the shirts with the imprint already on them...and cheaper, too. That helped a lot!

One valuable lesson I learned was you should always shop around before you make decisions about buying anything. I've said for years that anytime you are thinking about spending over $100 for an item, shop the price at least three places. We really started saving a lot of time and money after we discovered that company in Alabama.

We were getting real creative with designs and I have

copyrights on about a dozen designs for T-shirts and board games. I have made designs for dentists, pilots, pharmacists, a ruby mine in Franklin, North Carolina and others. My most popular shirt has been the one for nurses. Those of you who know a nurse or the family of a nurse might want to order one (or several) for them. Please see information about this shirt at the back of the book.

I have always loved the mountains so in 1976 we sold our home in Forest City and moved to Franklin, North Carolina. We bought a two and one-half acre homesite on top of a 3,500 foot mountain just outside of town. I then proceeded to build our dream home.

Kathy was working in town at the Angel Community Hospital. In early 1977, when she was about six or seven months pregnant, I dropped her off at the doctor's office for her weekly visit. I left to run some errands. When I came back to the doctor's office, the receptionist said the doctor needed to see me with Kathy. I sat down not knowing what he might have to say to us. They had done some X-rays and he wanted us to know we were going to have TWINS. Well, I had always heard women were the ones to carry the twinning capability but it usually skipped a generation. Kathy is a twin and it wasn't skipping anything with us! We were excited and couldn't wait to call our parents to tell them the DOUBLE good news.

That same day the doctor was seeing another patient and was holding one of those sound-amplifying devices so you can hear the babies' heart beat...a fetal heart monitor...on the tummy of a very pregnant woman. All of a sudden...where everyone in the room could hear it..."Come on good buddy!"...came out of the monitor. I guess somebody was outside on their CB radio and the monitor had picked up the signal. What a laugh we had!

On April 5, 1977 Kathy gave birth to our twins, Kimberly Irene and Jason Leon. Mom and the babies were all doing fine and in a couple of days, I took all three from the hospital to our home on top of the mountain.

I kept building the display panels in the basement of our home for a while but ultimately had to rent some warehouse space in town. We were selling them all over the country. I even shipped an order to an artist in Germany. Kathy and I were also still very much in the T-shirt business. The display business was not providing the steady income which we really needed to support our new twins so I finally sold it to a young fellow who worked for me. His name was Mark Kresal and the last I heard he was still in business. If you know of anyone who does art shows and wants a lightweight, all-aluminum display system, please have them call Mark Kresal with A.I.M. FIXTURES in Franklin, NC.

Kathy and I decided we would open up a candy store in Franklin. We found an empty shop next to the courthouse and opened..."KATHY'S KANDY & GIFTS". We bought homemade candy from Mrs. Magnus' Candies in Orlando and had a pretty good operation going. I probably ate up a lot of the profits because I love any type of candy. We had great candies but it was not making us enough money to live on, so after a few months of trying to make it work, we sold the equipment and closed the shop.

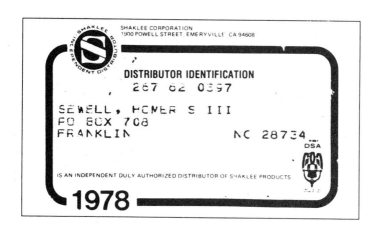

One day when the twins were about three months old, I was playing with them and the phone rang. A fellow from up north had been given my name and number. He started talking to me about becoming a Shaklee Distributor. He wasn't about to hang up the phone until I said yes, so I finally did. All I wanted to do was get him off the phone and go back to playing with my babies. I never did buy or sell any of their products.

LESSON TO BE LEARNED HERE IS: Don't ever let anyone talk you into something over the phone that you have absolutely no interest in doing. Don't ever give your credit card number over the phone to anyone you don't know. It is bad business to do that! There are those out there who could use your credit card numbers to charge all kinds of goods and services to your account! Make sure you know who you are dealing with before you ever give out your credit card number or Social Security number!

When the twins were about six months old, we sold our new house on top of the mountain and moved to Birmingham, Alabama. My brother-in-law, Dave, was the General Sales Manager for a big Toyota dealership and he offered me a job selling cars.

One day after having let several prospects leave the dealership ("walk"), Dave called me into his office and asked me why I hadn't sold them a car. I told him they would "BE BACK"! Dave said, "Homer, do you see the big barrel over there in the corner? That is our 'BE-BACK BARREL'! I want you to go over and stand in the barrel until they return!" The lesson I learned here was a "BE-BACK" was a rare item in the auto business!

I sold new and used cars for Dave for about six months but Alabama and selling cars were NOT for me.

In 1977 my dad was dying of cancer so after six months of living in Birmingham, we moved back to Altamonte Springs. Dad died in January of 1978. I bought the house I had grown up in from Mother. I continued to sell cars at a Toyota dealership in Sanford for a few more months. I made some money but I was not happy with what I was doing.

Please study this little article I wrote in 1978 while I was selling cars. It may save you a lot of those little bills with my (ABE's) picture on them!!

Bear in mind prices have changed a lot in the past 16 years. I am not taking the time now (1994) to update any figures used in this article. Even though the numbers may have changed, the basic ideas presented herein remain the same and will save you a lot of $$ the very next time you buy a vehicle.

C.A.R.S. REPORT (CARS AT REDUCED SPENDING)

WE NEED TO LEARN TO SPEAK THE LANGUAGE FIRST.

The following are some explanations of commonly used terms in the auto business:

A.P.R.: Annual percentage rate. The percentage amount of interest you will pay per year on your borrowed $$. It can be a big factor in what your monthly payments will be and your total $$ to be paid out over the period of the loan.

A & H: Accident & health policy. This will add as much as $200 or more to the total and $5 per month onto your payments. It is an insurance policy which will make your car payments for you if you or your spouse get sick and are unable to work. The dealership makes about 40% off this and the CREDIT LIFE POLICY. You don't need this additional expense unless you feel you might be in the position of not being able to make the payments due to illness.

CREDIT LIFE: An insurance policy to pay off the car loan if you or your spouse should die. Costs $200 or more. If you have adequate other life insurance, don't buy it. If you don't have another life policy that could pay off the car, get it. If you are married and want to leave a paid-off car for your mate, get it. Both CREDIT LIFE and A & H are optional and you don't have to get either one. The F & I man (or woman) or the salesman will automatically try to sell you these extras because he (she) does make money on them. THEY ARE NOT SUPPOSED TO DENY YOU CREDIT IF YOU REFUSE THESE POLICIES.

F & I: Finance and insurance person or business manager are one-in-the-same. His/her job is to sock it to you as much as he can. He usually gets a salary plus a percentage of the profits he earns for the dealership. Watch this person closely!! He will get into your pockets as badly as the salesman if you let him. I have seen the times when the F & I man makes more profit $$ for the dealership than the salesman did!

ACV: Actual cash value of your trade-in. This is the $$ figure the used car manager will put on your trade-in. It will be somewhere near what the black book or wholesale figure on your car is or what your car would be worth to a wholesaler. It is usually right near bank loan value and about $500 to $1,000 UNDER what the car could be retailed for.

DE-HORSE: To take you out of your trade-in car so you can't go around shopping for the best trade-in value at another dealership. Don't let yourself be DE-HORSED until you have looked at at least three lots.

DISCOUNT: The actual $$ reduction from the window sticker price. This will vary greatly from dealer to dealer. They all have to make a fair profit of at least $200 to $300 per car to stay in business. The discount available is directly affected by the amount of MARK UP on the car.

MARK UP: The amount of profit $$ built into the sticker price. It will run from only $200 for a small, bottom-of-the-line car to over $2,000 (or more) for the top-of-the-line loaded with extras. The amount of MARK UP will affect the amount of DISCOUNT a dealer could give you. Most dealers will add the DISCOUNT to the ACV on your trade to make you think you are getting more for your car. This is why it will be a big help for you to know in advance approximately what the ACV of your trade-in is.

TRADING DIFFERENCE: This is the difference in the dealer's sticker price and what he is allowing you for your car.

DRIVE-OUT or BOTTOM LINE $$: This is the figure you pay after TRADE-IN, STATE TAXES, TAG & TITLE, DOCUMENTARY SERVICE FEES, DEALER PREP and all other charges are totaled.

LOW BALL: What a dealer will do to you if he thinks you are going to leave him and go shopping elsewhere. He will give you a DRIVE-OUT or TRADING DIFFERENCE figure he will NOT be able to live with in order to keep you from beating his figures somewhere else. Most reputable dealers will not use this tactic. If you find out you have been LOW BALLED by one dealer, don't listen to his excuses about how he "must have made an error in addition" or whatever. If he will LOW BALL you, then he may get you later, too! Buy from a dealer who is HONEST and FAIR with you.

DEALER PREP: These charges will run from $100 to $300 and are really additional profit $$ built in for the dealer. It is supposed to cover preparing and checking out the car. This is a heavily-padded charge and should be part of the DISCOUNT you ask for.

DOC. SERVICE FEE or OFFICE CHARGES: This again is additional profit for the dealer. It is supposed to cover the cost of the office help doing all the necessary paper work.

STATE TAX & TAG, TITLE FEES: These all go to the

state or county. The dealer does not make any $$ on these charges so don't ask for them to be reduced or removed. Just pay them!

ADDITIONAL WARRANTY POLICIES: They run from $129 to $300 (or more) for up to 50,000 miles and five years coverage. Most are good to have but they are optional. They do add to your monthly payment. Study them carefully and if you feel you want it, you may want to pay for it separately so you don't have to pay interest on it for three to four years. You can usually add it later...up to six months after your purchase.

BUMP: No! This isn't the latest dance! This is when your salesman or his manager will try to get more $$ out of you when you have made an offer to purchase at a price too low for the dealer to make the profit $$ he wants. He may try to BUMP you back up!

DIP or SIDE POP: If you don't have enough $$ for the down payment, the salesman may be able to get you DIPPED or SIDE-NOTED at a local finance company. Watch out for these since their APR is very high. Try to get your own $$ for the DOWN PAYMENT.

DOWN PAYMENT: You will usually need 10 to 15% of the purchase price either in the form of your TRADE-IN or cash. The bank will usually only finance at or below the cost (what the dealer paid for the car) unless your CREDIT is very strong. So if you want to know about how much the car costs the dealer, ask the salesman how much total DOWN PAYMENT you will need to get financed. Subtract that figure from the sticker price and you will know approx. what the vehicle cost the dealer.

CREDIT: You will fill out a credit application to see if the bank will approve the loan for your car. The bank looks at several factors to determine if they want to lend you the money. Among other things: How long have you been on the job? (Six months or longer is good.) How long have you lived at your present address? Amount of income? Do you have a phone in your name? (This is important so if you don't have one, get it before applying for a car loan.) What other debts do you have and do you pay them in a timely fashion? Your auto insurance is a good reference for them to check, too. If you have good credit, work hard at keeping it.

NOW THAT WE HAVE SOME OF THE AUTO JARGON EXPLAINED, LET'S GO BUY YOUR CAR!

If you are going to trade your car, first call your banker and ask him what the wholesale value is on your car. He will be able to give you a rough figure from his NADA or BLACK BOOK. Another method of finding out what your car is worth is to take it to a lot that sells your brand of car. It is best if you go to another lot besides the one you intend to deal with. Tell them you want to sell it outright. Get a figure they will give you for the car right there on the spot. Get two or three of these figures and take an average. This is now your ACV to keep in mind.

The big decision is 'WHAT KIND OF CAR DO I BUY?' Read consumer reports on various autos and ask your friends about their brands of cars: dependability, service, gas mileage, etc. Then go looking and driving. Try out several. Don't get excited about a $15,000 car if you know you won't be able to afford the payments! Don't over-extend yourself on a car payment. Buy what you can really afford now and work your way up to a better one later.

Once you have decided on the type and brand of car you want, then you need to get the best possible price and service on that car. Plan to go to two or three dealers in your area who sell that type of car. Work them against each other.

When you have picked out a particular car, and you have taken it for a test-drive, your salesman will take you in to his desk to see what he can work up for you. DO NOT BE NERVOUS!! BE CALM AND IN COMPLETE CONTROL!! These are your $$ so spend them wisely! If you don't ask for a

DISCOUNT, you won't get it. If the salesman asks you to make a commitment to him about the car, tell him to give you his best price and then you will decide.

If you are trading in your car, you know what your ACV was so see what he is offering you. If you are buying a $10,000 car and your TRADE-IN is paid off and worth $3,000 and he offers to sell you the car for $7,000 then all he is giving you is ACV and NO DISCOUNT!! He will try to do this! Ask him for $500 or $1,000 more for your car. If he is offering you $3,500 for your TRADE-IN and your opinion is your ACV was $3,000, then ask for another $500 anyway. You may not get it all but anything you gain is $$ in your pocket instead of his.

Remember, your salesman is typically on a straight commission of about 25 to 30% of the profit $$ of the car he sells you. His commission will run from a low of $25 to as much as $1,000. So each $100 you get your TRADING DIFFERENCE lowered is approximately $25 out of his pocket.

If it is a straight sale and no trade involved, ask for a 10 to 12% discount from the sticker. You may not get it all but try for as much as possible. Don't show your ignorance by asking for a DISCOUNT for cash! They would rather finance you and make money on the finance charges. Just refer to what you are asking for as a DISCOUNT. It doesn't matter if you are paying cash out of your pocket, getting your own financing or having the dealership get it for you. You can still get a DISCOUNT from sticker price.

No one has to pay full sticker price unless prior to reading this report, you just didn't know you could get a DISCOUNT!

Whatever your salesman offers you for a DISCOUNT, ask for $300 to $500 more! He is going to hold out on you just as long as possible. Almost NO salesman can approve his own deals, so until he gets a manager to approve the deal, you've got nothing firm. Make sure the manager signs the buyer's order when you feel you've gotten your best deal. Tell him you want a copy to take to your credit union or bank to arrange financing. They won't usually give you a copy otherwise.

Now you can take this and go shop other dealers. Tell them you need to beat the price by $200 or you will buy from the other guy. Don't just settle for a $25 or $50 cut by one dealer. That little bit is not worth fussing over and your first salesman could get you that just to save the deal for himself.

If they are going to get your financing for you, call your banker to see what your APR would be with him. Your bank or credit union may be able to give you preferred rates. The cheapest rates are usually borrowing against your savings or CD's if you have them.

When you get face-to-face with your F & I man...BE ALERT! Here is where you can spend some $$ if you aren't careful! Tell him you don't want A & H and CREDIT LIFE, if that's what you decided. If you don't speak up, he will automatically have it added to your contract and you will sign for it before you realize what is happening. Make sure the APR he gives you is as low as your bank could have gotten you. You can KEEP or LOSE from $100 to $750 (or more) right here alone (on A & H, CREDIT LIFE and additional interest). Your monthly payments can be affected by as much as $20 or more.

One other important factor is WHEN TO BUY TO SAVE THE MOST $$? Near the end of the month they will give bigger DISCOUNTS than at the first of the month. You can get better DISCOUNTS at the end of the week and late at night right before closing time.

Whatever the BOTTOM LINE figure is, ask for the next lowest even dollar amount before you sign. For example: if the figure is $8,653.25, ask for it to be a nice rounded figure of $8,600! You can usually get it. Also ask for a tank full of gas before you sign the order. That is another $10-20 in your pocket. Always make sure anything you and your salesman agree to is in writing on the buyers' order and get a copy of everything you sign so there won't be any questions later.

I hope I have given you some facts you didn't know about and you have a more pleasant and rewarding experience the next time you buy a car.

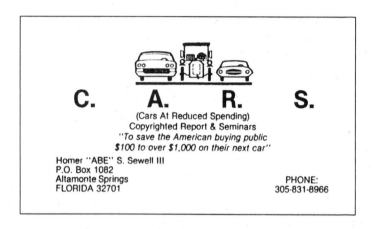

For a few months in 1978 I worked for a trucking company trying to convince businesses all over Central Florida they should use my company to handle their freight needs. It was a hard-sell competitive business to be in and I wasn't making much money at it. I was doing a lot of cold-calling all over Central Florida. For those of you NOT in sales, let me explain what COLD-CALLING means. When you don't have a specific appointment to see someone and you knock on doors hoping to present your wares...that's cold-calling. It is not fun! But, it is a necessary part of being a successful salesman regardless of what your product or service is.

One day while I was helping out in the warehouse, I moved a large, heavy crate of some kind and pulled my first hernia. I was in a lot pain and ultimately had to have my first of five hernia surgeries to repair the damage.

SEWELL ENTERPRISES

the **difficult**
we do
IMMEDIATELY

the **impossible**
takes a little
LONGER

BOARD GAMES.....
DESIGN • DEVELOPMENT •
MANUFACTURING •
DISTRIBUTION

Homer S. Sewell III
P.O. Box 1082,
Altamonte Springs,
Florida 32701
Phone: 305-831-8966

In 1978 while I was recovering from the surgery, I designed and copyrighted a board game about building houses. You play it like Monopoly except instead of buying up properties, you are given a fixed amount of money for a mortgage. The idea of the game is to see who can get their house built first without running out of money. It is a fun game to play and teaches people who have never built a house all about the major steps involved: from buying the land, building foundations, walls, roof, interior, windows, etc...to the landscaping.

I've got a thick file from all the major game companies I sent it to for them to consider manufacturing and marketing. Most big companies will not even look at anything submitted to them unless it comes through a broker they are already working with or their in-house design people. One of these days I will have enough money to have 1,000 of them printed and I will market them myself. It is also a good educational aid. I showed it to a mortgage company in Winter Park, Florida and they said if I ever did get it printed they would buy them to give to people applying for a construction loan so they could see what building a house was all about.

Don't ever give up on something you believe strongly in. I haven't totally written off getting this game marketed. It has just been placed on the BACK-BURNER for a few years while I go on to try other things.

106

I heard about Frank Messina, who had a shutter and window sales/manufacturing business in Longwood. He was looking for a salesman so I talked him into giving me a try. I would drive as much as 100 miles to show people what we had in the line of storm shutters for their homes, mobile homes, patios, etc. I would demo the samples I carried, measure their openings and give them prices. The prices ran from $1,000 to as much as $5,000 and I tried to get them to make a commitment to buy while I was there. I was closing a good percentage of them on the first call. Frank was happy with the job I was doing for him and the company. I liked meeting people in their own homes and showing them a good product at a good price. I worked for Frank off-and-on for several years. Frank, his family, and Polly the office manager, were super nice people to work with and I probably could walk back into Frank's office anytime and start working that same day.

A motto I learned early in sales and have encouraged others to follow is: "NOBODY CARES HOW MUCH YOU KNOW UNTIL THEY KNOW HOW MUCH YOU CARE!!" This is an important thing to remember for anybody in sales or any type of business where you deal with the public. I have always tried to live by this motto and show people that I DO CARE ABOUT THEM.

Custom-Designed
T-Shirts

Handcrafted Cypress
Clocks

Sewell Enterprises
"Call us for fast, personal service"
Wholesale/Retail

HOMER S. SEWELL III
Phone: 305-831-8966

P.O. Box 1082,
Altamonte Springs, FL 32701

In the meantime, I kept selling T-shirts and got into making custom clocks. I made them in cypress slabs and could make them out of almost anything you could think of. I even took business cards, had them photographically enlarged to about 12" x 24" and mounted a quartz clock movement into them. I sold a few of these all around Central Florida and still make clocks for special people out of pictures, posters or whatever. I made one for one of my nieces on the box of her favorite cereal...Fruit Loops.

I also began buying and selling items from the Orange and Seminole County School systems surplus warehouses. I would bid on and buy buses, desks, beds, computer consoles and lots of other items. I have had as many as two or three big, yellow school buses in my back yard at one time. I would buy them for $200 to $600, drive them home, place an ad in the *Truck Trader Magazine* and sell them for as much as $2,000. I didn't have to do anything except put enough gas in them to get to my house.

For those of you looking for a way to make some additional money, you might want to call your local school board and ask to be placed on their bid-mailing list for buses and other vehicles. Also ask them if they have a warehouse where you can buy surplus items. I probably sold over 500 school desks during one busy Christmas season. I bought them for 50 cents or less and sold them for $5. People would take them home, paint them and have a wonderful place for their children to do their homework.

Remember, what is one person's trash might very well be YOUR treasure!! There are a lot of people out there making a nice living buying up other people's throw-aways (from garage sales, etc.) and reselling them at flea markets.

HOMER WITH BUSINESS CARD CLOCK

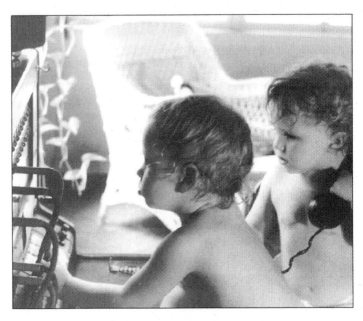

HOMER'S TWINS PLAYING WITH OLD SWITCHBOARD

I wasn't making enough money at anything I was doing and several friends suggested I might be good in the booming real estate market in Central Florida. I took the required 40-hour six weeks course and then passed the state exam in 1978.

I placed my license and went to work with a large firm in Altamonte Springs. Ann Pinnock was my office manager. About 20 years earlier I had dated one of her daughters. I did alright in real estate but I could see it was not what I really wanted to do the rest of my life.

I kept hoping I could make it work and be able to earn some good money. I wanted to follow in my grandfather's footsteps. He had been successful in real estate in Altamonte Springs for many years.

Buyers were not always loyal and you could take a family around in your car all day looking and not finding just what they wanted. A few days later you might find they had bought something with the help of another real estate salesperson. Again, this is strictly commission selling and you don't make a penny until you match up a buyer with a seller...and go to a closing. A couple of my deals fell through just hours before closing. At one time I had a $600,000 mobile home park listed but never could get it sold. That would have been a nice commission check! Don't ever spend your commission check before you have it in your hands! There can be a lot of disappointments in the real estate business.

In July of 1979, I was asked to ride on a float in a parade. It had a small log cabin as its central theme and with me there in front, it made the perfect Republican entry. Here is a short note written in the Orlando Sentinel about that parade. "Joining the parade?...Some Seminole County Republicans were slightly dismayed to find out the man portraying Abraham Lincoln on their recent parade float was---of all things---a Democrat. So they talked politics---and practicality---to him. And Homer Sewell agreed he would rather switch than fight. He registered as a Republican just before the parade. And the float won a first prize."

Over the years between 1978 and 1983 I worked for several real estate companies in Central Florida. In 1980 I went to school again and took the Broker's exam. I received my Broker's license and had my own operation for a while. I called my company PRESIDENTIAL PROPERTIES OF AMERICA.

One of the things I tried was taking 90-day options on mountain land in Tennessee and trying to sell the land to Central Florida buyers before the option expired. I knew a lot of people in Florida owned land in the mountains of either North Carolina or Tennessee. There was plenty of very cheap acreage if you knew where to look for it.

I placed ads in several east Tennessee newspapers and found some great parcels, tied them up with options but never could get them sold in time to make money. I had bought a very expensive, heavy VCR camera and shot footage of the properties. I then showed these to prospects in the Orlando area. I came close to putting a couple of deals together and one beautiful mountain-valley parcel I worked on would have netted me $20,000...but it fell through at the last minute. Nothing I did in real estate made me very much money.

I worked for a year for Barry Luckenbach and was his General Sales Manager for five Central Florida offices. I recruited, trained, motivated and inspired over 100 people while working for Barry. Barry was probably one of the most knowledgeable real estate people in the Orlando area and I learned a lot from him. If you ever need any help in real estate anywhere in Central Florida, I highly recommend Barry Luckenbach and his office of trained salespeople.

I read somewhere about a new, cheap aerosol-type fire extinguisher. Thinking I could make some money selling them, I bought the required 50 cases. I sold them through Boy Scouts and other fund raising groups. I would set up a meeting with a group looking for a way to raise money. I built a fire outside and then put it out with my handy little "Flame Out" extinguisher. I finally sold the last of them and made a few dollars in the process, but it was another bad experience. The man in Michigan who got me into the business went belly-up and ended up owing me about $250 which I never was able to collect. The fire extinguishers worked great on most types of fires. But I found out they had not been approved for sale in Florida, so that didn't help matters any.

I was trying to keep up with my real estate prospects and saw an ad in a magazine for a new portable phone. Since I had a communications background from the White House, I saw this as an opportunity to make some money and help people keep in touch with each other. I had to buy a minimum of three units at $500 each. Somehow I rounded up the money and bought my initial stock. They were the size of a small hand-held walkie-talkie with a touch-pad on the front. It worked great and I could make phone calls from my car or anywhere. This was before we came out with the new cellular phones of today, which work better and are less expensive to own. I finally sold those three phones and moved on to sweeter things.

In 1982 I became the distributor-salesman covering five Central Florida counties for World's Finest Chocolate of Chicago. It was a really sweet job! I had all the sample chocolate I could give away or eat! They have been around for a long time and have one of the best fund raising opportunities ever presented to any group. I called on churches, schools, Scouts, lodges, ball teams, bands, etc. all over Central Florida. I gave them free samples to see for themselves how good the chocolate really was and then wrote up orders. From the time I took an order to when the group had their chocolate delivered to them was less than a month.

I could have a custom-label printed up for their chocolate bars or boxes along with a promo from a local fast food place. One promo I put together was with Wendy's hamburgers...buy one single and get one free. They were selling for $1.29 then so the person buying the bar of chocolate not only helped the group doing the fund raising but also got back their money with the attached coupon. I had another promo with a local pizza store in Longwood...buy one large pizza and receive one free small cheese pizza valued at $3.50. What a deal! The group made about 50% profit from their sales and the company would buy back any unsold products. I still believe it to be one of the easiest ways a group can make money!

Bobby Coker/the little sentinel

'Coach, meet Mr. Lincoln'

Colonial High School coach Harry Nelson is introduced to 'Abraham Lincoln' at the school last week during a fund-raiser. Janette Copeland, center, a member of the school's Hero Club, made the introduction Wednesday during the club's chocolate sale, which raises money for trips and projects. Homer Sewell, who travels nationwide to portray Lincoln, is a distributor for World's Finest Chocolate Inc.

I had some labels made up by a friend in Longwood who had a label-making company. It said to "Eat the bar and save the wrapper. Call Homer for details about fund raising." I wrapped these around my little two inch long sample bars of chocolate and they became my "calling cards".

If your group needs a good fund raising event, I still recommend World's Finest Chocolate in Chicago. Tell them ABE said to call!

Now, I've got another even BETTER WAY FOR FUND RAISING and if you will call or write me, I'll tell you all about it.

116

COUNTY COMMISSIONERS, SEMINOLE COUNTY

SANFORD, FLORIDA

Whereas, the Board of County Commissioners of Seminole County, Florida,

does determine a need for

Seminole County Historical Commission, and

Whereas, this appointment is hereby designated to be held until *January 1985*

or until a successor is appointed.

Now, therefore, reposing especial trust and confidence in your loyalty, patriotism fidelity and prudence we the Board of County Commissioners of Seminole County, Florida, under and by virtue of the authority vested in us do hereby appoint

Homer Sewell III

for the aforesaid term, to have, hold and exercise the said position and all powers appertaining thereto, and to fulfill the duties thereof and to receive the privileges and emoluments, if any, thereof in accordance with the requirements of law.

In testimony whereof,

We do set our hands and cause to be affixed the seal of the Board of County Commissioners of Seminole County, Florida, at Sanford, Florida, this _____ *9th* _____ day of

February _____ A. D. 19 *82.*

_____ Chairman

Attest:

CLERK

117

World Book Opens the Way

For several months in 1982 I also sold World Book Encyclopedias. I sold enough sets to make some money and to earn a free set of encyclopedias and Book of Knowledge for my family. They are great books and are less expensive than some of the others on the market. We still use them and I recommend to ALL my students across the country that they read their entire set of encyclopedias...a few pages at a time. It will help you with ALL subjects and YOUR grades.

HOMER "ABE" SEWELL
INTERVAL OWNERSHIP
RES: 692-3682

MOUNTAIN RESORT
BIG CANOE, GEORGIA 30143
522-8437 (ATLANTA AREA)
404 268-3333 (REMAINDER OF GEORGIA)
1 800 241-9361 (SOUTHEAST)
1 800 342-7516 (GEORGIA)

In May of 1983 I saw an ad in the Orlando Sentinel about a resort in the mountains of North Georgia looking for salesmen. I called and got an interview with the sales manager, Mike Conners, who was to be in Orlando recruiting. Mike told me he was looking for experienced time share salespeople. I had lots of sales experience and had sold general real estate but had not yet sold any time sharing. I finally convinced Mike to give me a try for 30 days starting June 1.

On Memorial Day, I did a Lincoln program in DeLand, Florida and then headed for the mountains. When I finally arrived at the Big Canoe Resort, an hour north of Atlanta, I was in love. I have always loved the mountains of North Carolina and didn't even realize Georgia had such beautiful settings. After being trained how to present the resort to perspective owners, I was turned loose to do my own "TOURS".

I toured about 30 couples in those first two weeks and never made a sale! I was in serious trouble and getting a little discouraged! So was Mike! He called me outside one day and we had a long talk. He said, "Homer, I thought you told me you could sell!" I told him I could but just hadn't had any buyers yet. He was ready to send me back to Florida but I persuaded him to let me finish my 30-day-trial period. In those next two weeks I sold enough to make over $5,000 in commissions. I was finally making some really decent money!!

I bought a clean 1972 Mercedes 280SEL from my long-time friend, Ron Masten. It was a great car for touring with its big back seat and large windows for my prospects to look out at the mountains.

One of the couples I sold was from Marietta and the following is a letter their daughter sent to me after I had visited her school:

March 27, 1984

Dear Homer:

As you can tell from the enclosed letters, all of the students at Wood Acres thoroughly enjoyed your visit. I'm sure your visit and presentation will make any future studying of ABE LINCOLN more interesting and much easier...after all, they "saw" and "heard" ABE himself!

On behalf of the staff, I would like to say "thank you" for a truly wonderful program. We were all "captivated" by ABE.

Personally, I was thrilled to meet you because of all the wonderful things my parents, S.L. and Alice Nixon, have said about you. I understand now why they think so highly of you.

There were several things that conveyed the presence of ABE...the clothes, the beard and the stories. However, what really impressed me was your gentleness and calm manner. This is exactly how I've pictured ABRAHAM LINCOLN all of my life. I've always thought of him as a gentle person...calm and in complete control.

Mom and Dad have enclosed the newspaper article. I think it was a great "write up".

Hope to see you again.

Sincerely, Johnnie Preston

I toured over 3,000 couples in the five and one-half years I worked for Big Canoe Resort. I certainly did not sell something to all of them, but I sold my share. I had a chance to visit with a lot of nice people during those years and many are still close friends. I loved working outdoors and showing people around the beautiful mountains of North Georgia.

The next time you take a vacation, you might want to consider buying and using Time Sharing. I found it to be a nice way to take a vacation. I own one week and enjoy exchanging to resorts around the country.

I wrote the following article in 1984 to let people know

more about the Time Sharing industry. Things may have changed since 1984 but the basic information may be of some interest to you.

"IS THERE A TIME SHARE/INTERVAL VACATION IN YOUR FUTURE? or EVERYTHING YOU ALWAYS WANTED TO KNOW ABOUT TIME SHARING/INTERVAL OWNERSHIP...BUT WERE AFRAID TO ASK! (OR DIDN'T KNOW WHO TO ASK!)"

What is it and is it for you? Take time to read this article and you will have all the answers. The author has been selling at a 7,600 acre resort one hour north of Atlanta and will give you all the answers, pitfalls, what to look for, when to buy, where to buy and a lot of other good information which could be gained only from working in the business.

First, let's go into some detail with explanations of terms related to the industry. Before you can ever think about buying anything, you need to have enough knowledge to be able to make an intelligent decision. Understanding the terms as they relate to the industry will give you a better basis for your buying decision.

TIME SHARE WEEK: A week of vacation you own at a particular RESORT along with about 50 other people. There is usually one or two weeks set aside for maintenance of the unit and all other weeks are sold. You will be able to take your vacation at the RESORT where you own or you may be able to exchange it for a different RESORT and a different time through membership in an EXCHANGE CLUB. You are pre-paying, at today's prices, for the vacations you and your family will take from now on.

UP or PROSPECT: The person (single male or female or married couple) who is going to be shown the property. If you are married and show up without your spouse, you probably will not be toured! This is referred to as a "ONE-LEGGED PROSPECT".

WHEEL or LINE ROTATION: The salespeople who work at a RESORT have a system of determining who will see the next PROSPECT who comes in. That rotation is based on a lot of factors... from sales volume to when the REP finished his last tour. The next salesperson in line to see the next PROSPECT through the door is considered to be ON POINT.

PREMIUM or GIFT: The item you will be given as an incentive to go to the RESORT and take a tour. Once you have taken the tour, you will be entitled to that GIFT whether you buy or not. The GIFTS will range from small items worth less than $5 to black & white TV's, portable phones, luggage, tickets to tourist attractions and more...with values up to $100.

MOOCH: The people who go to RESORTS just to get whatever they can get FREE...with NO intention of ever buying ANYTHING! DON'T BE A MOOCH!!! You don't even want to know all the other names you will be called behind your back!

RESORT: This is the location you will be visiting. It can vary from a small spot on the beach that is a converted motel or hotel to a beautiful complete recreational area which could be as large as 7,000 acres or more.

TYPE OF OWNERSHIP: FEE SIMPLE or RIGHT-TO-USE? What type of ownership do you get when you buy? Some offer only the RIGHT-TO-USE for a period of time...from 10 to 20 years and then title reverts back to the owner/developer. Stay away from this type of ownership! FEE SIMPLE means you own title for an indefinite period of time and it becomes part of your will or estate just as your home ownership does. You will be able to sell it, lease it, rent it, exchange it, will it, deed it or give it away. This is the best type of ownership to have.

M & M FEES or MAIDS & MAINTENANCE FEES: The fees you will be charged on an annual basis to cover the costs of keeping your vacation villa/unit in top shape. These fees will cover taxes, insurance, utilities, replacing furniture, appliances, carpeting, etc. They will vary widely from a low of $125 to over $500 per year per week owned. Maids' fees may be listed separately and run from $25 to $50. These fees may increase slightly over the years but will always be less than it would cost your family to stay in a motel for a week.

EXCHANGE CLUB: This is the club, group or network that will enable you to give up the use of the week or weeks you own at your HOME BASE RESORT and exchange the time for use at another RESORT. Make sure your RESORT offers membership in a large, well established network such as RCI. RCI is the one the author of this article is involved with and it has over 900 RESORTS all over the world to choose from. (As of 1994 that number has risen to over 2,400.) They will be able to give you the exchange you want about 95% of the time. Smaller clubs may not be able to help you with exchanges at anywhere near this success rate.

ANNUAL DUES/FEES: What it costs to maintain your membership in the exchange club. This could vary from $50 to $99 a year. The exchange fees charged by the club could run from a low of approx. $12 for an internal exchange (for changing times within your own HOME BASE RESORT) to approx. $89 for external exchanges to resorts around the world.

EXCHANGE TIMING: You may be able to request a different resort up to 24 months ahead of time or as little as two days. The longer you give your exchange club the opportunity to place you someplace other than your HOME BASE RESORT, the better your chances of getting WHAT & WHERE you desire.

FRONT END: Not the front of your car!! This is the talk session you and your RESORT REP will have when you first get together. Just relax and listen to what you are being told about the RESORT. You may be asked a lot of questions which will help your REP guide you to a decision as to whether this program will work for your family. You may also be shown a film during the FRONT END or during the DRIVING TOUR. Ask questions as you think of things you want or need to know. Your REP will be happy to answer them for you and will be delighted to know you are interested enough to be involved and are staying awake during his presentation.

WARM-UP: The process during the FRONT END by which you and the sales REP will get to know each other better. You will be asked personal questions about your family and work so the REP will have a friendlier rapport with you. This also brings to mind the old adage: "Nobody cares how much you know until they know how much you care!" Those of you involved in any type of sales or dealing with people should never forget this!

TOUR GUIDE, SALESPERSON or REP: This is the man or woman who will be leading and guiding you down the path toward OWNERSHIP at that RESORT.

LAY-DOWN or COCONUT: This is a PROSPECT who falls in love with the RESORT and begs the REP to write it up! Perhaps this RARE person could also be called an "EASY SALE". I did have a few COCONUTS!

BURN: Could have two meanings. It could be what you will do if a SALESPERSON gives you a hard time and insults your intelligence. Or, it could also be what the REP will do to you if you are not a qualified PROSPECT. He can get rid of you in a few minutes without taking you on the tour. You will usually still receive your GIFT. Unless that RESORT has rules against giving GIFTS to "repeater-MOOCHES" who have been caught.

DRIVING TOUR: A tour of the property you are visiting. You will be shown all of the highlights and amenities offered for your use. During this time, see what is available that turns you and your family on for a week at a time. If there is nothing, then DON'T BUY at that RESORT! If there is nothing that excites YOU here, then it may not be able to excite potential exchanges either and it would be difficult to exchange out of this RESORT.

Do those amenities cost you or are they FREE for your family to enjoy while you're there? This is important! You don't want to have to be spending money all week for such things as golf, tennis, swimming, paddle-boats, canoes, water slides, etc. They should all be free except for the golf cart rentals.

BACK END: This is the conversational period after you have been toured. Now is the time the REP will try to CLOSE you. You will be shown available weeks of inventory. Prices, terms, down payments, etc. will all be discussed. At this time the decision is yours to either buy or not!

CLOSE: This is what the salesperson is paid to do. He/she is strictly on commission and will not earn any money if you do not buy. He will do his best to get you to say YES. If the salesperson does not feel he is making any progress with you, he may "T.O." you.

"T.O.": Turn over the PROSPECT to a sales manager who often has the capabilities to convince you to buy and to overcome any objections you may have.

BE-BACK: There is NO such thing in the Time Share business!! If you tell your REP you need time to think about whether you want to make the purchase and want to go home to "talk it over with your children, mothers and fathers, butcher, lawyer, fireman, policeman, candlestick-maker, doctor, CPA and the 99-year-old next-door-neighbor" and you will BE-BACK at a later date to make the purchase... YOU ARE NOT FOOLING ANYONE BUT YOURSELF!! Your SALESPERSON has been around the business long enough to know he can't feed his family on "BE-BACK sandwiches"! You might as well go ahead and tell him you don't want what he is offering you, because that's exactly what you mean! Very rarely does anyone ever come back later to purchase. If you like what you are being shown and feel comfortable about the purchase...based on all the criteria you learn about in this article...then go ahead and buy and take advantage of those FIRST DAY BENEFITS.

FIRST DAY BENEFITS: Knowing that buying a TIME SHARE WEEK is a difficult decision to make on the spot, the RESORT may offer a package of items which will help you make that important decision. They will vary...from discounts of $500 to over $3,500...to special referral programs worth money to you, or...perhaps paying for your EXCHANGE CLUB membership for a couple of years and much, much more!

LIST PRICES: The prices the units are normally sold for. There may be DISCOUNTS taken from these prices depending on how the RESORT has priced them and how badly they need your business today. These prices may vary from a low of $4,000 to over $20,000 for single weeks...depending on where the resort is located and what time of year you desire to own.

DISCOUNTS: The amount of reduction from the LIST PRICE will vary greatly from resort to resort. Typically, it will run from a minimum of $500 to as much as $3,000-$4,000 on a package of two or more weeks.

TERMS: You should be able to buy what you want for as little as 10% down and with eight-to-ten year financing programs. Don't worry about the interest rates since all the interest paid is tax-deductible. (It may not be anymore!)

P.O.R. or PROPERTY OWNER REFERRAL: After you become an owner, your new resort may offer you some type of REFERRAL PROGRAM which will enable you to send or bring your friends, business associates, church members, relatives, etc. up to visit the RESORT. These programs will vary greatly but they could be worth some dollars to you.

RED, WHITE & BLUE or GOLD & SILVER: These colors refer to how the weeks of ownership are handled in the exchange programs. EXCHANGE CLUBS color their weeks variously. RCI uses red, white & blue: red being the prime time use at that RESORT; WHITE being a swing time of medium desirability and use; and BLUE being the least demand or off-season time. RED time will always be the most expensive and

BLUE time the least costly.

CONDO DOCS: These are the legal documents which will tell you all about the type of ownership you have and will go into a lot of details about covenants and restrictions, management fees, etc. Read these very carefully.

UNIT SIZE: The units will vary from one room efficiency units converted from motels to large 1,200 square feet villas sleeping up to eight people. Be cautious about the size of your unit as this will greatly affect the exchangeability. The most desirable will be the free-standing villas.

INVENTORY/FURNISHINGS: What comes with your unit? Hopefully, it will contain everything you will need to have an enjoyable stay. It should contain all linens and complete kitchens. The only items you should have to pack for your trip should be toothbrushes, clothes, groceries and a box of your favorite soap for the washer/dryer your unit should have. Some units will also have spas, saunas and microwaves.

RESCISSION PERIOD: The period of time you have to rescind your contract...BY LAW!! This can vary from three to 15 days depending on your state laws. Don't buy in the first place if you intend to exercise this right. All you will do is cause a lot of heartbreak for some poor salesman who is trying to earn a living for his family! He would rather you say NO at the time of the BACK END and CLOSE than to think he has made a sale and then lose it a few days later. If some emergency arises and you really need to rescind your contract then you have the legal right to do so.

HAPPY TIMES: What you will see a lot of after you make your purchase!

Since we have the terms explained which will be used in your presence (or behind your back), let's discuss whether TIME SHARING is for you or not.

If you are able to answer YES to the following questions, then TIME SHARING may be just what you need for your family.

1. Do you like to take vacations for at least one week at a time?
2. Do you like to travel?
3. Are you tired of staying in motels/hotels and having nothing to show for those stays except pictures, memories, souvenirs and receipts?
4. Instead of throwing your money away, can you afford to set aside a monthly payment as low as $60 for a vacation savings program? Without taking food off the table?
5. Are you turned-on by the possibility of having over 2,400 resorts throughout the world to choose from for exciting vacations for the rest of your life?

If you answered YES to those five questions, then read on. If you answered NO to any question, then stop here because it is NOT for you.

Now that you think TIME SHARING might be for you, how do you go about deciding where your HOME BASE RESORT should be? You could start by asking friends where they own or have visited. Check out some of the mail you have been receiving from resorts. Check in your local phone books and Chamber of Commerce to find out what is around you.

Make an appointment to go see one or several nearby RESORTS. Before you go, make yourself a list of what you would like to find at the RESORT for your family to do during your week. Don't waste your time buying at a RESORT you wouldn't spend a week at if you couldn't exchange to another RESORT. You want your HOME BASE RESORT to be desirable. If it is not desirable to you, then it may not be desirable to anyone else either and you will have a hard time exchanging out of it.

You may have an opportunity to visit a RESORT as a P.O.R.; to visit by letter invitation to receive a gift; or, you may call the RESORT and ask to be admitted for a tour. Show up for your scheduled TOUR on time or call to re-schedule if you can't make it.

Be polite, attentive and ask questions of your REP. If the RESORT meets all of the criteria you have established, then buy a week or two!

Have the REP give you the best price he can for the week or weeks you would like to own. Sometimes you may be able to bargain for a lower price. You won't know until you ask! Back up your request for a discounted price with a deposit check. This will show the REP and his manager you are a serious buyer. Management will have a harder time turning down a signed worksheet with a deposit check than if you just verbally asked for it. Sometimes you can bargain for extra GIFTS or PREMIUMS to be thrown in with the package. Once you and the REP have agreed on the best possible price, terms and benefits to you, all of the contracts will be typed by a secretary. Usually, while the paperwork is being typed, you will be filling out a credit application.

Go over these contracts carefully with your REP. Make sure you are given copies of all documents you sign. You will also receive a copy of the RESORT'S CONDO DOCUMENTS and of the latest edition of the EXCHANGE CLUB directory showing all of the places you can visit in the years ahead. You will find yourself looking through this "DREAM BOOK or WISH BOOK" instead of watching TV some nights.

Once you have completed all of the paperwork, relax and know you are in store for a lot of exciting weeks of vacations away from motels/hotels.

Even as you drive home from your new RESORT, you may want to be making a list of your friends you could invite to see your RESORT. Call your REP with these names and let her start working to give you back some of your money through her REFERRAL PROGRAM. Make sure you have inquired about this before you made the final buying decision. A good REFERRAL PROGRAM could get you some nice gifts for sending your friends.

If you have purchased at a RESORT that gave you a FEE SIMPLE warranty deeded ownership (the only kind to buy), then you MAY be able to sell it in later years if you need or desire to do so. But, do you really want to give up something that brings you so much pleasure and gets CHEAPER as motels/hotels get more and more expensive?

Further proof TIME SHARING might be right for you is that one recent study indicates a one-week visit to a motel/hotel in 1999 will cost you over $1,500! Your cumulative cost for the next 15 years would be over $15,000! The Marriott Hotel people just bought four TIME SHARE resorts in Hilton Head and now own them in other places. This shows us that the hotel people know we are sick and tired of throwing away our $$ and they had better diversify their holdings.

HAVE A GREAT VACATION!

One of the people I sold a Time Share week to was a beautiful lady from Atlanta by the name of Jacque. At the time I sold her, she was working for Edwards Baking Company. Any time she would come to visit the resort, she would bring my friends and me lots of Edwards' pies. Those were some of the best store-bought pies I have ever eaten! She also needlepointed me something that has become my motto to live by: "BE A DREAMER, A STARGAZER AND A RAINBOW CHASER". I have since added..."AND SOAR WITH THE EAGLES!!" I use this on all of my brochures and stress it in all of my shows.

I toured airline pilots, business executives, doctors, lawyers, chicken farmers and people from all walks of life while at Big Canoe.

I was consistently in the top three or four of the 20 salespeople working there. In early 1984 I bought a nice lot for $3,000 in the resort next to Big Canoe called Bent Tree and made plans to build a home on it. Both resorts have great golf courses and for those of you who have never played on a mountain course, you would be in for a real treat.

My family came up after school was out the summer of 1984 and we've been here ever since. We all love it here in the mountains.

CEDARDALE LOG HOMES

"Call for an appoinment to see
our beautiful model home."

Homer "ABE" Sewell
P.O. Box 13,
Phone: 404-692-3682

3725 Shadowick Mt. Road,
Bent Tree Resort
Jasper, GA 30143-0013

I have always wanted to live in a log cabin so we built a 3-level 3,000 square foot log cabin during the spring and summer of 1984. We rented a cute little A-frame cabin off Burnt Mountain Road outside Jasper while I built our log cabin. I rented it from Curtis Mabie, who was with the Dawson County sheriff's department at the time. Now he is with security at the Atlanta airport and I see him nearly every time I fly somewhere.

I heard about a company that makes great log cabin kits from white northern cedar. I got in touch with them and did some Lincoln work for them at a big home show in Atlanta. In lieu of paying me for the job, I took a discount from the price of the log cabin kit. I made my cabin available for folks to come see and was probably helpful in getting some log cabin kits sold.

We lived in our new log cabin for a couple of years until we got tired of the 10-mile winding road drive to town several times a day. We sold it and bought a house on the west side of Jasper...only one-half mile from the airport and one mile from the four-lane highway.

Perhaps my other motive for being so close to the airport is someday I will realize my dream I've had since my first airplane ride in third grade. I've been working on it for 22 years and as of 1994 I have 20 of the 40 hours needed to get my pilot's license. It seems when I've had the money to pay for it, I didn't have the time. And, when I've had the time, I didn't have the money. Isn't that true of so many things in life? When I took my first lesson in 1972, the cost was only $19 an hour for the plane, fuel and an instructor. In 1993 the cost had risen to close to $50 an hour!

Sometime in the near future I hope to be able to finish getting my pilot's license. Then I can walk to the airport, get into a rented plane (or my own plane) and fly off to visit with family, friends or to be "ABE" somewhere.

I've gotten hundreds of letters from kids since 1975 and will put a collection of the best of them in my next book, DEAR PRESIDENT LINCOLN. Here is one I received in February of 1986 from a young student:

Dear President Lincoln:

Thank you for spending some of your time at Sardis Elementary School. We appreciate your concern on wanting us to learn about Lincoln. I enjoyed your speech. I hope everybody else did too. I learned a lot from the slavery speech. I learned that everybody should be free. If you had not told me you were Mr. Homer Sewell, I would have thought you were Lincoln. Come back soon.

Your friend, Lisa Nance.

"ABE" AT FT. SUMPTER, SOUTH CAROLINA

In September of 1986 I was invited by Dick Schreadley, Editor of the Charleston, South Carolina *News-Courier,* to come speak to the 40th Annual Convention of Newspaper Editors from all over the country. Dick even wrote my speech for me! I had the opportunity to visit Ft. Sumpter, where the Civil War had begun on April 12, 1861.

In 1988, while I was still with Big Canoe, I noticed the skating rink in Jasper was for sale so with some money Kathy inherited from her mother, (and against her better judgment) we bought it. Now we were $150,000 in debt...with a $1,800-a-month mortgage payment! And that was on top of a $800 monthly mortgage payment for our home!

I was determined we would make it work. We cleaned up the whole operation. No more drugs, alcohol or smoking were allowed! We added a large game room at one end with 30 video games and five pool tables. We rebuilt the skate storage room and built a three foot high 16' x 24' stage in the middle of the rink...for those who wanted to dance. We added a large double pizza oven. We could bake 12-16" pizzas at one time. I started making pizzas not only for the customers who came in, but started a delivery service for the Jasper area. Up until then, the only other pizza operation in town did not deliver.

There was now a clean, wholesome place for the young people of Pickens County to go on Friday and Saturday nights.

We also had special group skating parties during the week. I got the whole family involved. Kimberly, Jason and Chip helped out in the concession stand, made pizzas, gave out skates, took money at the door, did floor-guard duty and whatever else needed to be done to run the operation. Kathy was there to help whenever she could.

I put the word out around town that I needed someone who could repair skates and help with other responsibilities. Rhoda Warren stopped by one day to see what needed to be done. I hired her and Rhoda became a real asset around the rink. She kept all those 300+ pairs of skates in good working condition. She had a real knack for mechanical things and a lot of patience with the young people.

During the winter months, when there wasn't much else to do outdoors, we were busy and able to pay the bills. But, during the summer, our business died and after two years of struggling to make ends meet, we finally decided to shut down the skating rink. I had more $dollars$ going OUT than coming IN!

I should have known if the banker's daughter, who owned it before us, couldn't make it work, we probably couldn't either. We were in for a serious up-hill battle! But, I had to try! We finally sold the building and it is now a shirt manufacturing plant.

A lot of small towns all over the country have nothing for their teenagers to do except cruise the main street, go parking or looking for trouble. Students still come up to me in town wanting to know when I'm going to open "Flashers" back up, so they can have a place to gather and have fun.

When it was obvious the young people were not going to come in sufficient numbers to pay the overhead, I asked them what they wanted that they would support. Some of them said, "Build us a race track for motorcycles and four-wheelers". So that's exactly what I did.

We have eight acres with woods and pasture, a stream

down by the pasture, a waterfall and gorge across the street and lots of peace and quiet. I had never even visited a four-wheeler race track but had an idea of what one should look like. I had several cases of 2,500-foot rolls of copy paper a church in Atlanta had given me. I took a couple of those rolls and walked off the course...trailing paper behind me...to mark it.

I then hired a contractor with a bulldozer to build the track. It ended up being about one half-mile long with banked-turns, jumps, "table-tops" and lots of curves and switch-backs. I even put in an irrigation and sprinkler system to keep the track wet when there had been no rain. I bought trophies, printed flyers, fixed up a concession stand in the barn and put the word out all over North Georgia that we were now open for business. Rhoda was there to help run the track. She helped with concessions, kept score and took entrants' and spectators' money. I couldn't have done it without her.

At our peak, we had as many as fifty people coming to race and/or watch. Our only accidents were a broken wrist and a gashed leg. With as many as ten 4-wheelers or motorcycles racing at one time, there could have been some serious accidents. We were lucky! It was exciting watching folks race around the track!

Although it was self-sustaining and something fun to do on Saturdays and Sundays, I didn't have the money to promote it properly and after a few months of operation, I decided to shut it down.

It was fun while it lasted. The track is all grown up now with tall grass and trees but I still go down when I am in town and ride my twins' four-wheeler or motorcycle. I enjoy it and it's a way for me to relax.

In the fall of 1988, the Time Sharing business at Big Canoe was declining and the company decided to get out of it completely. They would concentrate on selling homes and lots. I was offered an opportunity to sell general real estate. I quickly decided it was not what I wanted and started looking for other opportunities.

In October, when I left Big Canoe, I had a job for a while doing part-time work for Georgia Temps. They placed people in temporary jobs in the 51-story headquarters building of Georgia-Pacific Company in downtown Atlanta. For several weeks I was the PBX operator on the 17th floor in the Wood Products Division. I was answering and routing as many as 800 calls a day to the 50 people on my floor. I did meet a lot of nice people there in Georgia Pacific and they featured ABE in their *Atlanta This Week* newsletter to employees. I drove the 55 miles each way for a few months until I realized it wasn't going to work out. They weren't giving me enough hours to support my family and I knew I needed to find something else.

Kathy worked as a nurse during all these years and it was her income which helped support the family when I wasn't working at all or not making very much money. Her favorite quote was, "When are you going to get a real job?" She has been a nurse for nearly 30 years and can get a good job in any state in the country. She always wanted me to go get a 40-hours-a-week punch-a-time-clock type job. It just wasn't me! The entrepreneurial spirit in me is too strong to punch someone's clock!

Chapter 8

Even More Jobs

Some interesting things happened while I was a good, HONEST lawyer in Springfield...

All these years since 1975 I was continuing to portray ABE part-time and studied more and more about his life. My ultimate dream had always been to find a way to support my family by being ABE full-time.

Mark, one of the guys who had sold real estate with me at Big Canoe Resort, called me from his home in south Florida one evening in 1989. Mark was into something big and wanted me to get into it too. He had discovered NSA water filters and its multi-level marketing (M.L.M.) plan. Mark had been one of our top salesmen at Big Canoe so I figured he must know what he was doing and if it was good enough for him, it was good enough for me too.

So I bought into NSA and started selling water filters. They are good filters and probably priced competitively with other filters that do the same job.

The demonstration we were taught to do was a real eye-opener! I had some chemicals you would use to test the chlorine level in your pool. I would go into a prospect's home which had chlorinated city water and fill a clear plastic tumbler with tap water. Then I would hook up the portable filter and run another tumbler full of filtered tap water. I then placed six drops of the chemical into both glasses of water. The unfiltered water turned "pee-yellow" real quick! The water with the chlorine filtered out remained clear. Then I turned to the prospect and asked, "Mrs. Jones, which water would you like to drink? Shall I leave this filter hooked up for you?"

For people who were interested in having good, clear, clean non-chlorinated water, the filter did the job. I recommend to everyone who has city water...get some type of water filter that filters out the chlorine and other impurities which are poisoning our bodies.

For a while I sold Electrolux vacuum cleaners around North Georgia. I also did some home shows for them as ABE. I sold a few and made some money in commissions. They are good vacuum cleaners and last a long time. I can remember Mom and me cleaning house in Altamonte Springs in the 50's with an Electrolux. I personally think some vacuum cleaners are over-priced. From my experience with Sears and Electrolux vacuums, I think the best buy on the market now is the Royal Dirt Devil Upright Deluxe. I bought one last year from WalMart (my favorite store) for about $129 with all the attachments. It works as well as vacuums selling for five times as much! You need to thoroughly evaluate what YOUR needs are and what is the best buy for you to accomplish those needs.

Mike Harrison, who had worked for me at Sears, had tried unsuccessfully in 1980 or 1981 to get me into selling insurance for A.L. Williams. I told him then I didn't like to sell non-tangible things like insurance. Again in early 1989, someone contacted me about selling term life insurance for A.L. Williams. I finally, reluctantly, agreed to give it a try. I went to school to take the necessary hours for my Georgia insurance license and passed the exam. Now I was a licensed insurance salesman. I still didn't like it!! I sold a few policies and even talked Vi Montgomery, a friend from Altamonte Springs, into getting her license.

MAY I SHARE SOME INFORMATION WITH YOU FOR 45 MINUTES?

IT MAY .....CHANGE YOUR WHOLE LIFE!!
    .....$AVE YOU $$$!!
    .....SHOW HOW YOU TOO CAN MAKE $$$!!

MY PROMISE TO YOU .....
NO OBLIGATION!   NO PRESSURE!

JUST GOOD INFORMATION . . . . PRESENTED HONESTLY!!
(PHONE: 404-692-3682   ABE

Both of us dropped out of it after a few months of cold-calling and not selling! They were a good company for term insurance but selling insurance is just not my "cup-of-tea".

I was hired in February of 1989 to be Systems Manager at the Marietta District Office for the Census Bureau. My job would be to set up a computer system with 15 terminals, two printers, etc., hire and train about 20 people and be responsible for the day-to-day running of this system. We would be handling payroll for 800 to 1,000 people on a daily basis. I would be there for a one year contract and then for an additional six months to end in September of 1990. This was the time I had already planned to go full-time as ABE so the timing would be great.

I did the job I was hired to do well enough that they had me helping train other Managers for other offices in North Georgia. I was always at work on time and put in my eight hours---five days a week. I worked overtime, if necessary, without complaining.

On Monday, February 12, 1990 (ABE LINCOLN'S birthday) I was scheduled to do a program in the Atlanta area.

The previous Friday I told my manager I would be off the following Monday to do this program. He reminded me to be sure to take a day of either sick leave or annual leave. I assured him I would. I would not want the Census Bureau to think I was at work and on their payroll while I was at a school as ABE.

I had several days of both sick leave and annual leave accumulated. During the weekend I was installing a hot water heater in my home and pulled something loose in my neck or back. I was in so much pain I couldn't lay down to sleep. I had to sit up in a chair to sleep.

It would be helpful for you to understand that when I make a commitment to appear at a school or other location as ABE, unless I am already dead, I will be there. Even though I was in extreme pain and was barely able to stand in front of all of those students, I was determined to be there. That Monday morning I called in and told one of the ladies who worked for me to tell my manager I was out sick. I gave her the number at the school so I could be reached in case she needed me. I told her to put me down on the time sheet for a day of sick leave. In fact, during my program later in the day, I was called to the school office to take a call from my Census office. I handled a small payroll problem which had come up and then continued with my program for the students.

I already had an appointment to see a chiropractor that Monday afternoon just as soon as I finished at the school. I felt since there was a medical problem, I should call my absence "sick leave" instead of "annual leave". Now, don't forget, I had plenty of both types of leave available to me!

I want to put in my two cents worth right here about chiropractic care. I strongly believe in what they do. If it weren't for Doctor Dan Smith here in Jasper and other chiropractors I've visited around the country, I would be in a lot of pain. I see him on a regular basis. Everyone should get adjustments by a good chiropractor frequently. One of these days our insurance companies will wake up and realize that if chiropractors were seen first, (became the "GATE-KEEPERS" for the medical profession) there would be a lot less money spent for expensive MRI's, CAT scans, drugs and unneeded surgeries. Drugs will only mask the problems if your spine is out of adjustment!

And speaking of chiropractors, I've got another friend who has been a pharmacist for several years and in 1993 graduated from Life College of Chiropractic in Marietta. Rick and his beautiful wife, Melissa, just had their first baby (a pretty little girl) in March of 1994. They've gone camping with us and we visit each other whenever we can. Rick is one of the most-fun-to-be-with friends I have. Regardless of how your day or night has been going, Rick will make you smile. Everyone needs a friend like him! May GOD continue to bless you, Rick.

If any of my readers have any doubts about what a good chiropractor can do to help you feel better all over...all the time...and without drugs...please give me a call. I will be happy to tell you how much I appreciate MY chiropractor!

I did my program and went straight to the doctor. In fact I went nearly every day for over a month. I was in so much pain I was not able to sleep except sitting up in a reclining chair. I still, to this day, have problems in the same area of my neck and back and have to have regular chiropractic care in order to be able to walk.

Even though I continued to be in extreme pain and made visits to the chiropractor almost every day, I was always at work and put in a full day of duties for the Census Bureau. I NEVER MISSED A DAY OF WORK!

"ABE LINCOLN GETS FIRED FROM CENSUS..."

On February 21, one of the supervisors from the Atlanta office came into my office and in front of several of my employees, directed me to come with him. We sat down in the

District Manager's office. He handed me a letter (copy on next page for your inspection) stating that "I had violated sick leave policy". He asked me for my ID badge and keys and fired me on the spot! No questions about anything nor did he offer to change the type of leave I had taken to ANNUAL instead of SICK. His statement to me was "If I was sick enough not to be there at work then I was too sick to be performing as ABE in front of school students".

Needless to say, I was devastated!! I had never been fired from a job and I wasn't going to take it lying down. I called an attorney friend and asked him what to do. I called the EEOC office and filed an EEOC complaint. After months of hearings and phone conversations back and forth between here, Washington, California and Atlanta. I ended up with nothing! I figured they owed me my pay for the six months I was told I would still be working plus something for all the pain and suffering my family and I had been through. We nearly lost our home! I tried to get unemployment compensation while I fought to get my job back but was turned down because they said I had violated company policy and therefore was not qualified.

If the man who fired me, because he saw an article in the newspaper about my being at the school, hadn't had it in for me for some reason, he could have said, "Well, Homer, let's change that to Annual Leave and everything will be alright." Everyone including my own boss, Mr. Frances Brooke, said I was doing an excellent job and did not want to see me fired.

UNITED STATES DEPARTMENT OF COMMERCE
Bureau of the Census
Regional Census Center
Atlanta, GA 30309-3112

February 21, 1990

Mr. Homer Sewell, III
P. O. Box 13
Jasper, GA 30143

Dear Mr. Sewell:

On February 28, 1989, you were given a Schedule A, Temporary Appointment not-to-exceed February 27, 1990, as an Assistant Manager for EDP Operations with the Bureau of the Census in the Marietta District Office.

I am terminating your temporary appointment for improper use of sick leave by requesting sick leave under false pretenses on February 12, 1990, when in fact you were appearing at Minor Elementary School, in Gwinnett County, playing the character of "Honest Abe." This fact was determined when your picture appeared in the Gwinnett Extra section of the Atlanta Journal on Tuesday, February 13, 1990. Your appearance at the school on February 12 was confirmed by school officials.

Since you hold a supervisory position, you are held to a higher standard of conduct. Your improper use of sick leave violates the basic trust in your honesty and truthfulness afforded you in hiring. Because of the seriousness of this incident, it is not considered in the best interest of the government to retain you in the Federal Service. Therefore, I am terminating your appointment as of the close of business on February 21, 1990.

If you believe the decision to terminate your appointment was based on race, color, religion, sex, national origin, age, or a physical or mental handicap, you may pursue a complaint through the Census Bureau's discrimination complaint process. Any such complaint must be filed no later than 30 calendar days after the effective date of termination. If you wish to do so, or would like additional information, you should contact Sharon Collins, your servicing EEO Specialist, at Bureau of the Census, 1365 Peachtree Street, NE Room 625, Atlanta, GA 30309-3147, telephone number (404) 347-5271 or Ms. Marilia Matos, the Census Bureau's EEO Officer. Ms. Matos' telephone number is (301) 763-7676, and her mailing address is Room 3071 FOB#3, Bureau of the Census Headquarters, Washington, DC 20233.

Please return all materials, equipment, and badges to Gene Wallace. If you have any questions about this matter, please call Gene Wallace or me at (404) 347-5443.

Sincerely,

JAMES F. HOLMES
Regional Director

145

If it weren't for a lot of help from my Pastor, Max Caylor, at the Jasper United Methodist Church, and my banker, Mark Whitfield, at the Jasper Banking Company, we would have lost our home. I really appreciate all they both did to help during these most trying times.

I have always had a strong belief in GOD and know HE will answer prayers and be there when we need HIM. I have tried to attend church as regularly as possible. These were some very hard times in my life and prayer and GOD helped us through it. There were times when I wondered if tomorrow would be a better day...but I never gave up.

I am often asked about ABE's religious beliefs and I want to quote what he said when someone asked why he never officially joined a church.

"I have never joined any church, but when any church will inscribe over its altar, as its sole qualification for membership, the words of the Savior, 'Thou shalt love the Lord thy GOD with all thy heart, and with all thy soul, and thy neighbor as thyself'; that church will I join with all my heart and with all my soul."

It was probably one of the worst times in my life. One of these days I hope to be able to find an attorney or someone who can help me fight the Census Bureau for their unfair labor practices. I was told if I had been an employee for JUST ONE MORE WEEK, I would have had a lot more rights because of being a military veteran. I think they also knew that! For now, I must go on with my life.

LESSON TO BE LEARNED HERE IS: Even when you are being HONEST, FAIR and ABOVE-BOARD, someone might still try to discredit you. But, don't EVER give up when you know you are right. Stand up and fight for what you believe in.

After the Census disaster in my life I did whatever I could the summer of 1990 to make ends meet. I worked for a while for

Digital Equipment Corporation in Alpharetta. I did word processing and answered phones for their Talent Tree Temp. Service. That was a part-time thing which did not give me very many hours.

During this same year, I developed stones in my gall bladder and it was decided my gall bladder needed to be removed. Knowing I was facing several days stay in a hospital, a lot of pain and being cut open in the belly, I was not excited! About that same time I saw an article in my favorite magazine, the *Reader's Digest*, about a relatively new type of surgery called Laparoscopic Laser that made gall bladder removal and other types of surgery a lot easier on the patient.

I called Emory University in Atlanta and asked who in the area was performing this type of surgery. They said Dr. J. Barry McKernan in Marietta had pioneered this type of surgery and was teaching it all over the world. I called his office, made an appointment and went to see this world famous doctor. I liked him right off the bat. He is a very warm, friendly and extremely knowledgeable man and it was easy to see he KNEW what he was talking about.

We scheduled the surgery for the following week and I had it done "out-patient". The doctor made five small incisions into my abdomen for instruments, TV camera, suction, etc. I got up and walked two miles the day after surgery! I've even got a video of the procedure.

Again in 1992, when I pulled another hernia, I called Doctor McKernan's office to see if he was doing hernia repairs with Laparoscopic surgery. There was so much scar tissue in my tummy from previous surgeries that I didn't relish the idea of going through it again the "old-fashioned way".

I was told he did perform hernia repairs using this new procedure so I had it done again on an "out-patient" basis. I highly recommend this procedure whenever you or a loved one need to have anything fixed or removed. Everyday there are new advances in this type of medical treatment and MY doctor is the leader in the field.

Because of Doc McKernan I was able to do my performances within a day or two of surgery instead of being out of work for a couple of weeks! THANKS DOC!

Early in 1994 I got a call from Doc McKernan's office asking if I would mind if they had their new PR person get in touch with me to do a human interest story about "ABE" and his surgeries. I told them I didn't have any objection and I got a call a few days later from Marilyn Pearlman of Atlanta. She came to see one of my school programs and has since been working up some PR releases for Doc McKernan. She also arranged for me to appear on an Atlanta TV talk show that had featured my doctor the week before.

For a while I placed my Georgia real estate license with two different companies in Jasper and tried general real estate again. I decided it still wasn't what I wanted to do.

I was trying to bring in enough money to live on until September when I would go full-time as ABE.

In late 1989 I had been on a flight somewhere and sat next to a lady who told me if I ever wanted to go full-time as ABE, she had a friend in Kansas who booked talent into schools all over the country. I got in touch with him and signed a contract for the school year 1990-91 to begin in September.

Right after a Labor Day family camping trip to our favorite place on the Blue Ridge Parkway in North Carolina, I hit the road as a full-time ABE. MY 19-YEAR DREAM HAD FINALLY MATERIALIZED! Would I be able to handle the stress of 10 shows a week (At that time I was still doing half-day shows. I've since decided I can give the schools and students more for their money by being there for an all-day program.) and being away from my family for weeks at a time?

In that first nine months of being ABE full-time, I did 333 appearances in 17 midwest states! I was doing more appearances in more locations than most any other type of public speaker, singer or other kinds of performer ever does!

My agent booked me all of those jobs and paid me in a timely fashion, but the man never bothered to come see my show or to meet me in person! I was within an hour of his office for two solid weeks and he never made an effort to come see my performances. I handed over $30,000 to him that school year 1990-1991! It was obvious he was more interested in what he could make...off my performances and those of the other 15 talents he handled...than of taking time to meet me!

If I gave you $30,000, wouldn't you at least come take me to lunch or dinner and say, "GREAT SHOW! And thanks for the money, Homer?"

At least it proved to me there was a need for my services and I could handle the schedule of being on the road all the time. My family didn't like my being gone but the money was good. I was getting a check for $1,500 a week, sending $1,000 home and catching up on a lot of debts.

If you are in an area of the country I haven't worked in yet and you want to make some money as my agent, please call or write. I will tell you how to book some shows and make yourself some commissions. I would love to get to the remainder of the states that aren't yet on the list at the end of the book.

Chapter 9

Off to Washington

I ran again in November of '60...for the big office...and guess what happened?...I won that one!!! I became your 16th President!

Right before that election I received the nicest letter from a little eleven year old girl who lived up in Westfield, New York. Her name was Grace Bedell. Miss Grace said she thought I would make a good president; if I had any little girls, would I ask them to write to her and I might look much more handsome if I grew some whiskers.

In all those miles of traveling, I've had a lot of interesting experiences and met quite a few people who encouraged me to write a book. I started gathering my notes.

I have wanted to write a book for years and now that it is done, I am fulfilling one of the dreams I have had. I came across a quote the other day and I would like for those of you who didn't see it to have a chance now.

This quote is taken from the May, 1993 issue of my favorite magazine, *Reader's Digest;* was quoted there from *Writer's Digest* and was written by one of my favorite writers, Tom Clancy. He has written such wonderful adventures as *Hunt for Red October, Clear and Present Danger, Red Storm Rising, Patriot Games* and *Without Remorse*, published by the Berkley Publishing Group. If you are looking for some adventurous reading and haven't yet read these books by Tom Clancy, you may want to do so.

"The foundations of successful writing are within anyone's grasp," says best-selling author Tom Clancy. "Writing is like golf or skeet shooting or any other human endeavor," he says. "The only way to do it is to DO it." Clancy considers his accomplishments:

"My greatest good fortune was that I didn't know that I was doing everything wrong. If I'd done a single thing right, I probably would have failed. If I'd known how hard---statistically speaking---it is to get a first novel published, I might have given up and done what my wife told me to do: sold more insurance".

"What success really means is looking failure in the face and tossing the dice anyway. You may be the only person who ever knows how the dice come up, but in that knowledge you have something that millions of people will never have---because they were afraid to try".

"Right-on Tom!!" I love what he says and what he writes! And to think that I used to sell insurance too!! I could only DREAM of ever selling as many books as Tom Clancy has but if we don't ever reach for our goals, we will NEVER ACHIEVE THEM!! I read somewhere that Tom now gets a $4,000,000 advance as soon as he is ready to start on another book!

By the way, if you aren't already subscribing to *Reader's Digest* and reading it cover-to-cover each month, you need to. It is a great little magazine and I have my copies all the way back to the 1960's.

This is a good place for me to repeat my favorite little motto...

"BE A DREAMER, A STARGAZER, A RAINBOW CHASER AND SOAR WITH THE EAGLES" ...YOU WILL HEAR ME SAY IT OVER AND OVER AGAIN!

I want you to write down, either on this page or another piece of paper, what ten things you most want to accomplish or achieve with your life in the next five years.

1. _____

2. _____

3. _____

4. _____

5. _____

6. _____

7. _____

8. _____

9. _____

10. _____

1. List them in order of their importance.
2. What do you need to accomplish these goals?
3. Break down your goals into small daily segments so you can achieve them daily. This will help build your personal self-esteem when you are able to accomplish goals each day.
4. Tell family or friends what you want to accomplish. This will force you to make them happen! You don't want to be a failure in front of friends. Post the list where you will see it every day...on your refrigerator or mirror.
5. Read all the self-help books and listen to all the tapes you can find.

SOME GOOD SUGGESTIONS:
See You at the Top by Zig Ziglar
The Greatest Salesman by Og Mandino
How to Win Friends and Influence People
        by Dale Carnegie
The Greatest Thing in the World by Henry Drummond
Acres of Diamonds by Russell Conwell
And there are lots, lots more out there.

Go to your library and check out autobiographies of successful men like Victor Kiam, Dave Thomas, Sam Walton and Conrad Hilton. Read and study about these people's successes and failures. Reading these books and others like them will motivate YOU to success!!

LESSON TO BE LEARNED HERE IS: If you can dream it, you can achieve it!

Chapter 10

Gettysburg

Some things happened in '63 that looked like they might cause the war to wind down a little.. on January first I issued the Emancipation Proclamation.

On July first, second and third...outside the town of Gettysburg, Pennsylvania there was a major battle. At that one battle over 60,000 troops from the North and the South were either killed, wounded or missing in action. It became a major turning point of the Civil War. As the townspeople of Gettysburg were burying those dead soldiers in a 17-1/2 acre portion of that battlefield, they decided since this had not been just any ordinary battle, this certainly could not be just any ordinary cemetery. It needed national dedication and national recognition. The date was set for November 19, 1863 and a lot of very important people were invited to attend.

My friend, Edward Everett, a great Senator and former Governor from Massachusetts, was asked to be the main speaker of the day. Finally, on November 2, just two weeks ahead of time, I received a telegram at the White House asking me if I could come speak "a few appropriate remarks, just a short talk"...with the emphasis on SHORT.

I wrote my little speech in the White House, revised it slightly on the train on the way to Gettysburg and then revised it again for the third time in the home of Judge David Wills, the family I stayed with in Gettysburg.

CIVIL WAR CANNON NEAR THE SITE
WHERE ABE DELIVERED HIS SPEECH

THE GETTYSBURG ADDRESS

Four score and seven years ago, our fathers brought forth on this continent a new nation, conceived in liberty and dedicated to the proposition that all men are created equal.

Now we are engaged in a great Civil War, testing whether that nation, or any nation, so conceived and so dedicated, can long endure. We are met on a great battlefield of that war. We have come to dedicate a portion of that field as a final resting place for those who here gave their lives that that nation might live. It is altogether fitting and proper that we should do this.

But, in a larger sense, we can not dedicate--we can not consecrate--we can not hallow--this ground. The brave men, living and dead, who struggled here, have consecrated it far above our poor power to add or detract.

The world will little note nor long remember what we say here, but it can never forget what they did here. It is for us, the living, rather, to be dedicated here to the unfinished work which they who fought here have thus far so nobly advanced. It is rather for us to be here dedicated to the great task remaining before us--that from these honored dead we take increased devotion to that cause for which they gave the last full measure of devotion--that we here highly resolve that these dead shall not have died in vain--that this nation, under GOD, shall have a new birth of freedom--and that government of the people, by the people, for the people, shall not perish from the earth.

Chapter 11

Mom, Look Who's Here!

Did I tell you about the nice family I stayed with in Gettysburg? Judge Wills fed me a couple of good meals and I enjoyed visiting with him and his family. I stayed with a lot of nice folks in my travels as an attorney.

When I travel around the country visiting schools and other locations, I prefer to stay with families. That way I am not staring at the four walls of a motel room and having to eat fast-food all alone. That gets old! I enjoy visiting with families and having a good home-cooked meal and I leave them a frameable certificate which says "ABE" stayed with them.

The times when I don't have a family to stay with, I look for one of my favorite places to eat...Cracker Barrel Restaurants. I can always count on a good "home cooked" meal with reasonable "down home" prices and great "Presidential" friendly service. When you're traveling next time and want a great meal, stop by a Cracker Barrel and tell them ABE sent you.

As I have traveled, I've met some very special people all over America. It would take a complete book to tell you about all of them but I do want to share a few of my experiences.

I took the title of this chapter from a young student who lives in Grandview, Missouri. When I finished my program at her school on a Friday afternoon, she, her sister and brother said, "Mr. Lincoln, why don't you walk us home and surprise Mom?" I didn't have anywhere I needed to be for the night or the weekend so I agreed to walk with them two blocks to their house. When we arrived at the front door, Tonya, Melissa and Timmy yelled inside, " M o m , look who's here! We brought Mr. Lincoln home to dinner." Terri and Mac invited me to supper and to spend the night. I accepted their invitation and we had a great time visiting.

When I arrived at the home of principal, Al, his wife, Pat and son, Scott, in Sheridan, Indiana, he asked me, "Would you like to eat tonight?" I told him I would love to. He then told me "that we were going to a Rotary Club supper meeting...and by the way...would you SPEAK for your dinner?" As much as I love food...and talking...I readily agreed and spoke for 30 minutes after dinner. I am always ready to eat a good meal or talk to folks...anywhere...any time.

While I was on a tour of the beautiful state of Colorado in 1990, I was having some trouble with my red, white and blue sports car. I pulled into the little town of Swink late one afternoon with my radiator boiling over. As I was trying to figure out what to do, a very nice lady stopped by to see if she could help. Dorothy turned out to be the librarian at the school I would visit the next day. She was gracious enough to take me to a parts store where I bought a thermostat. She took me back to the car and found a high school student she knew who installed it for me. That weekend I went with her to visit her friends, Jack and Lori, who were in the process of building a log cabin. I helped them put up some fencing for their animals. I then visited the fort where Jack works.

In Ripon, Wisconsin, I stayed with Leon, Barb, Jenny and Paul. Leon drives a big tanker and picks up milk from a lot of dairy farms to make some of that great Wisconsin cheese. They showed me the little building where the first Republican Party meeting had been held just a few years before ABE became President. Ripon is also the home of Rippling Good Cookies.

When I was in south Texas, I heard about a man who lived

in Ingram. I was going to be driving near his home. I called and was able to stop by for an hour or so to see Bill and Peggy. Bill is one of the few men still living who helped carve Mount Rushmore. He showed me around his home and shared some of the "small" pieces he had sculpted. I would imagine after working on Mount Rushmore, no other artistic endeavor could ever compare! He was a fascinating man and we had a nice visit.

Bea is a wonderful counselor at her school and I stayed with her and Phillip at their home in Amity, Arkansas. Phillip took me on a tour of his sawmill. It was interesting for me to see how they cut big logs down to small boards to make pallets. All that modern technology sure beats the way ABE used to split rails and sawed boards by hand! Bea cooked us a great southern meal.

I stayed in Westlake, Ohio with Don, Maria, their twins, Amanda and Nicholas and MANDY. Mandy may very well be our first lady President! She is studying hard and heading in that direction already. Don also showed me around one of his six temp. service offices and we talked about the possibility of me doing some TV commercials for his company.

Connie and Melba cooked me a great meal in their school cafeteria in Lyons, Kansas. I always enjoy eating a good meal in school and these two ladies KNOW how to cook! Their cherry pie was excellent!

I went to Neal's ice hockey game and stayed with Biri, Catherine, Colin and Neal in Olmstead, Ohio. I had never seen an ice hockey game and it was exciting watching all those youngsters flying around on the ice.

The award for living closest to the school I would visit goes to Anne in San Antonio, Texas. Her home was directly across the street. She took me on a boat ride at the River Walk in downtown San Antonio.

When I pulled into one little town in Wisconsin, I didn't know where I was going to stay. I don't like staying in motels but I didn't have a family to stay with for the night. As I was reluctantly checking into a motel, I met Karen. She invited me to stay with her, Wanda and their 25 cats. That evening she took me to visit a family who had a dairy farm. While we were watching the cows being milked, one of them in a nearby stall decided it was time to "pee". She did and it splattered all over my black pants and frock-tailed coat. For the next two days nobody would get anywhere near me at school! I smelled bad! I finally got my suit to a cleaners that weekend...and not a minute too soon!

I stayed in a big, beautiful log cabin in Montello, Wisconsin with Rich, Monica, Ricky and Christopher. ABE would have loved THIS cabin!

When I stayed with Wayne, Linda, Bryn, Jim and Katie in Plover, Wisconsin, Wayne got a call to go out to a farm. Wayne is a vet and he invited me to go along with him. So I changed clothes and helped him deliver a calf. That was an experience! There really are vets who still make house calls!

The award for the largest family I've ever stayed with goes to Bobbie in Dallas, Texas. Her husband died a few years ago and Bobbie is raising Junior, Nicole, Jana, Joshua, Jennifer, Jamie, Jesse, John, Jeff, Julie, Joy and Jordan ALL BY HERSELF. Yes, count them again...twelve kids. One dozen! She is quite a hard-working mother! And, she also does a lot of volunteer work in the community. GOD bless you, Bobbie.

One of the "sweetest" ladies I've ever stayed with was in Garland, Texas. Sweet (That's her real name!), Kenny, Kendall and Ivy feed me great meals and Sweet later wrote me two of the nicest letters I've gotten from anyone. She is the PTA President and they should be proud to have such a hard working lady on their team. Kenny and Sweet...thank you for everything.

I stayed with teacher, Carol and bank president, Randy, and sons Scott and Nathan in Troy, Ohio. Randy's bank paid me to ride on the bank's float in a big parade on Saturday. Then I ran into them again that summer while I was at Mount Rushmore. Great food! Great folks!

When we were on the way to Virginia in the summer of 1993, we stopped at a Wendy's to eat. I met a couple from Texas and they asked me to call them the next time I was in Irving, Texas. My next trip to that area, I stayed with Bob and Sheila for a weekend. Their children, Lindsey and Logan, are both very talented, beautiful models for TV and newspaper ads and they took me for a walk/bike ride to a park a few blocks from their home.

In Round Rock, Texas I stayed with Richard and Sara. She is a wonderful, talented and caring, principal at the school I visited and Richard designs computers for IBM. He is also a pilot and has his own plane. One weekend when I was in the Austin area, I helped him wash his plane and then we went flying for an hour or so. I loved it! I relish every chance I get to SOAR WITH THE EAGLES!

The award for the biggest in-home fish collection goes to James in Flat Rock, Indiana. He is the school superintendent and his beautiful old two-story home is full of fish tanks of various sizes and descriptions. He had fresh and salt water tanks and I don't even remember all the types of fish he had collected over the years. They were beautiful!

Oink! Oink! That's the noise I heard from a couple of hundred pigs I helped feed late one night when I stayed with Jim, Judy and John in Rockbridge, Illinois. We ate some great pork chops for supper! I wonder where they came from? After we ate, I put on some big rubber boots and helped Jim feed and give shots to some of his pigs.

I stayed with Ray and Ronnie in Attica, Kansas the same day that Ronnie had run over and broken off a valve to a natural gas line in their backyard. They were lucky there wasn't an explosion! Ray is the principal at the school.

I milked my first and ONLY goat when I stayed with Tom,

Sara, Kellen, David and Paul in Three Lakes, Wisconsin. Milking a goat is different than milking a cow and it wasn't easy to get the hang of it. Tom is principal and raises bees in his spare time. He gives all of his teachers and friends fresh honey for the holidays. Sara has about a dozen goats and sells the goats' milk. Wisconsin is a cold place to visit in the winter...but I had a warm family to be with... and eat great food!

Brad and Brenda are teachers in Westlake, Ohio and Brad took me for a ride on his motorcycle along the shores of Lake Erie. We ate a big pancake breakfast at an old Veteran's Home.

Tom, Sharon, J.D. and Josh in Ironton, Ohio, had a big spread of food for me and a lot of friends who stopped by to meet "ABE". Tom took me to Masonic Lodge with him that night. I enjoy visiting other Lodges whenever I can.

On a trip in Ohio, I was talking on my CB radio to a UPS driver. He invited me to come home and have a meal with his family that weekend. Steve, Delores, Steven, Sarah, Rachael and Gracie fed me a good home-cooked meal in Broadview Heights, Ohio and I had a nice visit. This was just one of the many, many cases of people taking me in and feeding me when I wasn't even going to their school. I must have an honest face or something that makes strangers feel comfortable around me!

I've had many interesting experiences with African-Americans but two stick in my mind. One time I was at the Atlanta airport and prior to departure, I was having my boots shined. A security guard came over to me and politely asked me to come with her after I was finished. I followed her and she introduced me to her boss. She said, "Mr. Lincoln, I just wanted to thank you for what you did for the black people. Would you please autograph something for me?" I was more than happy to autograph one of my brochures for her.

When I took a group of students to Mount Vernon in March of 1994, I had another moving moment. As we were headed back to get on our bus, we were passing a long line of buses. A black driver was standing outside of his bus and when he saw me coming up the sidewalk, he got down on his knees in front of me, stuck out his hand and said, "Mr. Lincoln, I appreciate what you did for us and just wanted to shake your hand." I take portraying ABE very seriously and these two simple gestures of sincerity meant a lot to me personally. I understood what they both meant and how the man I represent would have felt under the same circumstances.

I am sorry I can't mention ALL of the nice families who took me in and fed me good meals or I met and visited with along the way. There just isn't enough space to list all of you. Perhaps someday soon I will write another book just about my experiences with families across the country. I do appreciate your hospitality and I hope anytime you are anywhere near the mountains of North Georgia, you will give me a call so I can try to return the hospitality.

LESSON TO BE LEARNED HERE IS: "Do unto others as you would have them do unto you." Go out of your way to be friendly to a stranger TODAY. Your smile, friendliness, caring and compassion to others will reward you ten-fold in so many ways. Give someone a hug today.

Chapter 12

The Importance of Letter Writing

I wrote a lot of letters while I was president. Some were happy but a lot of them were very sad letters.

November 21, 1863...

Dear Madam:

I have been shown in the files of the War Department a statement of the Adjutant General of Massachusetts, that you are the mother of five sons who have died gloriously on the field of battle.

I feel how weak and fruitless must be any words of mine which should attempt to beguile you from the grief of a loss so overwhelming. But I cannot refrain from tendering to you the consolation that may be found in the thanks of the Republic they died to save.

I pray that our Heavenly Father may assuage the anguish of your bereavement, and leave you only the cherished memory of the loved and lost, and the solemn pride that must be yours, to have laid so costly a sacrifice upon the altar of freedom. Yours, Very Sincerely, A. Lincoln

I included this letter because it has become a classic around the world and speaks so much of Lincoln's compassion, caring and concern.

One of the projects I've been working on these past few years is to get the law changed that allows ANYONE to burn our flag. I have been encouraging my students around the country to write letters and I would like for you to do the same.

Please take time right NOW to write a letter and address copies of it to your Senator, Congressman, TV stations, newspapers and the President. Tell them as a red-blooded patriotic American citizen, you want to see the law changed right now that allows anyone to burn our flag for any reason other than if it is torn, soiled or damaged. And then it should be burned in a ceremony.

I've been told by people I've met from other countries that if you burned the flag of their country, you would be SHOT or HUNG on the spot! If enough of my audiences and my readers will take time to write, perhaps someday soon we can get the law changed. Please, for the sake of our flag, write a letter TODAY!

This might be a good place to quote something I recently read in a book I borrowed from Sally Smith. *In and Out of Rebel Prisons* was written in 1888 by Lt. Alonzo Cooper and published by R.J. Oliphant, Job Printer, Bookbinder and Stationer of Oswego, NY. Lt. Cooper was born in 1830 so he was 32 years old when he joined the Union Forces in 1862. His book is an excellent look at Rebel prisons and the way the officers were treated in those prisons. Enlisted men were kept in separate prisons from their officers. The following paragraphs came from near the end of his book as 2,000 prisoners were being exchanged near the end of the war.

"When the head of the column came under the shadow of 'OLD GLORY', both our cheers and our old dilapidated hats went heavenward with all the velocity that we were able to impart to them. Some were too feeble to more than faintly whisper their greeting to the dear old flag they loved so dearly, while tears of joy attested the genuineness of their affection for that beautiful emblem of liberty, the sight of which had so long been denied them.

"I never before realized how much I loved the dear old stars and stripes, or how much protection there was beneath its shining folds. How I longed to press it to my heart and lips. And not me alone, but of the nearly two thousand skeletons who that day saw it proudly waving high over their heads for the first time in many months; there were few indeed who would not have fervently kissed and caressed it had it been within their reach. As a mother's love goes out to her first born that has come to her amid suffering and pain, so that old flag seemed a thousand fold more beautiful and precious to us, for the sufferings and privations we had passed through in its defense.

"Cheer after cheer went up as the straggling column passed along, feeble hands were waived, and feeble voices joined in the huzzahs, with which we celebrated our return to 'God's country'."

It is too bad some of our young people today have no idea what patriots of our country have gone through to keep our flag flying high. There needs to be more respect for our flag from young and old!

And a couple of more interesting quotes from an old book. These came from one of a dozen books I bought in a small used book store while visiting Gettysburg, Pennsylvania in January of 1994.

This is a quote from a speech given in an address before the Union League of Philadelphia on February 12, 1938 by Joseph Fort Newton taken from his book, We Here Highly Resolve, published by Harper & Brothers in 1939.

"No one is really masterful until he has first been mastered by a great idea, a great cause, a great passion, a great purpose. Something outside himself, greater than himself, worthy of the utmost devotion is needed to unify his life, organize his energies, and give power to his genius."

THIS IS A STRONG MESSAGE FOR ALL OF US TO THINK ABOUT! It certainly fits Lincoln and probably fits me too! My CAUSE since 1975 has been to help our youth have a positive attitude about life, read more, stay off drugs, respect their parents and teachers and...NOW...more recently...do whatever they can to help stop youth violence in America.

Another quote from this same book. This one is from the sermon delivered by Mr. Newton at the 75th Anniversary of the Battle of Gettysburg, July 3, 1938.

This is from the very end of his sermon and speaks strong words for us today...

"'That we here highly resolve,' as one people, under one flag, that we join hearts in one faith, join hands in one purpose, uniting spiritual vision and political wisdom, and individual initiative with social obligation, for the safety and sanctity of our republic; for the rights of man and the majesty of the law; for the moral trusteeship of private property, public office, and social welfare; for the education of the young in the laws of life, the freedom of the truth, and the service of humanity; for the lifting of poverty, through self-help, to security, comfort, and nobility; for the holiness of the home and the altar; for a life more abundant, a liberty more responsible, and a happiness more abiding.

"May the God of our fathers, who has led us thus far down the ways of time, mercifully grant that our flag---symbol of blood-making not of blood-shedding--- may never again float over a field of war, but ever and forever over scenes of peace, honor, and progress; flag of unity and justice at home, of fraternity and good will among all nations; the ensign of a free people, uniting many races without rancor, many faiths without feud, many classes without friction; in a land where men not only live and let live, think and let think, but live and help live; that the high destiny of man and the holy will of God may be fulfilled in the history of our country. Amen."

It has now been 56 years since these words were uttered by a great speaker but they are words very fitting for our society today. Please pay particular attention to what he said about our flag. What would ABE have said about someone burning our flag? I don't think he would have tolerated it! Do you? Please do as I have suggested and take time to write a letter about changing the law that allows anyone to burn our flag.

I can't emphasize enough to my young readers the importance of learning letter writing at an early age. The ability to communicate with the rest of the world is something we all need to be able to do.

I learned very early about how to get results with letter writing. If you want to find out what a good letter can do in a hurry, go into your cupboard and get a box of your favorite cereal, cookies, soup or other products you really like to eat. Sit down and write a letter to the president of the company. Tell them how much you love their products and you and your family eat them all the time. Get Mom or Dad to show you how to address the envelope properly---if you don't already know--- and send the letter to the address listed on the package.

Within two or three weeks you will probably receive a nice letter from the company, along with some coupons good for FREE products. I've gotten lots of coupons good for free food and other items over the years by writing letters to companies. You can have fun doing it and writing the letters is a good experience for you.

I have taught my children to write letters when they liked a particular product or found something defective. My son, Jason, once bought a can of tennis balls with a defective lid. He wrote to the company and got two free cans of tennis balls. You need to take time to write whether it is a compliment or a complaint. A company's customer service department wants to hear from its customers...good or bad!

Here is probably a good place to say something about one of my pet peeves . . . answering correspondence. ATTENTION: CORPORATE EXECUTIVES AND ANYONE WHO RECEIVES MAIL...Please have the courtesy to answer your mail. Even if you aren't able to help or give the kind of results the writer might wish, at least acknowledge their letter. And do so as quickly as possible. I've sent letters to companies and executives who have taken a month or two to answer, or in some cases, never answered at all.

THE FOLLOWING PAGES CONTAIN COPIES OF LETTERS I'VE RECEIVED FROM PEOPLE ALL OVER THE WORLD.

LESSON TO BE LEARNED HERE IS: Take time to send a NICE letter or card to someone at least once a week. They will be glad to hear from you.

WALT DISNEY PRODUCTIONS

500 SO. BUENA VISTA ST. • BURBANK, CALIFORNIA 91503 • CABLE ADDRESS: DISNEY

August 2, 1967

Mr. Homer S. Sewell III
Post Office Box 265
Altamonte Springs, Florida 32701

Dear Mr. Sewell:

General William E. Potter has asked me to respond to
your letter of July 19, regarding our Disney World
project near Orlando, Florida.

Our Experimental Prototype Community of Tomorrow has
been projected for the second phase of the development,
and construction is not expected to begin until the
early 1970s. The first phase of the development will
include motels, outdoor recreation facilities and an
amusement theme park similar to our Disneyland in
California.

As a specific opening date for our EPCOT community has
not yet been set, we have not yet reached the point
where we will be considering products such as the
"Cutco" cutlery and tools you are offering. It will
be a number of months yet before a purchasing department is established to handle presentations such as
yours, however, I will place your letter in our files
for consultation at that time.

Thank you very much for your interest in Walt Disney
Productions.

Very truly yours,

James L. Stewart

JLS/jh

NO AGREEMENT WILL BE BINDING ON THIS CORPORATION UNLESS IN WRITING AND SIGNED BY AN OFFICER

 **EASTERN**

January 18, 1973

Mr. Homer S. Sewell III
P. O. Box 6426
Ft. Myers, Florida 33901

Dear Mr. Sewell:

Thank you for your recent inquiry regarding employment opportunities with Eastern Airlines. Your letter of December 31, 1972, which outlines your background and experience has been forwarded to me by Mr. S. L. Higginbottom.

We have reviewed your qualifications and, indeed, find them impressive. Currently, we are not adding to our work force and we project this situation to continue beyond the near future. We, therefore, must advise you that we cannot actively consider you at this time, but we are taking the liberty of keeping your file active for future consideration. Should an appropriate opening materialize, we shall notify you immediately.

We appreciate your interest in Eastern and look forward to the possibility of having further contact with you.

Sincerely,

Robert O. Hach
Specialist
Management Recruiting

ROH:mf

THE WHITE HOUSE

WASHINGTON

March 25, 1976

Dear Mr. Sewell:

President Ford has asked me to thank you for
your kind message of support and generous
offer of assistance in his election campaign.

As you may know, the President is determined
to maintain a clear separation between his
official duties and his role as a candidate,
in full compliance with Federal election law.
Therefore, he has directed that all campaign
activities be handled by the President Ford
Committee, and I am forwarding your letter
to the Committee. I am sure they will be in
touch with you shortly.

The President wants you to know he is grateful
for your willingness to assist in his campaign.

Sincerely,

Roland L. Elliott
Director of Correspondence

Mr. Homer S. Sewell III
Post Office Box 944
Altamore Springs, Florida   32701

THE WHITE HOUSE

WASHINGTON

March 24, 1977

Dear Mr. Sewell:

On behalf of President and Mrs. Carter, I wish to thank you for your kind invitation to visit your home.

The Carters are grateful for your expression of friendship and will keep your gracious invitation in mind for the future. They send their regards and warm good wishes.

Sincerely,

Jane S. Fenderson
Appointments Secretary to
Rosalynn Carter

Mr. Homer S. Sewell III
Post Office Box 708
Franklin, North Carolina   28734

Flea Training Certificate

DALLAS, TEXAS_____November 2,_____19 73

Read This Well ∿ Here's A Story To Tell

Let the whole world know that_____Homer S. Sewell lll_____is
a fully qualified--dedicated-- " Flea Trainer." By jumping out of the jar and refusing to
get cooked " in the squat", he is earning the rights and privileges this world has to offer.

Flea Trainers are people who are driven from within and are not "SNIOPS" (Susceptible to
Negative Influence of Other People). They have removed their own ceilings and are
teaching others to do the same.

Flea Trainers work at seeing people through-instead of seeing through people. They
teach others how to " get on"-instead of telling them where to " get off." They are con-
fident but not arrogant and know how to serve without being servile.

Flea Trainers seek " total" success and a well balanced life by building on honesty,
character, loyalty, faith and integrity. They know that dedicated effort is its own reward
and that what you get by reaching your objective is not as important as what you become
by reaching that objective.

_____Homer_____is going up with the knowledge that " he climbs highest
who helps another up."

Zig Ziglar

Zig Ziglar
America's No. 1 Flea Trainer

Ⓒ ZIG ZIGLAR 1975

174

Philip Caldwell
Vice Chairman of the Board

Ford Motor Company
The American Road
Dearborn, Michigan 48121

October 4, 1978

Dear Mr. Sewell:

Thank you for your congratulatory note, and
for your kind words about Ford Motor Company.
I trust that we will continue to merit your esteem.

Sincerely,

Philip Caldwell

Mr. Homer S. Sewell III
Realtor-Associate
Gale Associates
Real Estate One, Inc.
424 Semoran Boulevard
Altamonte Springs, Florida 32701

The First Baptist Church

553 CHURCH STREET / JASPER, GEORGIA 30143
February 11, 1985

Dear Homer,

Your presentation of Abraham Lincoln Sunday night was excellent.
Thank you so much for coming to be with us and giving this inspiring patriotic message. The music and speaking parts all fit together and made a very impressive and meaningful program.

Thanks again,

Charles O. Walker

COW/ms

CHARLES O. WALKER
PASTOR
DAVID M. STUART
MINISTER OF MUSIC-YOUTH

176

DEPARTMENT OF THE ARMY
MOBILE DISTRICT, CORPS OF ENGINEERS
OFFICE OF THE RESOURCE MANAGER, CARTERS LAKE
P.O. BOX 86, OAKMAN, GEORGIA 30732-9999
TELEPHONE 404/334-2248

November 9, 1988

REPLY TO
ATTENTION OF:

Resource Manager

Mr. Homer Sewell
P.O. Box 13
Jasper, Georgia   30143

Dear Mr. Sewell (Abe):

The U. S. Army Corps of Engineers' staff at Carters Lake would like to thank you for your concern, support, and participation in our first multi-high school Stay-in-School Program.

The program proved to be a big success only because of concerned individuals such as yourself. The teachers and counselors expressed many positive comments and thanks for everyone's active role in donating their time and interest in working with their students.

This year's Stay-in-School Program hosted approximately 255 students with teachers and counselors from five local high schools. With the drop out rate between 45% - 50% in Northwest Georgia, your participation in this program is greatly appreciated by all.

Once again, we appreciate your time and participation in this program. It proved to be most successful only because of the high quality of presentations and sincere interest of speakers like yourself.

Sincerely,

Jeffrey C. Pobieglo
Park Ranger
Carters Lake

177

Frenship
North Ridge Elementary School

". . . Making tracks together!"

Rod Davis
Principal

TO WHOM IT MAY CONCERN:

If ever the word "pride", "honor", "motivation", and "patriotism" could be extended to describe an individual, it would be proper and fitting in Homer Sewell's abilities to portray President Abraham Lincoln. Sewell's entertaining stories of Lincoln's life is a rare personal exposure to the human side of the man called "Abe". Sewell's unique touch with youngsters makes this program a true hands-on learning experience.

Sincerely,

Rod Davis

Principal

(806) 793-6686
6302 11th Street   Lubbock, Texas
Mailing Address: P.O. Box 100, Wolfforth, Texas 79382

178

Denver City Intermediate School

"Kids Under Construction"

Gerald F. Judd
Principal

February 3, 1991

Homer S. Sewell III
P.O. Box 13
Jasper, GA   30143-0013

Dear Homer,

Your portrayal of Abe Lincoln made a famous American come alive and history real and meaningful.

Our students were spellbound. When you are able to keep the attention of 4th, 5th, and 6th grade children for a full day you have accomplished a great deal.

I realized you had captured the audience from the quality of questions the children were asking.

I would say to any school person, if you book just one assembly program for the year . . . this is the one!

Thank you for making us proud to be Americans.

Gratefully,

Gerald F. Judd

GFJ/sjs

Denver City ISD   "The Key Is You"

1003 North Avenue F
Denver City, TX 79323-2599
(806) 592-2623

179

115 NORTH PRAIRIE STREET
GREENFIELD, IL 62044
(217) 368-2551

MARILYN SCHILD
PRINCIPAL

February 9, 1991

Mr. Homer S. Sewell III
P.O. Box 13
Jasper, GA 30143-0013

Dear "Abe,"

On behalf of the students and staff at Greenfield Elementary School, I would like to express our appreciation and gratitude for your visit to our school. The presentations you made during the assembly for students in grades 3-8 as well as the classroom visits for students in K-2 were educational, inspiring and enjoyable. Teachers as well as students have commented that your presentation was one of the best we have had.

We certainly will recommend your program to others and hope that we have the opportunity to visit with you again. Good luck as you inspire others to be dreamers and rainbow chasers who soar with the eagles as they "become!"

Sincerely,

Marilyn Schild

Marilyn Schild
Principal

180

MISTER ROGERS' NEIGHBORHOOD

Family Communications, Inc. 4802 Fifth Avenue Pittsburgh, PA 15213 (412) 687-2990 FAX (412) 687-1226

June, 1991

Mr. Homer Sewell III
P.O. Box 13
Jasper, GA 30143-0013

Dear Mr. Sewell,

It was a pleasure to get to know you from your thoughtful
letter, and we're sorry we weren't able to answer sooner.
In the past months we received so much mail from our viewers
that it's been difficult to respond as quickly as we'd like
-- nevertheless, we want to continue to be as personal as
possible in all of our communication. Unfortunately, that
causes some delays, but we hope you will understand.

Thank you for your kind comments about our program. We're
deeply grateful for your support of our work. It was
interesting, too, to know about your connections with
Rollins College.

It's good to know you've found your own creative way to help
children think about things like honesty, values, and
respect through your appearances as Abraham Lincoln. We
appreciated your offer to visit on our program, but it's not
likely that we could consider inviting you to be on our
program. We produce only 15 new programs a year to add to
our series; those are organized as three new weeks of
programs, each with a central theme into which all the
elements relate.

Nevertheless, I personally am very much interested in the
life of Lincoln. (I love Sandburg's collection.) I was
wondering if you have a videotape of your work which I could
view for my own pleasure. Of course, I will return it to
you. Thank you for thinking of us, and thank you for all
you do for others.

Best wishes to you from all of us here in the Neighborhood.

Sincerely,

Fred Rogers

MISTER ROGERS' NEIGHBORHOOD is underwritten by Public Television Stations and
The Sears-Roebuck Foundation which is funded by Sears | Allstate | Dean Witter | Coldwell Banker.

181

ESTABLISHED 1818

Brooks Brothers

CLOTHING

Furnishings for Men, Women & Boys

MADISON AVE. Cor. 44th ST., NEW YORK, N.Y.10017
(212) 682-8800

August 2, 1991

Mr. Homer S. Sewell III
P.O. Box 13
Jasper, GA 30143-0013

Dear Mr. Sewell,

Thank you for forwarding information on your services to Brooks Brothers; we are always interested in ways of tieing in our store's history with American history in general.

At the present time, there are no future plans for highlighting our special connection with President Abraham Lincoln. However, should the occasion arise, we will certainly consider your public speaking services.

Again, thank you for contacting us and the best of luck in your endeavors.

Sincerely,   THIS COMPANY SOLD SUITS TO ABE

Karen Pavone

Karen Pavone
Advertising and Public Relations

MAYFIELD ⬤ DAIRY FARMS

Mr. Homer S. Sewell, III
Post Office Box 13
Jasper, Georgia 30143-0013

Dear Mr. Sewell:

Thank you so much for writing to tell us how much you enjoy our ice cream and milk. We strive for excellence in our products and always enjoy receiving compliments from our customers, especially those who have just recently joined our "Mayfield" family.

There are other Mayfield dairy products available that you and your family might enjoy trying. To meet the needs of our customers who are trying to reduce the amount of fat in their diets, we have introduced a line of Fruit Stix in a variety of flavors, and Fudge Stix. They are sugar-free, low in fat, and are enjoyed by "young and old" alike. Our low-fat frozen yogurt is also available in six delicious flavors, and you and your family may find you enjoy it as much as ice cream. The enclosed brochure shows our other products that you may enjoy sampling.

You do have a striking resemblance to our sixteenth president, Abraham Lincoln, and it was interesting to read about the similarities between Abe Lincoln's life and your own. Your presentations are certainly a fun way to gain knowledge about Abe's life and the history during that time period. I will forward the information to our ad agency in Atlanta, and they will keep it on file in the event an occasion should arise for this type of marketing.

Again, thank you for taking the time to tell us how much you enjoy Mayfield products. We certainly appreciate your business and hope you and your family will continue to be Mayfield customers. The enclosed gift certificates are for your enjoyment.

Sincerely,

C. Scott Mayfield
Senior Vice President

CSM/af

Enclosures

P.O. Box 310, 806 E. Madison Ave., Athens, TN 37303   Phone (615) 745-2151   FAX (615) 745-9118

The Zig Ziglar ▨ Corporation

THE TRAINING COMPANY ™

Zig Ziglar
Chairman

October 30, 1991

Mr. Homer S. Sewell, III
Post Office Box 13
Jasper, Georgia 30143-0013

Dear "Abe":

Thanks for your note, your kind words about my work, and your offer to appear on a program with me.

I don't personally sponsor any of my public seminars, Homer, so I'm not involved in the selection of other personalities which might be featured on those programs. However, should an opportunity arise wherein I can recommend you be considered, I'll be happy to do so.

Thanks again. God bless you in what you're doing. Have a good forever, and I'll...

SEE YOU AT THE TOP!

Zig Ziglar
Zig Ziglar

ZZ/lm

November 13, 1991

Mr. Homer Sewell
P.O. Box 13
Jasper, GA 30143-0013

Dear Mr. Sewell,

On behalf of Smith School and the Smith School PTA, I would like to express our thanks to you for providing a most rewarding day for our children.

Your portrayal of Abraham Lincoln was marvelous! Your enthusiasm for the man and his life was transferred to each child. Both of my young sons came home from school and talked non-stop about what they had learned. Your advice to the children to be dreamers, stargazers, rainbow chasers and to soar with the eagles was a very valuable gift indeed.

I am enclosing copies of several articles that appeared in local Cleveland and Berea papers.

Again, many thanks for a wonderful day!

Sincerely,

Barbara m. norris

Barbara M. Norris
President, Smith PTA

bmn/s
encls.

THE READER'S DIGEST ASSOCIATION, INC,
READER'S DIGEST ROAD
PLEASANTVILLE, NY 10570-7000

ELINOR ALLCOTT GRIFFITH
Correspondence Editor

February 28, 1992

Mr. Homer S. Sewell III
P.O. Box 13
Jasper, GA 30143-0013

Dear Mr. Sewell:

Thank you for your letter to Kenneth Tomlinson telling us how you promote Reader's Digest in your talks as "Abe Lincoln" to students. We're certainly pleased you find the magazine so educational and want to share your enjoyment with others. It's always encouraging to hear from such an ardent supporter of the magazine -- especially one as trustworthy as "Abe" himself!

It was good of you to write. We appreciate your interest in Reader's Digest.

Sincerely,

Elinor Griffith

186

April 3, 1992

To: Mr. Homer Sewell
     a.k.a. Abraham Lincoln
     P.O. Box 13
     Jasper, Ga 30143-0013

From: Lynn Elms
      Chairperson The Big Top Performers
                  Lubbock Arts Festival
      4605 18th Street
      Lubbock, Texas 79416

To Whom It May Concern:

        I have had the fortunate opportunity to meet and participate in
Mr. Homer Sewell's sharing of Abraham Lincoln. This man is truly
"called" to characterize the sixteenth president of the United
States. I was with Mr. Sewell in two very different situations: one
at our area wide Arts Festival which drew approximately 90,000 people
and in three of our elementary schools. He was a wonderful addition
to our Festival. He took the time to give lectures, to hand out
signed Gettysburg addresses and meet people during the three day
event. At our elementary schools he was met with great enthusiasm.
I would especially like to share one event which was an example of
this man's character. We were walking down the primary wing of one
elementary school when six deaf education children saw him coming.
The faces lite up and hands flew in excitement. Their teacher
explained that they had been studying Lincoln since early November
and they could not believe that he was in their school. Homer
stopped and took time with each child. He allowed them to see his
watch, try on his hat and tug at his beard and all the while shining
a smile that was pure joy. This encounter was but one of many
unscheduled and unplanned events which Mr. Sewell graciously handled.
I would encourage every opportunity for children to experience what
Mr. Sewell so wonderfully and knowledgeably calls his work.

Sincerely,
Lynn Elms

187

Richardson Independent School District

February 10, 1993

To All RISD Elementary Principals

Dear Colleagues,

I just spent the day with Abe Lincoln. Actually, President Lincoln spent the day here at Yale interacting with our kids, teachers, and parents in a very unique way. He put in a full day (8:00 a.m. to 9:00 p.m.) storytelling, visiting, conducting assemblies and grade-level question & answer sessions...and even had a great time helping pull lunch recess. The sight of Abe Lincoln booming punts halfway across the Yale playground in his stovepipe hat is a sight to see. The kids loved him, and he obviously enjoyed working with them. He was outside to see them off at the end of the day as they left on buses and cars and he was back fresh and ready for the PTA meeting where he was just as good with the parents.

The man portraying Lincoln is Homer Sewell, an actor from Georgia who does this full time. He has been to about 830 schools over the past few years and has talked to many thousands of children. I believe he is very effective in delivering his message, which is a combination of patriotism, commitment to a drug-free life, and just good old American values. His fee can be funded by your PTA, your corporate sponsor, or it qualifies as an anti-drug program if you want to pursue that avenue.

I highly recommend this program and am attaching information in case you want to contact him about a possible engagement for your school.

Cordially,

John Phillips

Dr. John Phillips, Principal
Yale Elementary School

400 S. Greenville Avenue   Richardson, Texas 75081   214/238-8111

188

BUCKINGHAM PALACE

31st March, 1993.

Dear Mr. Sewell,

I am commanded by The Queen to write and thank you for your letter, and for the enclosures you sent.

Her Majesty thought it kind of you to tell her of your teachings on Abraham Lincoln to schools in the United States of America. I am afraid it would not be possible, however, for The Queen to help in the way you ask, owing to the very large number of letters and requests received each day.

Perhaps you could contact the Central Bureau for Educational Visits and Exchanges at Seymour Mews House, Seymour Mews, London, W1H 9PE, England; telephone 071 486 5101, who might be able to make some suggestions.

I am to thank you once again for your letter.

Yours sincerely,

Susan Hussey.

Lady-in-Waiting

Mr. H.S. Sewell, III.

The Dial Corp

John W. Teets
Chairman, President and
Chief Executive Officer
phone 602. 207 6060

The Dial Corp
1850 North Central Avenue
Phoenix, AZ 85077

August 18, 1993

Mr. Homer S. Sewell, III
P. O. Box 13
Jasper, GA 30143-0013

Dear Mr. Sewell:

Thank you very for your letter of July 12, and I'm pleased you enjoyed the article in <u>Scottish Rite Journal</u>.

I am sure your portrayal of Abraham Lincoln is very memorable and that students and parents alike learn much about his profound wisdom. Unfortunately, Dial does not have a budget to support such endeavors.

Again, my sincere thanks for your letter and good luck in your program.

Sincerely,

John W. Teets

rbf

190

2733 Woods Lane
Garland, Texas 75044
November 14, 1993

Homer S. Sewell III
P O Box 13
Jasper, Ga 30143

Dear Homer:

What a wonderful, educational, inspiring, and exciting day you provided for our school.
I am still hearing praises from teachers, parents, and children about our visit from
Abe Lincoln. I cannot begin to thank you enough for the work which you do and the
message that you present to a new generation of Americans.

Numerous parents have told me that their children have not stopped talking about
your visit. We probably spent thirty minutes from an hour long PTA Board meeting
praising you. After I elaborated about what a delightful individual you are, how
wonderfully the children responded to you, and how relevant and important your
message is the other officers piped up and said they had never seen their children so
excited about a program. Just yesterday a friend from church told me that her fourth
grader who never comments on anything talked for a full forty-five minutes about
Abraham Lincoln and your program. It would be a gross understatement to say that
the Big Springs Community was impressed.

I am enclosing a message which I intend to distribute to other schools and the few
individuals whom I know that are involved in service organizations both here and in
Alabama. You are welcome to use this letter for your own references in any way that
you would like.

On a personal note Kenny, Kendall, Ivy and I immensely enjoyed your stay in our
home. We are the only family I know who now has a Lincoln bedroom ,and we were
entertained and educated beyond our furtherest expectations. You have led an
incredibly interesting life. Homer, you will never know the lives that you have
touched and the individuals that you have inspired. Your genuine love of people and
your gift of demonstrating that sincerely is a trait to be treasured. I truly believe
that you in your own right are a contemporary American hero and a wonderful person
to exemplify the spirit and character of Abraham Lincoln.

If ever there is anything that we can do to advance your appearances please let us
know. It is a noble and inspiring profession.

Your friend,

Sweet Hopkins
PTA President
Big Springs Elementary

191

FEED THE CHILDREN

LARRY JONES INTERNATIONAL MINISTRIES, INC.

Post Office Box 36, Oklahoma City, OK 73101-0036 • 405/942-0228 • Larry Jones, President

February 23, 1994

Homer S. Sewell III aka
"ABE LINCOLN"
C/O Gwen Knight/Public Relations
P. O. Box 10157
Cocoa, FL 32927-0157

To Whom It May Concern:

Dr. Larry Jones and our entire staff are pleased that President Lincoln
has agreed to raise badly needed funds for Feed The Children by initiating
"penny drives" and other projects at various schools where he conducts his
marvelous presentations.

Your kind support of 1200 pennies will allow us to procure and deliver 100
pounds of staple food items to deserving American children. Therefore, we
would appreciate any courtesies and cooperation that you could extend
"Honest Abe" in his efforts to increase awareness of child hunger in
America and help feed hungry kids.

Please call if I can answer questions concerning our relationship with Mr.
Sewell or about Feed The Children.

For the Children,

Michael B. Man

Michael B. Man
Director of Special Projects

MBM/mw

REMINGTON
PRODUCTS COMPANY

60 Main Street
Bridgeport, Conn. 06604
(203) 332-9773
TELEX: 4750046
FAX (203) 366-6039

VICTOR K. KIAM II
Chief Executive Officer

March 31, 1994

Mr. Homer S. Sewell, III
Abe Lincoln's America
P. O. Box 13
Jasper, CA 30143-0013

Dear Mr. Sewell:

Thank you for the autographed picture you sent along with
your note, and your kind and gracious wishes for my family
and Remington Products. I also share your wishes for this
great country.

Good luck in your all your endeavors, and may your book be a
great success.

Sincerely,

[signature: Victor K. Kiam]

3314e

Chapter 13

Taking a Trip

When the war was finally over, Mary started talking to me about going to a theater to relax and forget about the war. I said, "Mary, I don't have time to go to any theater. I've got a country to put back together again." She kept after me until I finally agreed to go on Good Friday evening, April 14... just five short days after the war had ended!

Early in 1991, I was asked by the National Park Service at Mount Rushmore National Memorial to help them with their upcoming 50th Anniversary Dedication Celebration to be held during the week of July 4, 1991. I was excited about the prospect of being there as history was being made with this celebration.

I have always enjoyed visiting our National Parks and do so every chance I get. I hope that you and your family are able to spend time enjoying our great National Parks located throughout America.

As a Mason I was even more excited knowing one of our greatest Masons, President George Washington was also on the mountain and there would be a look-alike for him as well as the other two presidents.

As the time drew nearer it was mentioned to me that President George Bush had been invited to participate along with a lot of famous people. All four of the Presidents who are on the mountain would be represented during the upcoming celebration...GEORGE WASHINGTON, THOMAS JEFFERSON,

TEDDY ROOSEVELT and ABRAHAM LINCOLN. The lady in charge of the program was having a difficult time finding look-alikes for all of the Presidents and I was quick to be the first to say I would be there to help out however I could. She didn't know until just a couple of weeks ahead of time whether President Bush would be able to attend.

I decided even though it was a 1,550 mile drive to South Dakota, I would take my family. I wanted them to be a part of it, too. We packed the car and left Georgia on Thursday, June 27.

We made one stop in Tennessee and then spent Friday night with our friends, the Grays, in Springfield, Missouri. We did a little boating with them on Saturday morning and I rode a jet-ski for the first time. It was a lot more fun than riding a horse. We then continued on our journey.

We tried to find a place to spend the night Saturday night but after stopping at about two dozen motels all through Iowa, we finally gave up on getting a good night's sleep. I knew then how Joseph must've felt. There was no room in the inn! There must have been something big happening because there just weren't any motels with rooms available anywhere!

Finally, at about 6 AM Sunday, after I had been driving all night, we stopped at a little restaurant, just across the border into South Dakota, to have some breakfast. I was telling the waitress we had been driving all night and were really wanting a place to get a few hours sleep before going on to Mount Rushmore. She and her husband invited us to go to their home. We were able to shower and get a few hours sleep. There really are still people out there who will take in total strangers. We appreciated their hospitality.

We arrived Sunday evening, June 30, about 7:00 PM. Reservations had been made for us at the lovely First Lady Motel...in Keystone, just three miles from the memorial. As soon as we were checked into the motel, I drove the family the final three miles so we could see the mountain. I don't know about the rest of the family but I couldn't wait any longer. I just had to see the mountain right then! That night!

It was absolutely awesome! Beyond anything you could imagine! And all carved on the face of a mountain with air-driven-drills and dynamite...by a man with a dream!! You talk about NEVER GIVING UP! Mr. Borglum certainly didn't!

Monday morning, July 1, I got dressed and went to the park to meet with those in charge. I started walking around and being "mobbed" by visitors wanting to have their pictures taken with me. IT WAS GREAT!! I discovered that if I stood in just the right spot on the terrace at the visitor center, people could be in the picture with me with the memorial in the background behind and above us. I always pointed out they should be sure to get the guy on the right in the picture...that was ABE!!

I was there in character all day Monday and Tuesday. Wednesday, President Bush was there from 2:00 - 3:00 P.M. and the park was closed to the public. Only about 3,500 specially picked people were allowed to be there for the ceremonies which included President and Mrs. Bush, Tom Brokaw, Mary Hart, Mr. and Mrs. Jimmy Stewart, Barbara Eden, White Eagle and others. The Secret Service said the four look-alikes could NOT come in character! What a disappointment! I had hoped all four of us could have gotten our picture in front of the memorial shaking hands with the President. I still think he missed a great photo-opportunity! I don't know why the Secret Service doesn't allow someone who has already passed security checks to be anywhere near the President! So I was there in my jeans with my family to witness the official dedication.

Wednesday evening all four of us "presidents" were in a greeting line at a gala reception for about 500 VIP'S in Rapid City. We were able to meet and chat with Mr. and Mrs. Jimmy Stewart, Barbara Eden, Secretary of the Interior and others.

Thursday, the four of us were in a 260-unit parade in downtown Rapid City and then it was back to the mountain for more picture-taking and visiting with nice folks from all over the world. If I'd gotten a dollar for each time someone took my picture, I would be rich.

Friday, I was at the memorial for a full-day of picture taking and lots of just plain pride to be a part of it all! That evening my family and I stopped by Rapid City to speak to a group of about 75 people at a senior citizen village. This gave me another opportunity to visit with some of my favorite people...seniors. Then we headed out for the long drive back to Atlanta.

Oh! I've got T-shirts of the memorial, poster-pictures and lots of photos we took but the biggest souvenir I have was just being there!! There are no words to describe my feelings upon seeing the image of ABE and the others carved on that big mountain!

MR. BORGLUM (THE SCULPTOR) GEORGE, TOM, TEDDY AND ABE

LESSON TO BE LEARNED HERE IS: Nothing is impossible if you work at it hard enough!

"ABE" WITH SENIOR CITIZEN AT MOUNT RUSHMORE

United States Department of the Interior

NATIONAL PARK SERVICE
MOUNT RUSHMORE NATIONAL MEMORIAL
KEYSTONE, SOUTH DAKOTA 57751-0268

IN REPLY
REFER TO:

A-8215

July 22, 1991

Mr. Homer Sewell
P.O. Box 13
Jasper, Georgia   30143-0013

Dear Mr. Sewell:

What a pleasure it was to have you as Abe Lincoln at Mount Rushmore
National Memorial for the Golden Anniversary Celebration. You helped to
make the series of events in which you were involved even more memorable.

Homer, I know we had a busy schedule for you during your stay in the Black
Hills of South Dakota, but having you here was very key to all of those
events. You and the other three presidents and Gutzon Borglum were the
hit of the reception in Rapid City the evening of July 3. The parade
would not have been complete without all of you on July 4. And, the
evening program here at Mount Rushmore on July 4 was spectacular with an
estimated 4,000 people in attendance. The four presidents pulled together
and worked out a wonderful program, each talking about the reason they
were chosen to be a piece of this spectacular carving.

The Golden Anniversary Celebration and Formal Dedication of Mount Rushmore
National Memorial is the largest event in the history of South Dakota. We
are all very proud to have been a part of history -- and hope you are too.

Sincerely,

Daniel N. Wenk
Superintendent

Enclosure:
Certificate of Appreciation

With Grateful Recognition and Appreciatio

to

HOMER SEWELL
_____

for participating in
The Golden Anniversary Celebration
of
Mount Rushmore National Memorial
1941 - 1991

Daniel N. Wenk, Superintendent
Mount Rushmore National Memorial

Carolyn Mollers, President
Mount Rushmore National Memorial Societ

200

Chapter 14

Search for Family

Mary and I had four sons: Robert, Eddie, Willie and Tad. We loved our boys very much.

I've known all along I was adopted when I was ten weeks old. As I have gotten older I have wondered what my birth parents were like and did I have any brothers and sisters. Were my parents still living and if so, where?

I love my adopted family very much and have always felt proud to be part of the Sewell family and to have been adopted by a couple who gave me so much love. But I think all of us have a desire deep down inside to know about our roots and biological family background. As I have gotten older, the desire to find my roots has become stronger.

In 1981 I paid my dues and joined A.L.M.A. (Adoptees Liberty Movement Association) in hopes of finding a match between me and my birth parents, if they were looking for me. Nothing ever came of that.

When I made the decision in the summer of 1990 to go full-time as ABE and travel all over the country talking to students, I also started doing some serious looking in phone books for my birth name...FERENCY. The copies of correspondence on the following pages are just part of the intensive search that took me a couple of years to do.

DEPARTMENT OF THE ARMY

HEADQUARTERS. 24TH INFANTRY DIVISION (MECHANIZED) AND FORT STEWART
FORT STEWART. GEORGIA 31314-5000

January 31, 1986

REPLY TO
ATTENTION OF

Records Management Office

Homer S. Sewell III
Post Office Box 13
Jasper, Georgia 30143-0013

Dear Mr. Sewell:

This is our response to your January 11, 1986, request for information concerning your biological father.

This headquarters does not have any military personnel records dating back to the August 1943 time frame. Military personnel records are transferred to the National Personnel Records Center in St. Louis, Missouri.

We contacted Ms. French at the National Personnel Records Center and were informed that these records are not releasable to you under the Freedom of Information Act. However, for further assistance and information, you can contact Ms. French at the following address:

> National Personnel Records Center
> 9700 Page Boulevard
> St. Louis, Missouri 63132

Your biological father's full name and home of record may be listed on your birth certificate. Since you were born in Hinesville, your birth certificate should be on file at the Liberty County Probate Court. The Probate Court's address is as follows:

> Liberty County Probate Court
> Post Office Box 28
> Hinesville, Georgia 31313

To avoid delays, cite the Freedom of Information Act when requesting information regarding your biological father and cite the Privacy Act when requesting your birth certificate.

Sincerely,

Angela H. Williams
Second Lieutenant, AG
Deputy Chief, Administrative
    Services Division, Directorate
    of Information Management

September 20, 1991

Homer Sewell
Box 13
Jasper, GA 30143

Dear Homer,

Hi! I just wanted to let you know that I received the
information that you sent to me. We will see what we can
do to help you out.

Enclosed is a book that I thought you might be able to
use. Call me if you have any questions or problems at
1-800-933-2494.

Sincerely,

Jill Van Lokeren
The Maury Povich Show

"You, Too, Can Find Anybody"
by Joe Culligan

A Paramount Communications Company

221 West 26th Street • New York, New York 10001 • 212.989.8800

203

HOMER S. SEWELL III
P. O. BOX 13,
JASPER, GA 30143-0013
PHONE: 404-692-3682

SEPTEMBER 23, 1991

        Could you please search your files to see if you have any information
on the following persons:
                ALEXANDER FERENCY, U. S. ARMY SN # 355-34-659 stationed at
                              Ft. Stewart, GA in 1943. Approx. DOB-1920-26
                OR MILDRED FERENCY-Approx. DOB-1920-1926.

        I think that they were from the Youngstown, Ohio area.

        Could you please search your records of driver's license, accidents
reports, vehicle history or body film, birth or death certificates, marriage
licenses, wills on file, voters registration, hunting or fishing licenses or
records of any kind that might contain any information about either of these
people.

        If there is any fee involved, please let me know and I will remit same
by return mail. It is urgent that I locate these people ASAP.

        I appreciate any help that you may be able to give me in this matter.

        SINCERELY,

        Homer S. Sewell III   no record

        HOMER S. SEWELL III

204

OHIO DEPARTMENT OF NATURAL RESOURCES

Fountain Square
Columbus, Ohio 43224

Division of Wildlife
1840 Belcher Drive
Columbus, OH 43224-1329
614/265-7040

September 27, 1991

Homer S. Sewell III
PO Box 13
Jasper, OH 30143-0013

Dear Mr. Sewell:

This is in response to your recent request for hunting and/or fishing license information on Alex or Mildred Ferency. We do not computerize our licensing records and, therefore, are unable to ascertain if they have a license.

Sincerely,

William R. Page
License and Permit
Coordinator

WRP:dlm

Attorney General
Lee Fisher

September 27, 1991

Mr. Homer S. Sewell III
P.O. Box 13
Jasper, GA 30143-0013

Dear M. Sewell:

In response to your letter dated September 23, 1991, I must inform you that we are unable to assist you in your search. According to the Ohio Revised Code, a waiver signed by the person whose record is being searched must accompany the request.

I am sorry that we can not help you in this endeavor.

Sincerely,

Gregory Berquist,
Special Projects Director
For
John Lenhart,
Superintendent
Ohio Bureau of Criminal
Identification & Investigation

DEPARTMENT OF THE ARMY
UNITED STATES ARMY INFORMATION SYSTEMS COMMAND PENTAGON
WASHINGTON D C 20310 3010

October 1, 1991

Freedom of Information/
Privacy Act

Mr. Homer S. Sewell III
P.O. Box 13
Jasper, GA 30143-0013

Dear Mr. Sewell:

This responds to your letter dated September 23, 1991,
requesting information on Alexander Ferency or Mildred
Ferency.

We are forwarding your letter to the following agency for
appropriate action and direct reply to you:

　　　　Director
　　　　National Personnel Records Center
　　　　ATTN: Military Personnel Records Branch
　　　　9700 Page Boulevard
　　　　St. Louis, Missouri 63132

　　　　Sincerely,

　　　　Edith M. Miley
　　　　Chief, Freedom of Information/
　　　　　　Privacy Act Division

October 22, 1991

Homer S. Sewell III
P.O. Box 13
Jasper, GA   30143-0013

Dear Sir:

Enclosed is an uncertified copy of the birth certificate
for Alexander Ferency.

We have deposited $3.60 of your remittance to cover the
cost of our services.

Please note, as authorized by Ohio Revised Code Section
3705.24(B), an overpayment of two ($2.00) or less will be retained
and deposited in the State Treasury.

Sincerely,

Barbara Dawson
Mrs. Barbara Dawson, Supervisor
Bureau of Vital Statistics

BD/go

One evening during the summer of 1991 I got a call from Yvette Floyd in Orlando. I had recruited her into my real estate office when I was working for Barry Luckenbach in 1979. I had visited with her husband, Ron and their children on a couple of occasions and we kept in touch with each other after I moved up to the mountains of North Georgia in 1983.

Yvette had called to try to recruit me to sell some MLM products. I told her I probably wasn't interested but she sent me some samples to examine anyway. She also asked me if I had ever found my biological family. I told her I hadn't yet but was still looking. She said Ron had recently had an occasion to use a very good detective in Miami to help locate someone for him. His name was Joe Culligan and she said I should give him a call. I called him just as soon as we hung up.

I said, "Joe, I'm ABE LINCOLN and I am looking for my parents"! That got his attention! Joe told me he had recently finished a book, *You, Too, Can Find Anybody*, and he would have the Maury Povich Show send me a copy hot off the press. Joe has helped find long-lost family members for reunions on several talk shows. He told me I should follow his suggestions listed in the book and if I didn't find my father within 30 days he would find him for me FREE. That sounded like a great deal to me!

On Sunday afternoon, October 27, 1991 I got a call from Joe Culligan. He wanted to know how I was doing with my search for my family. I told him I had gotten a birth certificate for an Alex Ferency in Ohio. Joe asked me what his date of birth was and I told him it was 1927. He said it was the wrong Alex Ferency because my dad had been born in 1922. I knew then he knew something I didn't!

On October 28, 1991 at 5:05 PM, just as I was leaving the house to go pick up Kimberly from cheerleading practice, the phone rang. There was a man on the phone whose voice I did not recognize. He said, "Is this Homer Sewell?" I said it was. He told me he was Alex Ferency. I said, "THE Alex Ferency, the one who is my father?" He said, "Well, that's what they tell me."

We chatted for about 15 minutes. I found out he and my mother had gotten a divorce after giving birth to three more boys. So I had three brothers: Barry, born in 1944, lived in Long Beach, California; Stuart, born in 1947, lived in Hingham, Massachusetts; and Gershon, born in 1951, was in Israel, about 30 miles from Jerusalem. Dad was living in New London, Connecticut. Mom was remarried and living with her husband, Bill, in Dudley, Massachusetts, about two hours away from Stuart.

I found out I've got international blood-lines: Mom's side of the family is Russian and Dad's side of the family is Hungarian.

After the divorce, Mom and Dad did not maintain a close relationship so this made it more difficult to tell Mom I had found them and to put a reunion together. I asked when I would be able to see everyone and Dad said he would let me know later when it could be arranged. He was trying to figure out how to tell Mom.

Dad and I corresponded back and forth for six months. He would send me audio tapes he made while driving his taxi cab in the Hartford-New London area. I sent him a copy of a VCR tape of my ABE LINCOLN program so he could see what I looked like.

Finally, on April 25, 1992 Dad called me again. We chatted for a few minutes and then he said, "Would you like to talk to one of your brothers?" I said I sure would so he put Stuart on the phone. Dad had driven up to Stuart's house to break the news to him and his wife, Susan. We talked for a while. Stuart said he couldn't wait to call Barry in California and tell him HE wasn't the oldest brother anymore! They still hadn't told Mother I had found them and weren't sure how to go about doing it.

Five days later on April 30, 1992 I happened to be home when the phone rang. An unfamiliar female voice said..."I'm not sure you want to talk to me...but..." I interrupted her to say,

"Sure I do, Mom!" I just knew it was her! We cried and talked for a while. I think she was glad I had finally found her and the long-kept secret was out!

Finally I had located my long-lost family and now it was a matter of getting everyone together for a big reunion. We called back and forth every week or so. I even called to talk to my brother, Gershon, in Israel. Gershon is married to Rachel, an Israeli, and they have nine children. He has been a tour guide in the Holy Land for 15 years. I also talked to Barry in California.

Perhaps this is a good place for me to say something about how my adoptive mother (The only mother I'd known for 49 years!) took the news of me finding my birth-family. I guess she was happy for me when I told her I had found my "other family".

I don't know the correct way to refer to these TWO moms. I don't want to hurt anyone's feelings. One MOM gave birth to me on August 4, 1943 and I am sure, very reluctantly, gave me to the other MOM to be raised, nourished and provide for my needs from the time I was only ten weeks old. I know they BOTH love me and I love both of them very much.

Finding my birth-mother does not take away any of the love I have felt for the ONLY mother I'd ever known. Neither should it lessen the way I feel in my heart for the mother who carried me inside her for nine months and then ten weeks later went through the difficult decision of giving me up...not knowing whether she would ever see me again. I feel sure it has been a hard burden to bear all these years not being able to share "the secret" with anyone. I hope and pray someday soon both of these mothers will be able to meet so they can discuss my life with each other.

After waiting all these 49 years I didn't want to wait any longer and was anxious to meet everyone. I just didn't have the money to fly up to Boston, so I tried to get a talk show to pay for the reunion. We came close to doing it with the MAURY POVICH and the VICKI LAWRENCE SHOWS but just couldn't make it happen.

I was in Harrison, Arkansas renovating the 65 year old Lyric Theater and have devoted the next chapter to what happened there from May to November of 1992. Dad told me he was going to be in St. Louis, Missouri in early October for a church convention so I told him I would drive up there to meet him.

ABE WITH DAD

Photo by Gwen Knight

When I arrived at the Holiday Inn and went into the lobby, there was a tall, handsome man I instantly recognized from the pictures he had sent me. It was my father! I walked up to him, gave him a big hug and said, "Hello, Dad". At last, I was able to meet the man I'd sought for a long time. As we met for lunch, I discovered some of the similarities between us: we were each carrying identical briefcases, wearing the same black boots, had our beards trimmed the same and both of us had identical noses and eyes.

We visited for a few hours between his meetings. I had a million questions but there just wasn't time to get them all answered. I drove back two days later for another visit.

Finally, during the late summer I made the decision that my family and I would drive up to Boston for a Thanksgiving reunion.

I drove from Harrison to Georgia before Thanksgiving and picked up my family. We drove straight through the 1,200 miles from our home, one hour north of Atlanta, to Hingham, Massachusetts in the Boston area. I was tired but would not have been able to sleep in a motel if we had stopped. I was too excited about finally getting to meet Mom, two of my brothers and lots of other family members.

We finally arrived at Stuart's house about noon on Wednesday, the day before Thanksgiving. We met Stuart's wife, Susan, and their children, Fay and Alon and lots of other family members. Barry and his new wife, Urda, had flown in the weekend before from California. We all had a great time visiting and eating! The next day we drove about two hours up to Mom's house for the big reunion. There were 31 relatives there for the big dinner Mom had cooked.

I don't think I can put into words the feelings I had upon seeing my birth-mother for the first time in 49 years. The emotions were high and it was an exciting time for me, my family...and I am sure for Mom too. The pictures of Mom and me together for the first time say it all!

It was exciting finally getting to meet everyone. My NEW family instantly took us in as if we had never been separated. I met cousins, uncles, aunts, nieces and nephews and they all accepted me like a shepherd finding a little lost lamb. We all got along great!

My cousin, Jennifer, is an actress in New York so we had a lot in common. My step-dad is a Mason so we hit it off right away. One step-brother, Stephen, is a Rabbi in Yonkers, New York. I met other relatives who were attorneys, principals, teachers and doctors.

The only one missing was my youngest brother, Jerry. His Hebrew name is Gershon. Israel was a long way off for him to join us for this big reunion! We did call him on the phone and were able to chat for a few minutes. I know he would like to have been able to be with the rest of the family. We talked about the four of us brothers getting together in Israel as soon as we could arrange it.

On Friday, Dad came up from Connecticut with his teacher-friend, Susan, to Stuart's house and we had another big feast.

The three days we were there we did a lot of visiting and eating lots of good food. It was fun trying to catch up on all the family news of the past 49 years! Time passed too quickly! The Jewish side of the family sure knows how to cook!

If you ever need to find anyone, you might want to go to your library or a book store and get the book, *You, Too, Can Find Anybody* by Joseph J. Culligan. It is an excellent source of how to find people.

HOMER WITH MOM (MILLIE)

BARRY, HOMER AND STUART

DAD (ALEX), KIMBERLY AND HOMER

HOMER, BARRY AND STUART AT STATUE OF ABE
IN HINGHAM, MASS.

FAY, STUART, HOMER AND KIMBERLY

STUART'S FAMILY
FAY, SUSAN, STUART AND ALON

COUSIN JENNIFER AND HOMER

HOMER, MOM AND STEPDAD BILL

KIMBERLY, FAY, ALON AND JASON

JASON AND MOM

DAD AND CHIP

BARRY AND WIFE, URDA

COUSIN MICHAEL, HOMER AND JENNIFER

CHET, "ABE" AND COUSIN SANDY

Another exciting time as "ABE" was when I got invited by the Clinton Inaugural Committee to be part of the festivities in January 1993 for Bill Clinton's Inauguration. Even though our newest President is named after Jefferson, his favorite President is Abraham Lincoln. He is always quoting him and has a bust of ABE in his office.

I was at the Kennedy Center along with some other look-alikes to entertain children from around the country. I had hoped to be able to do my show for them but someone had dropped the ball and didn't make plans for me to speak. I did get to visit Chelsea Clinton's old classroom via TV/phone link to Little Rock. Again, the Secret Service would not let any of us in costume get near the President when he visited the Kennedy Center. Bill missed a chance to meet ABE.

I was mobbed as I strolled along the Mall area. I had the privilege of meeting some very interesting young students with VCR cameras... "U.S. KIDS TV". They interviewed me for their TV kids news program.

I was able to see Stuart for a couple of days while I was in Washington. I also met my cousin Sandy and her husband, Chet, while I was there. They both work for U.S.A. TODAY newspapers, so they took me on a tour of their offices. Sandy is in charge of SKY RADIO, a news and information service. It is broadcast directly to airplanes that have subscribed to the service. Chet is a political correspondent for several northern states and for Indian Affairs all over the country.

My family and I were able to spend some more time in late June of 1993 with Stuart, Susan, and daughter, Fay, in Virginia. We had a great time hiking and just getting to know each other better. Stuart and I went on a hike by ourselves and HE got us lost up on a mountain. We had a long hike bushwhacking our way back down to civilization but we had fun just being together.

SALUTE TO YOUTH

52nd PRESIDENTIAL

INAUGURAL

SERVICE

PIC   066492

Kid
(and proud of it)

The 52nd PRESIDENTIAL INAUGURAL

Hillary Clinton's Salute to Youth
Klutz Press / Kennedy Center / January 19 1993

INAUGURATION TIX AND PASS FOR KENNEDY CENTER

CROWD AROUND "ABE" AT INAUGURATION

Photo by Gwen Knight

223

STATUE OF LIBERTY FROM RIVER

The kids got along great with their newly-found cousin. Fay, 17, is one of the top cello players, for her age, in all of Massachusetts. Her brother, Alon, was not able to join us in Virginia because he was in Israel for the summer. He is now attending Harvard University.

In October of 1993, Stuart, Barry and I met in New York and flew to Israel to meet Gershon. Before we flew out of New York, Stuart and I took time to go for a nice boat ride with our step-brother, Rabbi Stephen Franklin. He showed us all around New York City via boat, I took some great pictures of the Statue of Liberty and then his wife, Karen, cooked us a great meal.

We four brothers spent two weeks together for the first time in 50 years! We had a marvelous time touring Israel from North to South, East to West and back again. I took over 400 pictures during the two weeks and I will share some of them with you.

In one 48-hour period, we swam in the Red Sea, the Dead Sea and the Sea of Galilee. The country is a beautiful place to visit and gave me the opportunity to find out more about my Jewish heritage. Gershon carried his M-16 rifle and/or pistol almost everywhere we went. I hope by the time this book comes out, there will be some real peace in Israel.

Since Gershon has lived there for 15 years and is an official tour guide, he really knows his way around. We visited so many interesting places, I can't even remember them all. We were able to stay a couple of nights inside the old walled city of Jerusalem. It was interesting seeing places over 2000 years old!

We visited Masada, the historic Jewish fortress that rises 1,400 feet above the nearby Dead Sea. In A.D. 73, 960 Jewish patriots died there after fighting off the Romans for several years. We visited the ruins of several temples including the Temple Mount where King Solomon's Temple had been. We saw remains of several battlefields and walked some of the same streets where Jesus had walked. It was exciting for me...being born Jewish, raised Protestant and the four of us brothers together for the very first time. We also visited with some of our distant relatives.

225

GERSHON

GERSHON, RACHEL AND THEIR NINE CHILDREN

HOMER, STUART, BARRY, GERSHON

HOMER, STUART, GERSHON, BARRY IN AUTHENTIC
BIBLICAL COSTUME

FISHERMEN ON RED SEA EARLY MORNING

RED SEA NEAR EGYPTIAN BORDER

TOWER AT SITE WHERE SAMUEL THE PROPHET IS BURIED...
WHERE RAINBOW APPEARED DIRECTLY OVER THE FOUR OF US

WALL AT TEMPLE MOUNT. NOTE DIVIDER WALL BETWEEN
MEN ON LEFT AND WOMEN ON RIGHT.

RUINS OF TEMPLE

WALL OF OLD JERUSALEM

VIEWS FROM MASADA

One day we visited the temple outside of Jerusalem where Samuel the Prophet is supposed to be buried. We were up on the roof admiring the view of the city when a storm started blowing towards us. We stood up there in the rain...and after the rain stopped, a beautiful rainbow moved directly over the top of where we were standing. It was an eerie feeling.

LESSON TO BE LEARNED HERE IS: Tell someone you love how much they mean to you...every day!

Chapter 15

A Bad Experience at the Theater

There was an actor by the name of John Wilkes Booth. He wasn't as famous as his brother Edwin, his father and uncle. In conspiracy with several others, John Wilkes Booth decided to do something to make a name for himself. Oh! I'm sure they had other reasons also. At first, they were going to kidnap me and hold me ransom to get us to release some of the rebel troops. When they failed at their kidnap attempt, John Booth decided to do something much more drastic.

"I am not afraid to die, and in fact, would be more than willing, but I have an irresistible desire to live until I can be assured that the world is a little better for my having lived in it."

"I had a rather bad experience the last time I was in a theater...."

That was the opening line for my performance from the stage of the 65-year-old Lyric Theater in Harrison, Arkansas.

On May 18, 1992 I was in the Houston, Texas area for a school program. When I finished, I decided to drive to Branson, Missouri and see what all the fuss was about in that town. My friends, Dana and Beverly Gray, live in Springfield, about an hour north of Branson, so I thought I would go visit them and check out Branson.

The Grays had been telling me about all the activity going

on in Branson and I had heard the segment on CBS's "60 MINUTES SHOW" where the comment was, "Would the last person leaving Nashville on the way to Branson, please turn out the lights!" It had gotten my attention along with millions of others. Now, admittedly I am not into country music but I did see the possibilities of being able to get off the road, settle down in one location and let folks come to me. I had already done over 500 shows all over the country in the two years since going full-time and liked the idea of settling down in one place.

When I arrived in Branson, I stopped by six theaters trying to see if they might like to have something in addition to country music. Finally, at the Cristy Lane Theater, my seventh stop...during a bad rain... I went in to talk to them. The man at the counter just happened to be Cristy's husband/manager and I said "I had a rather bad experience the last time I was in a theater but expected to have a much better experience soon" and I was looking for a place to do it.

The manager asked me, "What are you? A comedian?" I said, "I wasn't a comedian but a serious actor and was looking for a place with an open time-slot". He thought about it for a few minutes and then asked me how soon I wanted to start? I said, "ASAP". He said, "How about this Sunday at 4:00 PM?" I told him that was fine with me.

I shopped around in antique shops and rounded up an old table, chair, hat rack, books and a few other props I needed for a stage production of my one-man show.

I showed up on Sunday and every day that week. On three days of that week I was told I wouldn't be able to perform my show...due to sound or some other technical problems. They didn't do much to promote my shows and the 4 PM time slot had been a bad time for other performers who had tried it.

After a week of shows of less than 35 people per show, we parted company. I had to threaten to sue them to get what little money I had coming.

I had been staying about 40 miles south in Harrison, Arkansas and noticed the old Lyric Theater sitting empty on the courthouse square. I SHOULD HAVE STAYED AWAY FROM IT AND FROM THE TOWN OF HARRISON!

I did some checking around and found out who owned the old theater. I made arrangements for the owners, Kent and Glenna Regan, to show me the inside of the theater. I found out it had been closed for 18 years. I looked around and fell in love with it in spite of the fact that it was dirty, musky, full of pigeons and other varmits...and needed a lot of TLC.

I made some arrangements with the owners and signed a lease/option-to-buy contract good for one year. I figured if I couldn't make it work in one year, then I didn't need to be there.

I started organizing a major renovation project for the "OLD GAL" and worked day and night for weeks. I had to bring it up to 1992 codes for wheelchair access and many, many other requirements before I could open the doors to the public. I had a lot of volunteers come by to help haul out the trash and clean it all up.

Tom Lockett and his wife, Julie and their daughter, Wendy, came by early-on and were there helping every chance they had. Tom and Julie both worked for the newspaper, THE HARRISON TIMES, which was right next door to us. I could not have accomplished all of what needed to be done without their help and the help of others like Ruth Taylor, Darlene and Susan Farmer and many others.

I was determined to have the doors opened in time for the big July 4th celebration being planned on the courthouse square across the street. Everyone kept telling me it couldn't be done! That motivated me to work that much harder. I put in a lot of long hours and was able to get opened...in a fashion...for that weekend.

I had borrowed $25,000 from the owners to do all of the construction of new bathrooms and other things that needed to be done like painting and re-plastering the walls. I also borrowed another $25,000 from a friend.

From the very beginning, the town seemed to be supportive of what I was trying to do to get their old theater re-opened. They were all excited and dropped by everyday to see the progress I was making. Fay Hodge brought us donuts every morning. Avo McBee made some delicious pies and cakes and Ruth Taylor cooked some great meals. John Hudson helped me with my accounting records and he and his family were very supportive. I appreciated all of the people who were interested in what was happening to the Lyric.

When we did get open, we found out just how much Harrison DID NOT SUPPORT OUTSIDERS!! I did everything I could think of from a marketing standpoint to get the community to come see the show. I even offered FREE tickets but the townspeople just would not take an hour-and-a-half out of their schedules to come get motivated and inspired by "ABE".

The ticket was only $5. I billed it as "AN ABE FOR AN ABE"! I tried to get the local motels to offer special prices to their guests who had nothing else to do in the evenings. I had a total of about 20 people over a two month period who were sent from local motels. Before Christmas of 1992 I started realizing I was not going to get enough support to survive there in Harrison.

"ABE LINCOLN'S AMERICA"
LYRIC THEATER, COURTHOUSE SQUARE

Harrison, Arkansas
Phone: 501-741-4-ABE (4223)

ADMIT ONE — $5.00

Showtime is 7:00 P.M. • Tuesday Thru Saturday

LYRIC THEATER BEFORE WE REPAINTED THE MARQUEE

"ABE" WITH TWINS, KIMBERLY AND JASON

In contrast to today's theaters, this old theater had a lot of character you can't find anymore. It had three big, beautifulhand-painted murals approx. 12' x 12' along each wall, a big stage and a big balcony area. It was a perfect place for me to do my shows!

I had built a box up over one end of the stage to represent box 7 and 8 of the Ford's Theater and each night I climbed up into that box and had someone step in and shoot me. We really had a dramatic presentation! All of those who saw the show loved it! I had them laughing one minute and crying the next and we received great reviews from everyone who came to the theater.

I've said over and over again...if only I could pick up that beautiful old theater and move it anywhere EXCEPT Harrison, it would be a big success!

One of these days...the people of Harrison will wake up and realize they are in the 1990's and will start supporting things that come to town. There are millions of people driving right through town on their way to Branson. Those people could be spending some of their money in Harrison and I wanted to help them do that. WAKE UP HARRISON!! YOU MISSED A GOLDEN OPPORTUNITY TO HAVE ABE LINCOLN IN YOUR TOWN!

I had a lot of innovative ideas to help the town grow but they were not receptive to ANY "OUTSIDER'S" suggestions.

There are probably a lot of towns out there that would love to have ABE help them bring visitors and dollars to their town!

One day while I was working in the theater, J.D. Ramsey, a principal from a school I had visited in Missouri, stopped by to see me. He wanted to know about the possibility of using the theater for sales meetings on Monday nights. I wasn't doing my show on Mondays so I told him he could. He and some friends started conducting MLM meetings on a regular basis. The more I listened to them, the more interested I got. I finally signed up as a distributor/marketing executive. The company has great household products and a good marketing system. I've made a little money signing up some of my friends but I haven't taken the time to really work the business. I still buy the products each month and my family uses and enjoys them.

My most recent venture into the job market began in late July of 1993. I was talking to my newly-found brother, Barry, in California. I told him I was going to have to get some type of job to get some dollars coming in to pay the bills. I couldn't sit around all summer waiting for school to start and hoping to get some bookings for ABE. He said I should call a long-time friend of his in Atlanta. His name was Larry Human and he owned a bottled water business. I called Larry, arranged for an interview and he hired me on the spot.

Larry had been running his water business for three years by himself. He really needed someone who could help and give him some time off. I started on August 2 and spent the week of my 50th birthday loading and unloading 42-pound 5-gallon bottles of spring water in and out of vans. With my back prone to get out of shape easily and the fact that I've had five hernia-repair surgeries, I didn't need to be lifting anything heavy. But, in the water business, it is hard to be in the warehouse and NOT get involved in lifting or moving one-ton pallets of 54 bottles of water around with a manual pallet-jack! NOT FUN!!

There was a fellow by the name of Tommy who had been working with Larry off and on for several years. He was one hard-working guy and I tried to help him however I could. All companies need more dedicated, conscientious employees like Tommy who never complain about anything and do what they are asked to do without questioning.

I was kept busy doing payroll, posting payments, balancing checkbooks, checking drivers and their load sheets in and out and fielding customer service complaints. I'd go in about 7 AM and didn't get out of there until 5 PM. Those 10-hour days were hard on this old man!

239

I finally left Larry and the water business in October of 1993. I had enough of this type of work to last a lifetime!

In January of 1994 I had an opportunity to visit some schools in Ledford and Hartford, Connecticut area. This gave me another chance to spend some time with my dad. It was nice to be able to visit and catch up on some of the things I had missed growing up. Dad showed me some pictures, some listings of family ancestors and other information he had about our family. Perhaps someday soon I will be able to sit down with him or Mom and take a close look at family albums I wasn't there to be a part of.

Dad and Susan took me on a tour of New York City. After eating some good Italian food at a restaurant near the hotel where we were staying, we were getting on an elevator to head up to our rooms. A man and woman came up to the elevator just as the doors were starting to close. She said, "Is there room for two more?" I said, "Sure, come on in". The woman said to us, "Hi, I'm Hattie Jackson and I sell Hattie's Sauce". Pretty quickly the doors were opening to let us off at our floor and as I was getting off the elevator, I turned to her, handed her one of my business cards and said, "Hattie, I'm ABE LINCOLN and I'm here to help you!"

She was one of the most bubbly, vivacious ladies I'd met in a long time. She invited us to come up to her room a little later to tell us all about her sauce. I was impressed with her and the sauce she's cooked up to bring new life to hot dogs, hamburgers, salads and other foods. I told her I would do whatever I could to help her get her company up and running. Here was a lady who had never given up on trying to get this sauce marketed...17 years since the idea was first conceived. I was inspired by her faith in herself and in American Free Enterprise. She will go places and I hope to be able to help her get there! She is going to give away some college scholarships from profits of her new company.

I also took time to run up to Dudley, Massachusetts to have lunch and dinner with Mom and my step-dad, Bill. We had a chance to visit for a few hours and catch up a little more on all those long-lost years. Mom sure knows how to cook some good meals. In fact, both of my moms are great cooks!

As you can see from reading this book, I take what I do as ABE pretty seriously. I feel there is a real need for our young people to hear the messages I have for them. I started doing ABE back in 1975 just a few months after Kathy and I were married. She knew I always dreamed of being ABE full-time and was not happy about the prospect.

A lot of times since going full-time in 1990, students have asked me if I had a wife and family back home. I usually joked with them and said, "Yes, I am married. Or, at least I was the last time I was home!" Kathy didn't like the idea of me being away so much and leaving her to raise the twins by herself. I know it was hard on them but I tried to get home as often as I could and make something special of those times we had together.

Christmas of 1993 our family was in Utah skiing at our favorite place and Kathy told me she had gotten tired of me being on the road all the time and wanted a divorce! What a Christmas present that was! So, as of March 10, 1994, we are both single again.

The kids and I must go on with our lives and Kathy will go on with hers...without me in it. Jason has decided he wants to go to a different high school so he is now living with Kathy 35 miles away and closer to her office. Kimberly is still with me in our home in Jasper.

For any of you who have recently gone through a divorce, or are contemplating one soon...it will be hard on you but you WILL survive. Life is too short to remain in a relationship if you are not happy. My Pastor, Hoyt Jenkins, has been an inspirational help to me during these trying times of being single again after 19 years.

I did one of my programs in January for the Fairglen Elementary School in Cocoa, Florida. They mentioned they would be taking a sixth grade class trip to Washington the last week of March and invited me to go with them. I've always wanted to escort students on just such a trip so I agreed to go with them.

One of the teachers, Ms. Donna Welton, has been taking students on these trips to Washington for eight years and she has it all very well organized. I flew from Atlanta to Orlando on the new ValuJet Airlines and met the 29 students and their nine chaperones at 2:30 PM on Sunday, March 27, at the old Sears parking lot on US One in Cocoa. We loaded all our luggage into the bus and left promptly at 3 PM. Our two bus drivers, Elvin and Rick, with Destiny Tours, were a lot of fun to be with.

Our first stop was just north of Jacksonville for supper at Long John Silvers and McDonald's restaurants at about 6 PM. At about 10 PM we stopped at a truck stop in South Carolina so everyone could wash faces, brush teeth and get ready for a long night's ride on the bus.

Two hours out of Washington on Monday morning, we stopped for the breakfast bar at Shoney's. Everyone was excited we were almost to our destination.

At 10 AM we arrived at the Doubletree Hotel in Arlington, Virginia. We got all the students and their luggage settled into their rooms...four students to the room...with two adults in the adjacent rooms. The first thing everyone wanted to do was take a shower and change clothes.

We then met our Washington tour guide, Mrs. June Humphrey. She has been touring folks around Washington for 24 years and really knows where everything is. I met her husband, Capt. Bill Humphrey, who had worked for Admiral Rickover. I would love to spend some time with Capt. Humphrey. I'll bet he has some interesting stories to tell about his times spent working for one of our country's greatest

Admirals.

Our first stop was at the Vietnam, Nurses', Soldiers', Jefferson and Lincoln Memorials. Everyone wanted their pictures taken with "ABE" at the Lincoln Memorial. From there we had lunch at the Old Post Office building. Some of us took a trip to the clock and bell tower at the top of this beautiful old landmark.

We then went to the Ford's Theater and the Petersen Boarding House across the street. This was a very interesting but sad time for me. There were lots of visitors who wanted to have their pictures taken with "ABE" so I obliged them. The students also had a chance to buy some souvenirs from the street vendors.

From there we went to the Smithsonian Museum of Natural History and the group I was with got a special "Presidential" tour from one of the employees in charge of that building.

We drove past the White House, Old Executive Office Building, several embassies and other government buildings. We ate at the Crystal Station and then rode the Metro train to the Rosslyn Station which contains the second highest escalator in the world. The students enjoyed their train and escalator rides. We then took a night driving tour and a quick trip through the Kennedy Center.

On Tuesday after a breakfast at Roy Rogers Restaurant or McDonald's, the students took a tour of the National Cathedral. While they did that and the zoo, I went back to the Ford's Theater and met with the "U.S. Kids TV" film crew for about three hours.

The National Park Service personnel are responsible for the day-to-day operation of the Ford's Theater and they saw the reaction I was getting from visitors on Monday and Tuesday mornings. They asked me if I would like to perform some of my show. It was a pleasant surprise for me to be invited to speak from the same stage ABE had witnessed the play, *Our*

American Cousin on that fateful Good Friday night, April 14, 1865. It brought tears to my eyes when I thought about what had happened to ABE that night.

I did perform about 30 minutes of my show for approximately 500 people and then posed with several groups of visitors for picture-taking with ABE. I ran into a family from Florida who had been my next door neighbors when I lived in Altamonte Springs thirteen years ago.

When I finished at the Ford's Theater, I boarded the Metro train to try to catch up with my tour group. I went to the zoo, Union Station and the Smithsonian but kept missing them. I finally decided to go back to the hotel and wait for them there. They all came back about 4:30 and got dressed to go to a dinner theater to see "Annie Get Your Gun". All the students were looking mighty handsome and pretty in their fancy clothes. One young student told me she "would much rather be in her jeans!"

Wednesday we packed up all of our belongings and checked out of the hotel at 8 AM. After breakfast, we went to the Arlington National Cemetery. We saw the changing of the guard at the Tomb of the Unknown Soldier and visited the JFK grave site. I took four students with me and visited the tomb of Robert Lincoln, the only member of the family not buried in the Oak Ridge Cemetery in Springfield, Illinois.

We went to the House of Representatives and the Capitol and the students enjoyed seeing where our nation's laws are being made. Our Senators and Congressmen were out on spring break.

Some students asked me why the flags were flying at half-mast all over Washington and we found out it was because Rep. William Natcher of Kentucky had died of a heart attack at the age of 84.

I would like to quote some lines from an article about him by Leslie Phillips in the *USA TODAY* newspaper. "He will be remembered for his extraordinary voting record during his 42 years in the House. His last recorded vote, the 18,401st consecutive one, occurred on March 2. An austere gentleman, Natcher eschewed the ways of Washington from the moment he was elected in 1953. He never hired a press secretary, never paid consultants nor solicited campaign contributions, and he routinely returned 70% of the allowance members are given to run their offices. He sent out one press release a year to tout his voting record".

I quote this article because it sounds to me that Rep. Natcher was one of a rare breed of HONEST Representatives in Washington! We need more people like him who are doing what they were sent to do...government of, by and for the PEOPLE. MORE ABOUT THIS LATER!

We took a trip south to Mt. Vernon, George Washington's home, and then back to D.C. to the Smithsonian National Air and Space Museum. There just wasn't enough time to see it all!

We dropped June off about 5:30 PM and headed back to Florida. We drove straight through and arrived in Cocoa at noon on Thursday. It was a very rushed but educational trip for everyone.

I am now giving some serious thoughts to taking some other school groups to Washington myself. If your school would like to have "ABE" escort you to Washington and show you around for either a 3-day or 5-day trip, please get in touch with me for all the particulars.

Perhaps this is what my newest card will look like for taking students on tours to Washington. It is from a business that never quite got off the ground in 1981. I had bought an old school bus with a wheelchair-lift-elevator. I didn't have the money to properly promote the business.

In March of 1994, my friend, Tom Lockett, got me into marketing electronic security. It's a great company with a lot of potential and in my spare time, I will buy and sell their products. It might be something you are interested in having to protect you and your family plus a new business opportunity. Write me and I will send you information about distributorships available in your area.

LESSON TO BE LEARNED HERE IS: Even when today is NOT going your way, remember to make the most of it and "THE SUN WILL COME OUT TOMORROW".

Chapter 16

P.S. My Suggestions for Change

I may make some enemies with this chapter but I feel it needs to be said. I want to express my personal opinion about what needs to be done to take back our government from the politicians who are TRYING to run it now.

Our government has NOT...for many, many years... been a government OF THE PEOPLE, BY THE PEOPLE and FOR THE PEOPLE as Lincoln wrote in his famous speech. I feel our government is still the best anywhere in the world but it needs to be as it was in Lincoln's time. It needs to be run OF, BY and FOR the PEOPLE!

My solution would be for everyone to let their Senators and Congressmen know that they should either vote NOW to get rid of and abolish ALL Political Action Committees (P.A.C.s) or they will elect someone else who will!! Our politicians are being controlled by these P.A.C.s and are not voting for the issues best for US...the people who elected them. They are taking a lot of expensive gifts and trips at the expense of these P.A.C.s. When the time comes to vote on an issue, their votes are controlled by which P.A.C. showed them the most personal gain!

Once these P.A.C.s are eliminated and the elected officials start voting the way WE want them to vote, we will get some major changes in Washington. We will never get anything worthwhile accomplished as long as the P.A.C.s are running the country!

One of the first things they then need to vote for is to get rid of the I.R.S. and all of the $BILLIONS OF DOLLARS$ THEY ARE WASTING EVERY YEAR! They should then approve a FLAT TAX for EVERYONE! And I mean EVERYONE! There should be no more exemptions for big or little businesses to lie about. Everyone...little or big...should pay the same FLAT TAX.

I spoke to a young man a couple of years ago who had studied this matter pretty thoroughly for college and he said a FLAT TAX of ONLY 5% would give our government more money than they could ever spend. I think it could be somewhere between 5 & 10%. There are a lot of big companies out there that haven't been paying anything and they would have to start paying their fair share.

One of the places I want to see MORE of our dollars spent is on education. Our youth of today ARE tomorrow's leaders of this great nation and they are not getting the education they need! Part of the problem is our teachers are not being paid what they should NOR are they allowed to discipline students when necessary. Teachers deserve more credit for the number of years they spent in college, their patience and the amount of time and effort they put in every day and night at schools across this country.

Our teacher's salaries should be raised to be more in line with what private industry would pay someone as skilled and who puts in the number of hours teachers do. There are a lot of very dedicated men and women out there teaching OUR children and they deserve to be paid more than they are getting!

One place more dollars could be raised very easily and quickly and given to our teachers is to look at the school superintendents' salaries across the country. I have seen things in these past 19 years that amaze and astound me!!

Every governor needs to look at his/her state educational systems NOW! What they will find is a lot of over-paid people out there with the title of "SCHOOL SUPERINTENDENT" or other positions we could do away with.

I have seen superintendents who had only one or two schools they were being paid $50,000 to $60,000 to supervise. What a waste of dollars! The principal of those little schools could just as easily do his/her own administrational duties. Instead of having a superintendent for each little town or district, why not do as they do in Florida and in Georgia and have a superintendent for the WHOLE county.

When I asked one superintendent about this, he said they might have to do too much driving to cover a large, spread-out area. Isn't that why he/she is earning those big bucks? And it's not as if they have to drive the whole district every day!

I won't make any of my school superintendent friends very happy with what I've said here but something needs to be done about this situation. One superintendent in Texas told me a couple of years ago "there was such a good-old-boy-network out there that you couldn't ever get them dislodged from these plush 'no-work' jobs!" Well! Governors...Go for it!! How many fat and happy superintendents do you have in your state who could be taken off those fat payrolls? The millions of dollars each state would save could be divided among the teachers who are DOING THE WORK in the classrooms.

Another place we could easily come up with more money to help education (without increasing our taxes) is to eliminate ALL the subsidies the government is giving away to such industries as tobacco and many, many others they should get their hands out of. Let them survive or die on their own! Why should we subsidize the tobacco industry with our tax dollars on one hand and on the other hand tell us that tobacco is killing off Americans who smoke? This has got to rank as one of the worst government-give-aways EVER! I say give the money to our educational systems instead! We need to INSIST that Washington look at ALL subsidies NOW!

Our teachers of today are having to deal with more serious problems than years gone by...drugs and more and more violence in the classrooms. There are guns, knives and drugs being brought to the classrooms. YOUTH VIOLENCE NEEDS TO BE STOPPED!

I met with a group of kids while I was in Washington recently who are trying to help curb youth violence. They are being guided by Jim Halley and call themselves and the news reports they handle..."U.S. KIDS TV." I was impressed with the job they are doing!

I told them I would do whatever I could to help curb youth violence. As of the time we are taking this book to the publisher, we are trying to organize a "NATIONAL STOP YOUTH VIOLENCE IN AMERICA WEEK" and an essay writing contest. The winner from each state will be flown to Springfield, Illinois and ride the train to Washington to present these essays, "What I think needs to be done to STOP YOUTH VIOLENCE in America", to President Clinton on ABE's birthday in February 1995. I hope and pray we can get it all put together very soon.

I want to help kids however I can and have told two other groups I would be glad to help in their efforts to raise money: FEED THE CHILDREN and the PEDIATRIC AIDS FOUNDATION. Please do whatever you can to help these and other worthwhile youth organizations. I appreciate whatever you can do and I am sure they will also.

LESSON TO BE LEARNED HERE IS: Do what YOU can to help make our world a better place to live. Let's start with our government and our educational systems and stopping youth violence in America.

"ABE LINCOLN'S AMERICA"

Homer S. Sewell III

P.O. Box 13
Jasper, GA 30143-0013
(706) 692-3682

National
STOP
Youth Violence
in America

1-800-U-S-KIDS-94
(1-800-875-4379)

FOR MORE INFORMATION, PLEASE CALL OR WRITE.

National
STOP
Youth Violence
in America

1-800-U-S-KIDS-94
(1-800-875-4379)

251

North Ridge Elementary School
Lubbock, Texas

◆

Principal's Award

Presented to

H O M E R   "A B E"   S E W E L L

You're my **P.A.L.** because you've shown

a

Positive Attitude toward Learning

Enjoy this special day honoring your accomplishment.
Keep up the good work...it's great having you here!
I'm proud of you!

Awarded   September 20, 1990

Rod Davis   **Principal**

SCHOLASTIC

Chapter 17

Coincidences and Travel List

COINCIDENCES BETWEEN ABE LINCOLN AND HOMER S. SEWELL III

1. I delivered the Gettysburg Address on radio in Florida in Sixth grade.
2. Exactly 100 years, to the minute, after Lincoln was shot, I was working for the White House Communications Agency. (Switchboard operator)
3. The President I worked for was Lyndon Johnson. Lincoln's successor was Andrew Johnson.
4. The statue of Lincoln in the Lincoln Memorial was carved from marble taken from the county (Pickens) where I live in North Georgia.
5. Lincoln's first election to public office (Legislator) was 8/4/34. I was born 8/4/43.
6. Lincoln's hat size was 7-1/4. So is mine.
7. Lincoln's boot size was 12. So is mine.
8. Lincoln loved to read and needed glasses to do so. So do I.
9. Lincoln had blue eyes. So do I.
10. Lincoln had long, black, unruly hair. So do I.
11. Our weight is about the same...175 to 180 pounds.
12. Lincoln was raised in the Baptist Church. So was I.
13. I have a mole on my face in almost the same place Lincoln had one.
14. Lincoln was a storekeeper, an inventor and a poet. So am I.
15. Both of us had a lot of store failures. I've probably had more than he did!

16. Lincoln was in the Army in the Black Hawk Indian War for three months in '32. I was in the Army in the Vietnam War for three years starting in '64.

17. Lincoln was a great public speaker. So am I.

18. My twins, Kimberly and Jason, were born in Macon county, North Carolina. When Lincoln first moved to Illinois he lived in Macon county.

19. Lincoln's youngest son was born the day before my twins-April 4.

20. Lincoln's oldest son was born the day before my oldest son, Chip-August 1.

21. Lincoln's oldest son, Robert, was born in August of 1843. I was born in August of 1943.

22. Lincoln's four sons were born during a ten year period. My three children were born during a ten year period.

23. Both of us built and lived in log cabins.

24. Both of us walked to school.

25. Both of us love people...any age, any color, anywhere!

26. Both of us had two mothers.

27. Lincoln was shot by John Wilkes Booth. I had some surgery done in 1989 by Dr. Arthur Booth of Atlanta.

28. Lincoln was chosen to be one of the four presidents carved onto Mount Rushmore. I was chosen by the National Park Service to be part of the 50th Anniversary Celebration during the week of July 4, 1991.

29. Neither of us ever drank any type of alcohol or smoked anything.

30. Right before his death, Lincoln told Mary he wanted to take a trip to the Holy Land. I spent two weeks in Israel in October of 1993.

31. I recently found out I was born Jewish and have 17 generations of Rabbis in my family. Lincoln loved Jews and had a lot of Rabbis for friends.

32. My newly-found brother, Stuart, lives in Hingham, Massachusetts, next door to a Lincoln descended from the Lincolns who settled there in 1636.

COINCIDENCES BETWEEN ABE LINCOLN AND JOHN KENNEDY

1. Both Lincoln and Kennedy were concerned with civil rights.
2. Lincoln was elected President in 1860. Kennedy in 1960.
3. Both were slain on a Friday and in the presence of their wives.
4. Both were shot from behind and in the head.
5. Their successors, both named Johnson, were Southern Democrats and both were in the Senate.
6. Andrew Johnson was born in 1808. Lyndon Johnson in 1908.
7. John Wilkes Booth was born in 1839. Lee Harvey Oswald in 1939.
8. Booth and Oswald were Southerners who favored unpopular ideas.
9. Both Presidents lost children through death while in the White House.
10. Lincoln's secretary, whose name was Kennedy, advised him not to go to the theater.
11. Kennedy's secretary, whose name was Lincoln, advised him not to go to Dallas.
12. John Wilkes Booth shot Lincoln in a theater and ran to a warehouse.
13. Lee Harvey Oswald shot Kennedy from a warehouse and ran to a theater.
14. The names Lincoln and Kennedy each contain seven letters.
15. The names Andrew Johnson and Lyndon Johnson each contain 13 letters.
16. The names John Wilkes Booth and Lee Harvey Oswald each contain 15 letters.
17. Both assassins were killed before being brought to trial.
18. Lincoln was shot in the Ford's Theater. Kennedy was shot in a Ford car. (And, as a matter of fact...it was a Lincoln!)

The following pages contain a listing of the places I've visited since 1975 and up until the time we went to press. I thought it might be interesting for you to see if you recognize any of these places.

For my students who are still in school, the list might become a fun geography lesson as you get a large United States map and try to locate all the places I've visited.

SMALL U.S. MAP HERE TO FILL IN...

#	DATE	LOCATION	TOWN	STATE	APPROX. #
1.	Oct 75	ALOMA ELEM SCHOOL	WINTER PARK	FL	500
2	Oct 75	LAKE COMO ELEM SCHOOL	ORLANDO	FL	400
3	Jan 76	J. B. MCCAWLEY LOG CABIN 83rd	SANFORD	FL	250
4	Apr 76	RED BUG ELEM SCHOOL	CASSELBERRY	FL	350
5	Jul 76	WINTER PARK MALL	WINTER PARK	FL	300
6	Jul 76	BICENTENNIAL PARADE	FRANKLIN	NC	9000
7	May 77	COWEE ELEM SCHOOL	FRANKLIN	NC	400
8	Feb 78	MIDFIELD TOYOTA	BIRMINGHAM	AL	100
9	Jul 4 78	FESTIVAL IN THE PARK	PUNTA GORDA	FL	15000
10	Aug 78	SEMINOLE COUNTY LIBRARY	CASSELBERRY	FL	50
11	Jan 1 79	ST. MARK AME CHURCH	ORLANDO	FL	1200
12	Feb 79	DREAM LAKE ELEM SCHOOL	APOPKA	FL	400
13	Feb 79	SPRING LAKE ELEM SCHOOL	ALTAMONTE SPRIN	FL	500
14	Feb 79	APOPKA JR HIGH SCHOOL	APOPKA	FL	500
15	Feb 79	PHYLLIS WHEATLEY ELEM SCHL	APOPKA	FL	800
16	Feb 79	BOY SCOUT EAGLE CT of HONOR	LONGWOOD	FL	100
17	Apr 79	MILWEE MIDDLE SCHOOL	LONGWOOD	FL	400
18	Jul 4 79	REPUBLICAN PARADE FLOAT	MAITLAND	FL	8000
19	Jul 4 79	MALL CELEBRATION	ALTAMONTE SPRIN	FL	1000
20	Jul 4 79	FESTIVAL IN THE PARK	PUNTA GORDA	FL	12000
21	Jul 79	REPUBLICAN PARTY DANCE	ALTAMONTE SPRIN	FL	250
22	Sep 79	REPUBLICAN PARTY PICNIC	WINTER PARK	FL	500
23	Oct 79	BOY SCOUT CAMPOREE	DeLAND	FL	300
24	Nov 79	VETERAN'S DAY PARADE	ORLANDO	FL	3000
25	Feb 80	LAKE SYBELIA ELEM SCHOOL	MAITLAND	FL	500
26	Feb 80	GRINDLE for SENATE KICKOFF	FIVE CENTRAL FL	FL	2000
27	Feb 80	RESERVE OFF.'S ASSN DINNER	ORLANDO	FL	500
28	Feb 80	SWEETWATER ACADEMY	LONGWOOD	FL	100
29	Feb 80	CONWAY METH. KINDERGARTEN	ORLANDO	FL	100
30	Feb 12 80	FLA. FESTIVAL,SEA WORLD	ORLANDO	FL	20000
31	Mar 80	TV COMM-DON REID FORD	MAITLAND	FL	10
32	Apr 80	STAND UP FOR AMERICA	ORLANDO	FL	5000
33	Apr 80	CHURCH CONVENTION	WILLIAMSBURG	VA	200
34	May 80	LAKE MARY DAY CofC PARADE	LAKE MARY	FL	1000
35	Jun 80	REAL ESTATE CO. SALES MEET	MAITLAND	FL	100
36	Jun 80	CENT. FL. ZOO FUND RAISER	SANFORD	FL	250
37	Jul 27 80	CP BENEFIT	ALTAMONTE SPRIN	FL	200
38	Aug 2 80	BENEFIT FOR MDA	DAYTONA BEACH	FL	300
39	Aug 31 80	CP TELETHON AT SHERATON	ORLANDO	FL	500
40	Sep 12 80	KIWANIS BREAKFAST MEETING	ALTAMONTE SPRIN	FL	50
41	Oct 30 80	WINTER SPRINGS ELEM SCHOOL	WINTER SPRINGS	FL	400
42	Jan 31 81	RESERVE OFFICERS ASSOC	ORLANDO	FL	250
43	Feb 9 81	FERNCREEK ELEM SCHOOL	ORLANDO	FL	300
44	Feb 11 81	WOODLANDS ELEM SCHOOL	LONGWOOD	FL	400
45	Feb 12 81	PERSHING ELEM SCHOOL	ORLANDO	FL	350
46	Feb 12 81	ST. MARKS KINDERGARTEN	ALTAMONTE SPRIN	FL	200
47	Feb 12 81	ALL AMERICAN SKATING RINK	ALTAMONTE SPRIN	FL	500

48	Feb 20 81	LINCOLN DAY DINNER	ALTAMONTE SPRIN	FL	300
49	Feb 22 81	HUMANE SOCIETY BENEFIT	LONGWOOD	FL	60
50	Mar 15 81	ST. JOHN'S MISSIONARY BAPT.	SANFORD	FL	150
51	Apr 4 81	"STAND UP FOR AMERICAN"	ORLANDO	FL	8000
52	May 1 81	GOOD SHEPHERDCHURCH	S ORLANDO	FL	500
53	May 5 81	S. SEMINOLE MIDDLE SCHOOL	CASSELBERRY	FL	500
54	Jun 23 81	CUB SCOUTS AT NAVAL BASE	ORLANDO	FL	250
55	Jul 2 81	SEMINOLE COUNTY LIBRARY	CASSELBERRY	FL	100
56	Sep 9 81	FL ASSN. of CHRISTIAN SCHOOLS	DAYTONA BEACH	FL	1000
57	Sep 10 81	FIRE PREV WEEK CELEBRATION	ORLANDO	FL	300
58	Sep 15 81	TOM SKINNER CLUB	ORLANDO	FL	50
59	Oct 19 81	WARNER CHRISTIAN SCHOOL	SOUTH DAYTONA	FL	60
60	Oct 21 81	U. N.DAY, ALTAMONTE M ALT	ALTAMONTE SPRIN	FL	200
61	Nov 3 81	WOMEN'S SORORITY	LAKE MARY	FL	30
62	Nov 7 81	BOWL AMERICA LANES	SANFORD	FL	150
63	Nov 14 81	STS. PETER & PAUL CATH. CH.	GOLDENROD	FL	1000
64	Nov 17 81	IVEY LANE ELEM SCHOOL	ORLANDO	FL	800
65	Nov 21 81	TRAVELERS PROTECTIVE ASSN	ORLANDO	FL	50
66	Nov 21 81	HOME SHOW AT FAIRGROUNDS	ORLANDO	FL	500
67	Dec 10 81	SERTOMA CLUB	COLLEGE PARK	FL	30
68	Jan 9 82	FL MUSIC ED ASSN CONV	DAYTONA BEACH	FL	2000
69	Jan 13 82	COLONIAL HIGH SCHOOL	ORLANDO	FL	2000
70	Jan 15 82	LYMAN H. S. CIVICS CLASS	LONGWOOD	FL	30
71	Jan 20 82	Rolling Hills MORAVIAN CHURCH S	LONGWOOD	FL	50
72	Jan 24 82	RONALD MCDONALD'S HOUSE	ORANGE CITY	FL	500
73	Jan 29 82	CHARLOTTE CO. REPUBLICANS	PUNTA GORDA	FL	400
74	Feb 4 82	MILWEE MIDDLE SCHOOL	LONGWOOD	FL	200
75	Feb 6 82	PRIVATE BIRTHDAY PARTY	ORLANDO	FL	25
76	Feb 7 82	HERITAGE BAPTIST CHURC	FOREST CITY	FL	50
77	Feb 8 82	PINE HILLS CHRIST. CHURCH SCH	ORLANDO	FL	50
78	Feb 8 82	WHEATLEY ELEM SCHOOL	APOPKA	FL	900
79	Feb 9 82	WEKIVA ELEM SCHOOL	LONGWOOD	FL	350
80	Feb 10 82	ST. MARKS KINDERGARTEN	ALTAMONTE SPRIN	FL	200
81	Feb 10 82	GENEVA ELEM SCHOOL	OVIEDO	FL	300
82	Feb 10 82	PACE SCHOOL	FOREST CITY	FL	80
83	Feb 11 82	AUDOBON PARK ELEM SCHOOL	ORLANDO	FL	500
84	Feb 11 82	LONGWOOD TOURIST CLUB	LONGWOOD	FL	80
85	Feb 12 82	CHENEY ELEM SCHOOL	ORLANDO	FL	500
86	Feb 12 82	CAROLE NELSON TV SHOW	ORLANDO	FL	NA
87	Feb 12 82	OSCEOLA CTY REPUBLICAN S	OSCEOLA	FL	200
88	Feb 12 82	PRIVATE PARTY FOR NURSES	LONGWOOD	FL	30
89	Feb 22 82	CUB SCOUT PACK 540	CASSELBERRY	FL	300
90	Mar 3 82	ACTION YEARS SENIORS	MAITLAND	FL	30
91	Mar 4 82	35-LIVE SHOW,TV CH. 35	ORLANDO	FL	NA
92	Mar 6 82	ANNUAL GOLDENROD PARADE	GOLDENROD	FL	5000
93	Mar 13 82	FOUNDER'S DAY PARADE	ORANGE CITY	FL	6000
94	Mar 13 82	LEE CO. REPUBLICAN PARTY	FT. MYERS	FL	400
95	Mar 18 82	SOUTH SEMINOLE SENIORS	CASSELBERRY	FL	80

96	Mar 24 82	HOME SHOW LOG CABIN DISPLAY	TAMPA	FL	5000
97	Apr 2 82	FL REAL ESTATE EXPO	ORLANDO	FL	3000
98	Apr 17 82	HISTORIC KINGSTON FESTIVAL	KINGSTON	GA	3000
99	Apr 30 82	"I LOVE AMERICA WEEK"	MAITLAND	FL	500
100	May 17 82	ACTION YEARS SENIORS CLUB	ORLANDO	FL	30
101	May 25 82	ST. JOHN VIANNEY SCHOOL	ORLANDO	FL	400
102	May 31 82	DeLAND JR. HIGH SCHOOL	DeLAND	FL	800
103	May 27 82	PINE HILLS CHRISTIAN SCH	ORLANDO	FL	300
104	Jun 13 82	"STAND UP FOR AMERICA"	ORLANDO	FL	8000
105	Jul 4 82	Rolling Hills MORAVIAN CHURCH	LONGWOOD	FL	200
106	Jul 17 82	"Here's to the RED,WHITE & BLUE	TITUSVILLE	FL	200
107	Aug 15 82	ORLANDO GEN. HOSPITAL	ORLANDO	FL	300
108	Aug 24 82	COLLEGE PARK LIONS CLUB	ORLANDO	FL	30
109	Sep 24 82	FIRST PRES. CHURCH SENIOR'S	Mt DORA	FL	25
110	Nov 6 82	MUSICAL VARIETY SHOW A	ORLANDO	FL	100
111	Nov 18 82	CUB SCOUT PACK 629	MAITLAND	FL	200
112	Nov 20 82	HOLIDAY PARADE	WINTER SPRINGS	FL	3000
113	Nov 29 82	WORLD BOOK STATE CONV.	ORLANDO	FL	150
114	Dec 14 82	LIBERTY NATIONAL BANK	LONGWOOD	FL	300
115	Dec 21 82	KIWANIS MEETING	ORMOND BEACH	FL	40
116	Jan 26 83	JACKSON HGHTS MIDDLE SCHL	OVIEDO	FL	350
117	Feb 2 83	CUB SCOUT PACK 234	LONGWOOD	FL	20
118	Feb 7 83	PHYLLIS WHEATLEY ELEM SCHL	APOPKA	FL	500
119	Feb 8 83	ORLANDO JUNIOR ACADEMY	ORLANDO	FL	300
120	Feb 8 83	BROWNIE SCOUT TROOP 774	ALTAMONTE SPRIN	FL	30
121	Feb 9 83	APOPKA ELEM SCHOOL	APOPKA	FL	700
122	Feb 9 83	ST. MARKS KINDERGARTEN	ALTAMONTE SPRIN	FL	200
123	Feb 9 83	ALTAMONTE ELEM SCHOOL	ALTAMONTE SPRIN	FL	100
124	Feb 10 83	APOPKA JR HIGH SCHOOL	APOPKA	FL	1000
125	Feb 10 83	DREAM LAKE ELEM SCHOOL	APOPKA	FL	700
126	Feb 11 83	SOUTHLAKE ELEM SCHOOL	TITUSVILLE	FL	700
127	Feb 12 83	ALL AMERICAN SKATING RINK	ALTAMONTE SPRIN	FL	300
128	Feb 14 83	BANQUET,FIRST BAPTIS	ORMOND BEACH	FL	60
129	Feb 24 83	HIGHLANDS ELEM PTA	DAYTONA BEACH	FL	100
130	Feb 28 83	NEWCOMERS & SOCIAL CLUB	MT. DORA	FL	50
131	Mar 5 83	FRONTIER DAY PARADE	ORANGE CITY	FL	5500
132	Mar 21 83	APOPKA ELEM SCHOOL	APOPKA	FL	700
133	Apr 15 83	TEAGUE MIDDLE SCHOOL	FOREST CITY	FL	400
134	May 25 83	LaPETITE ACADEMY GRADUAT	MAITLAND	FL	50
135	May 31 83	DeLAND JR HIGH SCHOOL	DeLAND	FL	1000
136	Jul 4 83	PATRIOTIC PROGRAM	BIG CANOE	GA	1000
137	Sep 17 83	EDWARDS BAKING CO. PICNIC	ATLANTA	GA	700
138	Feb 7 84	CEDARDALE LOG HOMES	MARIETTA	GA	10
139	Feb 10 84	BROCKETT ELEM SCHOOL	ATLANTA	GA	500
140	Feb 10 84	MTN. PARK ELEM SCHOOL	ATLANTA	GA	500
141	Feb 12 84	CHURCH ST STATION DEPOT	ORLANDO	FL	2000
142	Feb 13 84	ALTAMONTE ELEM SCHOOL ·	ALTAMONTE SPRIN	FL	200
143	Feb 13 84	ST. MARKS KINDERGARTEN	ALTAMONTE SPRIN	FL	300

144 Mar 84	WOOD ACRES SCHOOL	ROSWELL	GA	750
145 Mar 84	CEDARDALE LOG HOME SHOW,WCC	ATLANTA	GA	100000
146 Dec 84	McEVER ELEM SCHOOL	GAINESVILLE	GA	750
147 Jan 85	ARTS COUNCIL MEETING	GAINESVILLE	GA	10
148 Feb 85	FIRST BAPTIST CHRUCH	JASPER	GA	200
149 Feb 85	JASPER ELEM SCHOOL	JASPER	GA	1100
150 Feb 85	FAIR STREET ELEM SCHOOL	GAINESVILLE	GA	650
151 Feb 85	ENOTA ELEM SCHOOL	GAINESVILLE	GA	800
152 Feb 85	LANIER ELEM SCHOOL	GAINESVILLE	GA	650
153 Feb 85	JONES ELEM SCHOOL	GAINESVILLE	GA	210
154 Feb 85	TADMORE ELEM SCHOOL	GAINESVILLE	GA	500
155 Feb 85	LOCHMAR ELEM SCHOOL	PALM BAY	FL	900
155 Feb 85	MTN. PARK ELEM SCHOOL	STONE MOUNTAIN	GA	400
157 Feb 85	MARBLE VALLEY HIST. SOCIET	JASPER	GA	30
158 May 85	WARREN ROAD ELEM SCHOOL	AUGUSTA	GA	500
159 May 85	VISIT with BASE COM. THOMA	FT. GORDON	GA	100
160 May 85	LAWRENCEVILLE ELEM SCHOOL	LAWRENCEVILLE	GA	1000
161 Jun 85	BENT TREE RESORT CLUB DINNER	JASPER	GA	50
162 Jul 85	JULY 4 CELEBRATION	BIG CANOE RESORT	GA	1000
163 Oct 85	MGM GRAND HOTEL	LAS VEGAS	NV	5000
164 Nov 85	PICKENS TECH COL. REAL ESTAT	JASPER	GA	30
165 Nov 85	LYNDHURST FOUNDATION	CHATTANOOGA	TN	25
166 Dec 85	LOCKHEED MANAGEMENT ASSN	ATLANTA	GA	1000
167 Dec 85	CAIN & BULTMAN-YORK A/C MEET.	ATLANTA	GA	150
168 Feb 86	RIVERSIDE ELEM SCHOOL	MABLETON	GA	500
169 Feb 86	POWDER SPRGS ELEM SCHOOL	POWDER SPRINGS	GA	500
170 Feb 86	SARDIS ELEM SCHOOL	GAINESVILLE	GA	500
171 Feb 86	OAKWOOD ELEM SCHOOL	GAINESVILLE	GA	700
172 Feb 86	WAUKA MT ELEM SCHOOL	GAINESVILLE	GA	550
173 Feb 86	PINE STREET ELEM SCHOOL	CONYERS	GA	750
174 Feb 86	GWIN OAKS ELEM SCHOOL	LAWRENCEVILLE	GA	200
175 Feb 86	JASPER ELEM SCHOOL	JASPER	GA	100
176 Feb 86	SEVENTH DAY ADVENT. SCHOOL	ELLIJAY	GA	100
177 Feb 86	SARAH SMITH ELEM SCHOOL	ATLANTA	GA	500
178 Feb 86	CUB SCOUT PACK 225	GAINESVILLE	GA	100
179 May 86	PICKENS H. S. BAND CONCERT	JASPER	GA	200
180 Jul 86	LINCOLN BOYHOOD AMPHI DED	LINCOLN CITY	IN	250
181 Jul 86	COMMUNITY CARE CENTER	DALE	IN	50
182 Aug 86	"INDIANA ADVENT. '86" TOURISM	INDIANAPOLIS	IN	500
183 Sep 86	NAT. CONF. EDITORIAL WRITERS	CHARLESTON	SC	500
184 Oct 86	LOOK-ALIKE CONTEST	HODGENVILLE	KY	1000
185 Dec 86	PIZZA EXPO,LINCOLN FOODSERV.	ORLANDO	FL	5000
186 Feb 87	ANNISTOWN ELEM SCHOOL	ANNISTOWN	GA	1000
187 Feb 87	MT. PARK ELEM SCHOOL	LILBURN	GA	600
188 Feb 87	B.B. HARRIS ELEM SCHOOL	DULUTH	GA	900
189 Feb 87	ST. MATTHEWS CATH. SCHOOL	MT. VERNON	IN	120

190 Feb 87	MT. VERNON JR HIGH SCH.	MT. VERNON	IN	400
191 Feb 87	MT. VERNON HIGH SCHOOL	MT. VERNON	IN	1100
192 Feb 87	MEDCO CTR NURSING HOME	MT. VERNON	IN	150
193 Feb 87	HEDGES ELEM SCHOOL	MT. VERNON	IN	400
194 Feb 87	WEST ELEM SCHOOL	MT. VERNON	IN	300
195 Feb 87	MARRS ELEM SCHOOL	MT. VERNON	IN	300
196 Feb 87	FARMERSVILLE ELEM SCH.	MT. VERNON	IN	300
197 Feb 87	GEN. ELECTRIC "ELFUN SOCIETY	EVANSVILLE	IN	80
198 Feb 87	SENIORS LUNCHEON	FREEHOME	GA	30
199 Feb 87	FLOWERY BRANCH ELEM SCH.	FLOWERY BRANCH	GA	500
200 Feb 87	ST. JOHN NEWMAN CATH. SCHOOL	LAWRENCEVILLE	GA	200
201 Feb 87	LILBURN ELEM SCHOOL	LILBURN	GA	800
202 Mar 87	KENNESAW COLLEGE HIST. CLASS	KENNESAW	GA	40
203 Apr 87	JR. ROTC DRILL MEET	MARIETTA	GA	1000
204 May 87	MTN. LAUREL FEST., 23RD ANNU	CLARKESVILLE	GA	5000
205 May 87	S.W. ATLANTA CHRIST.ACA	ATLANTA	GA	100
206 Jun 87	UNITED METHODIST CHURCH	FIELDS CHAPEL	GA	100
207 Sep 87	RIVERSIDE ELEM SCHOOL	MABLETON	GA	500
208 Sep 87	TADMORE ELEM SCHOOL	GAINESVILLE	GA	600
209 Sep 87	CREDIT CARD SOFTWARE MEET	ORLANDO	FL	200
210 Oct 87	MASONIC LODGE 96	ATLANTA	GA	50
211 Oct 87	SCOTTISH RITE K.C.C.H. MEETING	ATLANTA	GA	50
212 Feb 88	JONES ELEM SCHOOL	GAINESVILLE	GA	330
213 Feb 88	SUGAR HILL ELEM SCHOOL	BUFORD	GA	450
214 Feb 88	HARMONY ELEM SCHOOL	BUFORD	GA	350
215 Mar 88	A HIKE WITH ABE	BIG CANOE RESORT	GA	25
216 Mar 88	JASPER ELEM SCHOOL	JASPER	GA	200
217 Aug 88	JASPER LIONS CLUB	JASPER	GA	50
218 Oct 88	MARBLE FESTIVAL PARADE	JASPER	GA	2000
219 Oct 88	GOLD RUSH DAYS PARADE	DAHLONEGA	GA	50000
220 Oct 88	ROYAL ARCH MASONIC MEETING	JASPER	GA	15
221 Oct 88	LIONS CLUB LADIES' NIGHT	CANTON	GA	100
222 Oct 88	LITTLE COUNTRY STORE PROMO	DAHLONEGA	GA	210
223 Oct 88	"STAY IN SCHL" PROGRAM, CORPS	CARTER'S LAKE	GA	300
224 Oct 88	LITTLE COUNTRY STORE PROMO	DAHLONEGA	GA	250
225 Feb 89	MARBLE VALLEY HIST. SOCIET	JASPER	GA	50
226 Feb 89	BERKELEY LAKE ELEM SCHOOL	DULUTH	GA	1200
227 Feb 89	ELECTROLUX PROMO, GWIN. MALL	DULUTH	GA	5000
228 Feb 89	ARCADO ELEM SCHOOL	DULUTH	GA	950
229 Feb 89	MURDOCK ELEM SCHOOL	MARIETTA	GA	1300
230 Mar 89	KNOLLWOOD ELEM SCHOOL	DECATUR	GA	630
231 Mar 89	A.L. WILLIAMS INS. SALES RALLY	ATLANTA	GA	2000
232 Jun 89	PICKENS MIDDLE SCHOOL	JASPER	GA	250
233 Jun89	CENSUS BUREAU OFFICE	MARIETTA	GA	50
234 Jul 89	PICKENS STAR MASONIC LDGE 220	JASPER	GA	25
235 Jul 89	SUWANEE METHODIST CHURCH	SUWANEE	GA	100
236 Oct 89	AMER. PRESIDENT INTERMODAL C	ATLANTA	GA	250
237 Oct 89	"STAY IN SCHOOL" PROG., CORPS	CARTER'S LAKE	GA	600

238 Nov 89	HIGH MEADOWS SCHOOL	ROSWELL	GA	300
239 Feb. 90	WINSTON ELEM SCHOOL	WINSTON	GA	500
240 Feb 90	LANIER MIDDLE SCHOOL	BUFORD	GA	1000
241 Feb 90	REBECCA MINOR ELEM SCHOOL	LILBURN	GA	1400
242 Feb 90	DACULA ELEM SCHOOL	DACULA	GA	800
243 Feb 90	N. HALL MIDDLE SCHOOL PTA ME	GAINESVILLE	GA	50
244 Feb 90	SMYRNA PRESBYTERIAN SENI	SMYRNA	GA	50
245 Feb 90	1st UNITED METHODIST CHURCH	MARIETTA	GA	450
246 Mar 90	JASPER ELEM SCHOOL	JASPER	GA	1000
247 Apr 90	BAGLEY MIDDLE SCHOOL	CHATSWORTH	GA	750
248 Apr 90	R.D. HEAD ELEM SCHOOL	LILBURN	GA	950
249 May 90	INT'N INTERMODAL EXPO	ATLANTA	GA	10000
250 May 90	BELLS FERRY ELEM SCHOOL	MARIETTA	GA	750
251 May 90	MASONIC DIST. DEPUTIES MEET	MACON	GA	50
252 May 90	MASONIC CHILDREN'S HOME	MACON	GA	50
253 May 90	CHAM. OF ROSWELL RETIREMENT	ROSWELL	GA	100
254 May 90	KNIGHTS OF MECCA MASONIC	SAVANNAH	GA	50
255 Jun 90	EASTERN STAR 479 MEETING	JASPER	GA	50
256 Jul 4 90	SALUTE TO AMERICA PARADE	ATLANTA	GA	450000
257 Jul 90	WOODRUFF BOY SCOUT CAMP	BLUE RIDGE	GA	400
258 Jul 90	CIVIL WAR ENCAMPMENT, ATL. HIST	ATLANTA	GA	2000
259 Jul 90	MASONIC LODGE 154	CALHOUN	GA	30
260 Jul 90	LIFE CHIROPRACTIC CLASS P	MARIETTA	GA	50
261 Aug 90	COHUTTA MASONIC LODGE	COHUTTA	GA	20
262 Aug 90	PALESTINE MASONIC LODGE 486	ATLANTA	GA	50
263 Aug 90	SUPER SINGLES GROUP, J.U.M.C.	JASPER	GA	20
264 Aug 90	WING DING CONTEST JUDGE	STONE MOUNTAIN	GA	5000
265 Aug 90	RABUN GAP MASONIC# 265	LAKE BURTON	GA	50
266 Sep 90	MT. PLEASANT HIGH SCHOOL	MOUNT PLEASANT	TN	300
267 Sep 90	WALDRON MIDDLE SCHOOL	WALDRON	AR	600
268 Sep 90	GLOVER ELEM SCHOOL	BROKEN BOW	OK	100
269 Sep 90	BOWIE ELEM SCHOOL	ENNIS	TX	600
270 Sep 90	CROSS ROADS ISD SCHOOL	MALAKOFF	TX	400
271 Sep 90	BURKEVILLE ELEM SCHOOL	BURKEVILLE	TX	300
272 Sep 90	GROVES ELEM SCHOOL	GROVES	TX	450
273 Sep 90	LAURA REEVES ELEM SCHOOL	SILSBEE	TX	650
274 Sep 90	SILSBEE MIDDLE SCHOOL	SILSBEE	TX	600
275 Sep 90	READ TURRENTINE ELEM SCHOOL	SILSBEE	TX	650
276 Sep 90	REDD SCHOOL	HOUSTON	TX	200
277 Sep 90	DEEP WOOD ELEM SCHOOL	ROUND ROCK	TX	650
278 Sep 90	WINDCREST ELEM SCHOOL	SAN ANTONIO	TX	600
279 Sep 90	JOURDANTON JR HIGH SCHOOL	JOURDANTON	TX	1000
280 Sep 90	CHINA INTERMEDIATE SCHOOL	BRADY	TX	300
281 Sep 90	GRANDFALLS SCHOOL	GRANDFALLS	TX	250
282 Sep 90	NORTHRIDGE ELEM SCHOOL	LUBBOCK	TX	650
283 Sep 90	WILLIAMS ELEM SCHOOL	LUBBOCK	TX	500
284 Sep 90	ESTACADO JR HIGH SCHOOL	PLAINVIEW	TX	450
285 Sep 90	MAEDGEN ELEM SCHOOL	LUBBOCK	TX	500

286 Sep 90	METHODIST HOSPITAL VISITS	LUBBOCK	TX	100
287 Sep 24 90	CHILDRESS ELEM SCHOOL	CHILDRESS	TX	600
288 Sep 25 90	VALLEY SCHOOL	TURKEY	TX	300
289 Sep 25 90	NOTRE DAME ELEM SCHOOL	WICHITA FALLS	TX	200
290 Sep 26 90	RANCHWOOD ELEM SCHOOL	YUKON	OK	400
291 Sep 26 90	CHOCTAW ELEM SCHOOL	CHOCTAW	OK	500
292 Sep 27 90	JUSTICE SCHOOL	WEWOKA	OK	120
293 Sep 27 90	WETUMKA SCHOOL	WETUMKA	OK	320
294 Sep 28 90	LEE ELEM SCHOOL	TULSA	OK	400
295 Sep 28 90	J.F. KENNEDY SCHOOL	OILTON	OK	300
296 Oct 1 90	FREDONIA HIGH SCHOOL	FREDONIA	KS	250
297 Oct 1 90	FREDONIA ELEM SCHOOL	FREDONIA	KS	250
298 Oct 1 90	ARKANSAS CITY HIGH SCHOOL	ARKANSAS CITY	KS	600
299 Oct 2 90	ATTICA PUBLIC SCHOOL	ATTICA	KS	250
300 Oct 2 90	SOUTH HAVEN SCHOOL	SOUTH HAVEN	KS	250
301 Oct 3 90	GRABER ELEM SCHOOL	HUTCHINSON	KS	350
302 Oct 3 90	CHASE SCHOOL	CHASE	KS	200
303 Oct 4 90	LYONS KIWANIS BREAKFAST	LYONS	KS	25
304 Oct 4 90	LYONS HIGH SCHOOL	LYONS	KS	500
305 Oct 4 90	SOUTH ELEM SCHOOL	LYONS	KS	200
306 Oct 4 90	LYONS SENIORS CENTER	LYONS	KS	50
307 Oct 4 90	LYONS ELEM SCHOOL	LYONS	KS	200
308 Oct 4 90	RICE COUNTY HOSPITAL VISITS	LYONS	KS	50
309 Oct 5 90	RUPPENTHAL MIDDLE SCHOOL	RUSSELL	KS	250
310 Oct 5 90	CLAFLIN ELEM SCHOOL	CLAFLIN	KS	150
311 Oct 9 90	NORCROSS ELEM SCHOOL	NORCROSS	GA	1200
312 Oct 10 90	SOUTH BARBER HIGH SCHOOL	KIOWA	KS	250
313 Oct 11 90	MULLINVILLE JR HIGH SCHOOL	MULLINVILLE	KS	200
314 Oct 11 90	MEADE ELEM SCHOOL	MEADE	KS	300
315 Oct 12 90	STRAIGHT SCHOOL	STRAIGHT	KS	40
316 Oct 12 90	PRITCHETT SCHOOL	PRITCHETT	CO	100
317 Oct 15 90	SWINK ELEM SCHOOL	SWINK	CO	130
318 Oct 15 90	SWINK HIGH SCHOOL	SWINK	CO	200
319 Oct 15 90	SWINK COMMUNITY	SWINK	CO	50
320 Oct 16 90	COLORADO BOY'S RANCH	LAJUANTA	CO	50
321 Oct 17 90	EAST MIDDLE SCHOOL	AURORA	CO	750
322 Oct 17 90	SOUTH ELEM SCHOOL	CASTLE ROCK	CO	600
323 Oct 18 90	PROSPECT ELEM SCHOOL	KEENESBURG	CO	100
324 Oct 20 90	PICKENS CO. MID. SCHL PARADE	JASPER	GA	3000
325 Oct 22 90	B.B. HARRIS ELEM SCHOOL	DULUTH	GA	200
326 Oct 25 90	R.B. STEWART ELEM SCHOOL	LEOTI	KS	400
327 Oct 25 90	SHARON SPRINGS SCHOOL	SHARON SPRINGS	KS	400
328 Oct 26 90	WAKEENEY ELEM SCHOOL	WAKEENEY	KS	500
329 Oct 29 90	PHILLIPSBURG MID./HIGH SCHL	PHILLIPSBURG	KS	450
330 Oct 29 90	CALLAWAY PUBLIC SCHOOL	CALLAWAY	NE	250
331 Oct 30 90	CHAMBERS PUBLIC SCHOOL	CHAMBERS	NE	200
332 Oct 30 90	SPALDING SCHOOL	SPALDING	NE	150
333 Oct 31 90	NORRIS ELEM SCHOOL	OMAHA	NE	500

334 Oct 31 90	NORTHSIDE ELEM SCHOOL	NEBRASKA CITY	NE	350
335 Nov 1 90	SKYLINE ELEM SCHOOL	ELKHORN	NE	400
336 Nov 1 90	PAWNEE ELEM SCHOOL	OMAHA	NE	500
337 Nov 2 90	ST. WENCESLAUS CATHOLIC SCHL	OMAHA	NE	400
338 Nov 2 90	G. STANLEY HALL ELEM SCHOOL	LAVISTA	NE	400
339 Nov 5 90	GRANT CITY HIGH SCHOOL	GRANT CITY	MO	200
340 Nov 5 90	GRANT CITY ELEM SCHOOL	GRANT CITY	MO	300
341 Nov 6 90	CAMERON HIGH SCHOOL	CAMERON	MO	500
342 Nov 6 90	LATHROP ELEM SCHOOL	LATHROP	MO	600
343 Nov 7 90	SPRING GARDEN MIDDLE SCHOOL	ST. JOSEPH	MO	400
344 Nov 7 90	LUCY FRANKLIN ELEM SCHOOL	BLUE SPRINGS	MO	600
345 Nov 8 90	ST. REGIS ELEM SCHOOL	KANSAS CITY	KS	400
346 Nov 8 90	DOBBS ELEM SCHOOL	KANSAS CITY	KS	575
347 Nov 9 90	LOUISBURG ELEM/JR HIGH SCHL	LOUISBURG	KS	850
348 Nov 9 90	TURNER ELEM SCHOOL	KANSAS CITY	KS	450
349 Nov 12 90	SANTA FE TRAIL JR HIGH SCHOOL	OLATHE	KS	200
350 Nov 12 90	RAYMORE ELEM SCHOOL	RAYMORE	MO	800
351 Nov 13 90	OSAWATOMIE MIDDLE SCHOOL	OSAWATOMIE	KS	300
352 Nov 13 90	PLEASONTON ELEM SCHOOL	PLEASONTON	KS	500
353 Nov 14 90	PRAIRIE VIEW ELEM SCHOOL	PARKER	KS	150
354 Nov 14 90	HUMBOLDT HIGH SCHOOL	HUMBOLDT	KS	300
355 Nov 15 90	YATES CENTER ELEM SCHOOL	YATES CENTER	KS	450
356 Nov 15 90	YATES CENTER HIGH SCHOOL	YATES CENTER	KS	150
357 Nov 16 90	FLORENCE MIDDLE SCHOOL	FLORENCE	KS	100
358 Nov 16 90	ABILENE ELEM SCHOOL	VALLEY CENTER	KS	500
359 Nov 19 90	ST. MARY'S SCHOOL	SALINA	KS	500
360 Nov 19 90	DWIGHT ELEM SCHOOL	DWIGHT	KS	300
361 Nov 20 90	CUSTER HILL ELEM SCHOOL	FT. RILEY	KS	250
362 Nov 20 90	WESTMORELAND HIGH SCHOOL	WESTMORELAND	KS	100
363 Nov 27 90	RIVERBEND ELEM SCHOOL	GAINESVILLE	GA	400
364 Nov 28 90	GLADDEN ELEM SCHOOL	BELTON	MO	550
365 Nov 29 90	SOUTHWOOD ELEM SCHOOL	RAYTOWN	MO	450
366 Nov 29 90	ROBINSON ELEM SCHOOL	KANSAS CITY	MO	500
367 Nov 30 90	BUTCHER-GREENE ELEM SCHL	GRANDVIEW	MO	450
368 Nov 30 90	BELVIDERE ELEM SCHOOL	GRANDVIEW	MO	400
369 Dec 3 90	MCINTIRE ELEM SCHOOL	FULTON	MO	350
370 Dec 4 90	CAMBRIDGE ELEM SCHOOL	BELTON	MO	650
371 Dec 4 90	WARFORD ELEM SCHOOL	KANSAS CITY	MO	600
372 Dec 5 90	LANSING MIDDLE SCHOOL	LANSING	KS	400
373 Dec 5 90	OSKALOOSA ELEM SCHOOL	OSKALOOSA	KS	500
374 Nov 6 90	POTWIN ELEM SCHOOL	TOPEKA	KS	300
375 Nov 6 90	MCCLURE ELEM SCHOOL	TOPEKA	KS	350
376 Dec 7 90	TECUMSEH SOUTH ELEM SCHOOL	TECUMSEH	KS	450
377 Dec 7 90	MEADOWMERE ELEM SCHOOL	GRANDVIEW	MO	350
378 Dec 10 90	WATERVILLE ELEM SCHOOL	WATERVILLE	KS	450
379 Dec 10 90	NEMAHA VALLEY SCHOOLS	SENECA	KS	380
380 Dec 11 90	ST. CHARLES CATHOLIC SCHOOL	KANSAS CITY	KS	350
381 Dec 11 90	INDIAN TRAIL JR HIGH SCHOOL	OLATHE	KS	500

382 Dec 12 90	LEBANON JR HIGH SCHOOL	LEBANON	MO	850
383 Dec 12 90	HIGHLANDVILLE ELEM SCHOOL	HIGHLANDVILLE	MO	350
384 Dec 13 90	MOUNTAIN VIEW ELEM SCHOOL	MOUNTAIN VIEW	MO	750
385 Dec 13 90	PLEASANT VIEW ELEM SCHOOL	SPRINGFIELD	MO	800
386 Dec 14 90	DORA SCHOOL	DORA	MO	250
387 Dec 14 90	GAINESVILLE ELEM SCHOOL	GAINESVILLE	MO	400
388 Dec 17 90	ST. THERESA ELEM SCHOOL	GLENNONVILLE	MO	70
389 Dec 17 90	SCOTT COUNTY CENTRAL ELEM SCH.	SIKESTON	MO	250
390 Dec 18 90	CENTRAL ELEM SCHOOL	HARRISBURG	AR	300
391 Jan 3 91	SNYDER PARK ELEM SCHOOL	SPRINGFIELD	OH	350
392 Jan 3 91	MALINTA ELEM SCHOOL	MALINTA	OH	175
393 Jan 4 91	EASTWOOD JR HIGH SCHOOL	PEMBERVILLE	OH	400
394 Jan 4 91	LONGFELLOW ELEM SCHOOL	FOSTORIA	OH	350
395 Jan 7 91	EAST PALESTINE MIDDLE SCHOOL	EAST PALESTINE	OH	550
396 Jan 7 91	S.C. DENNIS ELEM SCHOOL	TORONTO	OH	280
397 Jan 8 91	PARKSIDE MIDDLE SCHOOL	WESTLAKE	OH	380
398 Jan 8 91	CEDARBROOK ELEM SCHOOL	PAINESVILLE	OH	350
399 Jan 9 91	HOLDEN ELEM SCHOOL	KENT	OH	350
400 Jan 9 91	CENTRAL ELEM SCHOOL	KENT	OH	400
401 Jan 10 91	ROOSEVELT ELEM SCHOOL	AKRON	OH	400
402 Jan 10 91	WALLS ELEM SCHOOL	KENT	OH	550
403 Jan 11 91	HAZEL HARVEY ELEM SCHOOL	DOYLESTOWN	OH	550
404 Jan 14 91	LIBERTY ELEM SCHOOL	N. RIDGEVILLE	OH	600
405 Jan 14 91	ST. MARY'S SCHOOL	AVON	OH	200
406 Jan 15 91	LAKEVIEW SCHOOL	LORAIN	OH	550
407 Jan 15 91	MAPLETON MIDDLE SCHOOL	NOVA	OH	200
408 Jan 16 91	BAKER MIDDLE SCHOOL	MARION	OH	500
409 Jan 16 91	CLINTON MIDDLE SCHOOL	COLUMBUS	OH	550
410 Jan 17 91	MCARTHUR ELEM SCHOOL	MCARTHUR	OH	450
411 Jan 17 91	MEIGS JR HIGH SCHOOL	MIDDLEPORT	OH	500
412 Jan 17 91	MEIGS HIGH SCHOOL	MIDDLEPORT	OH	500
413 Jan 18 91	CAMPBELL ELEM SCHOOL	IRONTON	OH	300
414 Jan 18 91	HAGER ELEM SCHOOL	ASHLAND	KY	300
415 Jan 19 91	BOAT/SPORTS SHOW	CINCINNATI	OH	10000
416 Jan 21 91	LEXINGTON CHRIST. ACADEMY	LEXINGTON	KY	275
417 Jan 21 91	PAINT LICK ELEM SCHOOL	PAINT LICK	KY	260
418 Jan 22 91	MEECE MIDDLE SCHOOL	SOMERSET	KY	400
419 Jan 23 91	MUNFORDVILLE ELEM SCHOOL	MUNFORDVILLE	KY	550
420 Jan 23 91	SOUTHERN/NORTHERN JR HIGH	SOMERSET	KY	500
421 Jan 24 91	MORTON'S GAP SCHOOL	MORTON'S GAP	KY	350
422 Jan 24 91	CLAY ELEM SCHOOL	CLAY	KY	530
423 Jan 25 91	CLARK ELEM SCHOOL	PADUCAH	KY	750
424 Jan 25 91	HARRISBURG JR HIGH SCHOOL	HARRISBURG	IL	750
425 Jan 28 91	FRANKLIN PARK ELEM SCHOOL	SALEM	IL	700
426 Jan 28 91	ALTAMONT ELEM SCHOOL	ALTAMONT	IL	600
427 Jan 29 91	ESTELLE KAMPMEYER ELEM SCHL	O'FALLON	IL	700
428 Jan 29 91	GRANT ELEM SCHOOL	FAIRVIEW HEIGHT	IL	400
429 Jan 30 91	COLUMBIA ELEM SCHOOL	COLUMBIA	IL	500

430 Jan 31 91	FESTUS ELEM SCHOOL	FESTUS	MO	1100
431 Jan 31 91	LINCOLN ELEM SCHOOL	ST. CHARLES	MO	250
432 Feb 1 91	BIERBAUM ELEM SCHOOL	ST. LOUIS	MO	800
433 Feb 1 91	KOCH ELEM SCHOOL	ST. LOUIS	MO	500
434 Feb 2 91	MARY KAY CSMTICS SALES MEET	ST. LOUIS	MO	300
435 Feb 4 91	LEWIS & CLARK ELEM SCHOOL	ST. LOUIS	MO	500
436 Feb 4 91	OAKVILLE ELEM SCHOOL	ST. LOUIS	MO	500
437 Feb 5 91	IMMACULATE CONCEPTION SCHL	COLUMBIA	IL	300
438 Feb 5 91	NIEDRINGHAUS ELEM SCHOOL	GRANITE CITY	IL	500
439 Feb 6 91	ST. MONICA CATHOLIC SCHOOL	ST. LOUIS	MO	480
440 Feb 6 91	RIVERBEND ELEM SCHOOL	CHESTERFIELD	MO	450
441 Feb 7 91	GREENFIELD ELEM SCHOOL	GREENFIELD	IL	550
442 Feb 7 91	NORTH GRADE SCHOOL	MT. STERLING	IL	500
443 Feb 8 91	MACON JR & SR HIGH SCHOOL	MACON	IL	450
444 Feb 8 91	LINCOLN ELEM SCHOOL	MONTICELLO	IL	450
445 Feb 11 91	LANIER ELEM SCHOOL	GAINESVILLE	GA	750
446 Feb 11 91	NORTH HALL MIDDLE SCHOOL	GAINESVILLE	GA	750
447 Feb 13 91	JEFFERSON PARK ELEM SCHOOL	EL PASO	IL	450
448 Feb 13 91	WOODROW WILSON PRIMARY SCHL	PEORIA	IL	600
449 Feb 14 91	CARRIE BUSEY ELEM SCHOOL	CHAMPAIGN	IL	500
450 Feb 14 91	JOHN GREER ELEM SCHOOL	HOOPESTON	IL	300
451 Feb 15 91	ROBESON ELEM SCHOOL	CHAMPAIGN	IL	700
452 Feb 15 91	DR. HOWARD ELEM SCHOOL	CHAMPAIGN	IL	550
453 Feb 18 91	CENTENNIAL SCHOOL	EL PASO	IL	300
454 Feb 18 91	IRVING ELEM SCHOOL	BLOOMINGTON	IL	500
455 Feb 19 91	GRANVILLE ELEM SCHOOL	GRANVILLE	IL	250
456 Feb 19 91	CORNELL GRADE SCHOOL	CORNELL	IL	150
457 Feb 20 91	HENNEPIN ELEM SCHOOL	HENNEPIN	IL	150
458 Feb 20 91	ROOSEVELT ELEM SCHOOL	PERU	IL	330
459 Feb 21 91	WALNUT GRADE SCHOOL	WALNUT	IL	300
460 Feb 21 91	NORTHLAWN JR HIGH SCHOOL	STREATOR	IL	600
461 Feb 22 91	KISHWAUKEE ELEM SCHOOL	GARDEN PRAIRIE	IL	220
462 Feb 22 91	CONKLIN ELEM SCHOOL	ROCKFORD	IL	500
463 Feb 25 91	LONGFELLOW ELEM SCHOOL	CLINTON	IA	500
464 Feb 25 91	LASALLE HIGH SCHOOL	CEDAR RAPIDS	IA	250
465 Feb 26 91	EUGENE FIELD ELEM SCHOOL	ROCK ISLAND	IL	320
466 Feb 26 91	SILAS WILLARD ELEM SCHOOL	GALESBURG	IL	400
467 Feb 27 91	VAN ALLEN ELEM SCHOOL	CHARITON	IA	350
468 Feb 27 91	HEDRICK COMMUNITY SCHOOL	HEDRICK	IA	250
469 Feb 28 91	CARLISLE JR HIGH SCHOOL	CARLISLE	IA	100
470 Mar 1 91	COLLINS-MAXWELL MIDDLE SCHL	COLLINS	IA	300
471 Mar 1 91	MANSON HIGH SCHOOL	MANSON	IA	250
472 Mar 4 91	SMITH ELEM SCHOOL	SIOUX CITY	IA	300
473 Mar 4 91	CRESCENT PARK ELEM SCHOOL	SIOUX CITY	IA	430
474 Mar 4 91	SIOUXLAND SENIORS CENTER	SIOUX CITY	IA	50
475 Mar 5 91	EVERETT ELEM SCHOOL	SIOUX CITY	IA	300
476 Mar 5 91	EMERSON ELEM SCHOOL	SIOUX CITY	IA	250
477 Mar 6 91	JOY ELEM SCHOOL	SIOUX CITY	IA	300

266

478 Mar 6 91	MORNINGSIDE CHRISTIAN SCHL/	SIOUX CITY	IA	250
479 Mar 7 91	ST. BONIFACE CATHOLIC SCHOOL	SIOUX CITY	IA	100
480 Mar 7 91	ROOSEVELT ELEM SCHOOL	SIOUX CITY	IA	250
481 Mar 7 91	WESTWOOD NURSING HOME	SIOUX CITY	IA	50
482 Mar 8 91	LINCOLN ELEM SCHOOL	SIOUX CITY	IA	400
483 Mar 8 91	IRVING ELEM SCHOOL	SIOUX CITY	IA	400
484 Mar 11 91	WHITTIER ELEM SCHOOL	SIOUX CITY	IA	350
485 Mar 11 91	AKRON WESTFIELD ELEM SCHL	AKRON	IA	500
486 Mar 12 91	LYND SCHOOL	LYND	MN	200
487 Mar 12 91	CLARKFIELD ELEM SCHOOL	CLARKFIELD	MN	250
488 Mar 13 91	V.L. REISHUS MIDDLE SCHOOL	BIWABIK	MN	450
489 Mar 13 91	CHISHOLM MIDDLE SCHOOL	CHISHOLM	MN	500
490 Mar 14 91	ST. ANTHONY CATHOLIC SCHOOL	WATKINS	MN	100
491 Mar 14 91	ST. MICHAEL'S SCHOOL	WEST ST. PAUL	MN	250
492 Mar 15 91	DURAND HIGH SCHOOL	DURAND	WI	350
493 Mar 15 91	HOWE ELEM SCHOOL	WISCONSIN RAPID	WI	500
494 Mar 18 91	FRANKLIN ELEM SCHOOL	LACROSSE	WI	350
495 Mar 18 91	LAWRENCE-LAWSON ELEM SCHL	SPARTA	WI	350
496 Mar 19 91	MONTELLO SCHOOL	MONTELLO	WI	800
497 Mar 19 91	TRI COUNTY ELEM SCHOOL	PLAINFIELD	WI	550
498 Mar 20 91	WAUPACA ELEM SCHOOL	WAUPACA	WI	1000
500 Mar 21 91	SUGAR CAMP ELEM SCHOOL	SUGAR CAMP	WI	130
501 Mar 21 91	THREE LAKES ELEM SCHOOL	THREE LAKES	WI	300
502 Mar 21 91	THREE LAKES HIGH SCHOOL	THREE LAKES	WI	250
503 Mar 22 91	ROTHSCHILD ELEM SCHOOL	ROTHSCHILD	WI	450
504 Mar 22 91	NORTHLAND PINES MIDDLE SCHL	EAGLE RIVER	WI	350
505 Mar 25 91	WAUSAUKEE ELEM SCHOOL	WAUSAUKEE	WI	450
506 Mar 25 91	MCARTHUR ELEM SCHOOL	MCARTHUR	WI	450
507 Mar 26 91	WASHINGTON ELEM SCHOOL	STEVENS POINT	WI	600
508 Mar 26 91	ST. PAUL LUTHERAN SCHOOL	STEVENS POINT	WI	100
509 Mar 26 91	BEN FRANKLIN JR HIGH SCHOOL	STEVENS POINT	WI	500
510 Mar 27 91	LINCOLN-ERDMAN ELEM SCHOOL	SHEBOYGAN	WI	250
511 Mar 27 91	LINCOLN ELEM SCHOOL	HARTFORD	WI	600
512 Mar 28 91	TRAVER SCHOOL	LAKE GENEVA	WI	100
513 Mar 28 91	EDGEWOOD ELEM SCHOOL	GREENFIELD	WI	300
514 Apr 4 91	ALICE CALLAN ELEM SCHOOL	RIPON	WI	140
515 Apr 4 91	CENTRAL ELEM SCHOOL	RIPON	WI	250
516 Apr 5 91	EDGERTON MIDDLE SCHOOL	EDGERTON	WI	400
517 Apr 8 91	KOLMAR ELEM SCHOOL	OAKLAWN	IL	400
518 Apr 8 91	ST. MARGARET MARY SCHOOL	ALGONQUIN	IL	250
519 Apr 9 91	WILLIAMS BAY ELEM SCHOOL	WILLIAMS BAY	WI	250
520 Apr 9 91	GIFFORD ELEM SCHOOL	ELGIN	IL	500
521 Apr 10 91	ST. WALTERS SCHOOL	ROSELLE	IL	450
522 Apr 10 91	ST. PAUL LUTHERAN SCHOOL	CHICAGO	IL	150
523 Apr 10 91	ABE LINCOLN BOOK STORE	CHICAGO	IL	5
524 Apr 11 91	ST. MONICA ELEM SCHOOL	CHICAGO	IL	400
525 Apr 11 91	HYNES ELEM SCHOOL	MORTON GROVE	IL	250
526 Apr 12 91	MARION HILLS ELEM SCHOOL	DARIEN	IL	250

527 Apr 12 91	CAROLINE BENTLEY ELEM SCHOOL	NEW LENOX	IL	650
528 Apr 12 91	CIVIL WAR RND TABLE DINNER MTG	CHICAGO	IL	150
529 Apr 15 91	WHITTIER ELEM SCHOOL	KENOSHA	WI	400
530 Apr 15 91	JOHNSON ELEM SCHOOL	AURORA	IL	350
531 Apr 16 91	LIMESTONE-WALTERS SCHOOL	PEORIA	IL	125
532 Apr 17 91	NOTRE DAME SCHOOL	MICHIGAN CITY	IN	250
533 Apr 17 91	CRETE ELEM SCHOOL	CRETE	IL	700
534 Apr 18 91	MT. MORRIS ELEM SCHOOL	MT. MORRIS	IL	400
535 Apr 18 91	WHEATLAND ELEM SCHOOL	NAPERVILLE	IL	450
536 Apr 19 91	JEFFERSON ELEM SCHOOL	KENOSHA	WI	450
537 Apr 19 91	WESTVIEW ELEM SCHOOL	ROCKFORD	IL	500
538 Apr 22 91	LINCOLN JR HIGH SCHOOL	PLYMOUTH	IN	800
539 Apr 22 91	BOONE GROVE ELEM SCHOOL	BOONE GROVE	IN	350
540 Apr 23 91	RIVER FOREST ELEM SCHOOL	HOBART	IN	350
541 Apr 23 91	HOLY TRINITY SCHOOL	GARY	IN	250
542 Apr 24 91	LAKE PRAIRIE ELEM SCHOOL	LOWELL	IN	375
543 Apr 25 91	TURKEY RUN ELEM SCHOOL	MARSHALL	IN	300
544 Apr 25 91	SHELBURN SCHOOL	SHELBURN	IN	300
545 Apr 26 91	CLARK MIDDLE SCHOOL	VINCENNES	IN	800
546 Apr 26 91	CHANDLER ELEM SCHOOL	CHANDLER	IN	600
547 Apr 29 91	SOUTHWESTERN ELEM SCHOOL	SHELBYVILLE	IN	400
548 Apr 29 91	SHELBYVILLE JR HIGH SCHOOL	SHELBYVILLE	IN	300
549 Apr 30 91	WEBB ELEM SCHOOL	FRANKLIN	IN	450
550 Apr 30 91	EASTSIDE ELEM SCHOOL	BRAZIL	IN	400
551 Apr 30 91	SHERIDAN ROTARY DINNER MEETING	SHERIDAN	IN	25
552 May 1 91	MARION-ADAMS JR/SR HIGH SCHOOL	SHERIDAN	IN	300
553 May 1 91	LAPEL SCHOOLS	LAPEL	IN	850
554 May 2 91	HAGERSTOWN ELEM SCHOOL	HAGERSTOWN	IN	700
555 May 2 91	LIBERTY MIDDLE SCHOOL	LIBERTY	IN	300
556 May 3 91	FAIRVIEW ELEM SCHOOL	CINCINNATI	OH	650
557 May 6 91	VAIL MIDDLE SCHOOL	MIDDLETOWN	OH	600
558 May 6 91	MONROE MIDDLE SCHOOL	MONROE	OH	400
559 May 7 91	ONIEDA ELEM SCHOOL	MIDDLETOWN	OH	300
560 May 7 91	AMANDA ELEM SCHOOL	MIDDLETOWN	OH	600
561 May 8 91	ROOSEVELT ELEM SCHOOL	MIDDLETOWN	OH	800
562 May 8 91	BROADWAY ELEM SCHOOL	TIPP CITY	OH	700
563 May 9 91	MIAMI EAST JR HIGH SCHOOL	TROY	OH	200
564 May 9 91	FT LORAMIE ELEM/JR HIGH SCHOOL	FORT LORAMIE	OH	500
565 May 10 91	VERITY MIDDLE SCHOOL	MIDDLETOWN	OH	250
566 May 10 91	FT. RECOVERY ELEM SCHOOL	FT. RECOVERY	OH	400
567 May 11 91	MAYFEST PARADE	SIDNEY	OH	25000
568 May 13 91	SOUTHEASTERN HIGH SCHOOL	S. CHARLESTON	OH	250
569 May 13 91	NEW KNOXVILLE SCHOOL	NEW KNOXVILLE	OH	450
570 May 14 91	ST. MICHAEL SCHOOL	SHARONVILLE	OH	400
571 May 15 91	BOTKINS SCHOOL	BOTKINS	OH	700
572 May 15 91	WOODROW WILSON SCHL, O.V.C.H.	XENIA	OH	200
573 May 17 91	BURNESON MIDDLE SCHOOL	WESTLAKE	OH	1000
574 May 20 91	WYOMING MIDDLE SCHOOL	WYOMING	OH	300

575 May 21 91	LADYFIELD ELEM SCHOOL	TOLEDO	OH	250
576 May 22 91	INDIAN HILLS ELEM SCHOOL	ROSSFORD	OH	300
577 May 22 91	ST. CATHERINE SCHOOL	TOLEDO	OH	400
578 May 23 91	SOUTH VIEW ELEM SCHOOL	MUNCIE	IN	650
579 May 23 91	COLLEGE CORNER ELEM SCHOOL	ANDERSON	IN	400
580 May 24 91	ZION-IMMANUEL LUTHERAN SCHL	MATTESON	IL	225
581 Jun 12 91	T.E.P.S.A. CONVENTION	AUSTIN	TX	2000
582 Jul 1 91	MT. RUSHMORE NAT'L MEMORIAL	KEYSTONE	SD	2000
583 Jul 2 91	MT. RUSHMORE NAT'L MEMORIAL	KEYSTONE	SD	2000
584 Jul 4 91	MT. RUSHMORE NAT'L MEMORIAL	KEYSTONE	SD	2000
585 Jul 4 91	MT. RUSHMORE NAT'L MEMORIAL	KEYSTONE	SD	5500
586 Jul 4 91	INDEPENDENCE DAY PARADE	RAPID CITY	SD	50000
587 Jul 5 91	MT. RUSHMORE NAT'L MEMORIAL	KEYSTONE	SD	2000
588 Jul 5 91	WEST HILLS VILLAGE SR. CENTER	RAPID CITY	SD	75
589 Jul 15 91	G.A.E.L ,GA. ASSOC. of EDUCATION	JEKYLL ISLAND	GA	1500
590 Jul 20 91	CIVIL WAR ENCAMPMT., ATL HISTORY	ATLANTA	GA	1500
591 Jul 21 91	CIVIL WAR ENCAMPMT., ATL HISTORY	ATLANTA	GA	1500
592 Jul 28 91	LITTLE RIVER UNITED METH. CHURCH	WOODSTOCK	GA	100
593 Aug 3 91	STANFORD CTR RETIREMNT. HOME	ALTAMONTE SPRIN	FL	100
594 Aug 4 91	HOWELL PLACE RETIREMENT CTR	SANFORD	FL	150
595 Aug 14 91	SCOTT. RITE ASSN DINNER MEET	DECATUR	GA	30
596 Aug 19 91	ALBANY HIGH SCHL STAFF ONLY	ALBANY	GA	100
597 Sep 7 91	GWIN. CULTURAL ARTS WRKSHP.	LAWRENCEVILLE	GA	25
598 Oct 2 91	ANNUAL SCHL SUPERINTENDENT'S	DAWSONVILLE	GA	50
599 Oct 3 91	SOUTHLAND ACADEMY SCHOOL	AMERICUS	GA	1000
600 Oct 4 91	SUMTER COUNTY ELEM SCHOOL	AMERICUS	GA	1400
601 Oct 5 91	HIST. ANDERSONVILLE PARADE A	ANDERSONVILLE	GA	5000
602 Oct 6 91	KANSAS SCHL FOOD SERV. ASSN.	WICHITA	KS	400
603 Oct 16 91	TATE ELEM SCHOOL	TATE	GA	350
604 Oct 19 91	JASPER TRU-VALU HRDWRE STORE	JASPER	GA	100
605 Oct 24 91	"STAY IN SCHL" PROG., CORPS	CARTER'S LAKE	GA	1000
606 Nov 4 91	FAIRWOOD ELEM SCHOOL	BEREA	OH	350
607 Nov 5 91	PARKNOLL ELEM SCHOOL	BEREA	OH	450
608 Nov 6 91	SMITH ELEM SCHOOL	BEREA	OH	300
609 Nov 6 91	WEST. RESERVE CIVIL WAR RND	BEREA	OH	50
610 Nov 7 91	RIVEREDGE ELEM SCHOOL	BEREA	OH	350
611 Nov 8 91	PERRY MIDDLE SCHOOL	PERRY	OH	450
612 Nov 8 91	PERRY ELEM SCHOOL	PERRY	OH	450
613 Nov 11'91	ST. MARY OF THE FALLS SCHOOL	OLMSTEAD FALLS	OH	300
614 Nov 12 91	FALLS ELEM SCHOOL	OLMSTEAD FALLS	OH	400
615 Nov 14 91	FIRST BAPT. CHURCH "LUNCH & LEARN "	ROSWELL	GA	300
616 Dec 3 91	LILBURN ELEM SCHOOL	LILBURN	GA	1200
617 Dec 9 91	MT. VERNON ELEM SCHOOL	MT. VERNON	TX	800
618 Dec 10 91	MALTA ELEM SCHOOL	MALTA	TX	60
619 Dec 11 91	QUEEN CITY ELEM SCHOOL	QUEEN CITY	TX	450
620 Dec 12 91	HOOKS ELEM SCHOOL	HOOKS	TX	425
621 Dec 13 91	AVERY ELEM SCHOOL	AVERY	TX	200
622 Dec 13 91	AVERY JR & SR HIGH SCHOOL	AVERY	TX	200

269

623 Jan 8 92	ELLIJAY ELEM SCHOOL	ELLIJAY	GA	600
624 Jan 9 92	EAST FANNIN MIDDLE SCHOOL	MORGANTON	GA	250
625 Jan 9 92	EPWORTH MENS CLUB	EPWORTH	GA	25
626 Jan 10 92	COMPTON ELEM SCHOOL	POWDER SPRINGS	GA	950
627 Jan 11 92	TAYLORSVILLE LIBRARY	TAYLORSVILLE	MS	25
628 Jan 13 92	SOUTHSIDE ELEM SCHOOL	ANGLETON	TX	600
629 Jan 13 92	WESTSIDE ELEM SCHOOL	ANGLETON	TX	500
630 Jan 14 92	FRONTIER ELEM SCHOOL	ANGLETON	TX	450
631 Jan 14 92	RANCHO ISABELLA ELEM SCHOOL	ANGLETON	TX	550
632 Jan 15 92	NORTHSIDE ELEM SCHOOL	ANGLETON	TX	600
633 Jan 16 92	FERGUSON ELEM SCHOOL	LEAGUE CITY	TX	950
634 Jan 17 92	STEWART ELEM SCHOOL	KEMAH	TX	550
635 Jan 20 92	PITTSBURG INTERMEDIATE SCHL	PITTSBURG	TX	500
636 Jan 21 92	ROXTON SCHOOL	ROXTON	TX	200
637 Jan 21 92	SULPHUR SPRINGS MIDDLE SCHL	SULPHUR SPRINGS	TX	300
638 Jan 22 92	BOWIE ELEM SCHOOL	SULPHUR SPRINGS	TX	450
639 Jan 22 92	AUSTIN ELEM SCHOOL	SULPHUR SPRINGS	TX	250
640 Jan 23 92	HOUSTON ELEM SCHOOL	SULPHUR SPRINGS	TX	300
641 Jan 23 92	DOUGLAS ELEM SCHOOL	SULPHUR SPRINGS	TX	250
642 Jan 24 92	TRAVIS ELEM SCHOOL	SULPHUR SPRINGS	TX	450
643 Jan 24 92	LAMAR ELEM SCHOOL	SULPHUR SPRINGS	TX	300
644 Jan 27 92	CIMARRON ELEM SCHOOL	HOUSTON	TX	850
645 Jan 28 92	HOLMSLEY ELEM SCHOOL	HOUSTON	TX	1000
646 Jan 29 92	SAM HOUSTON ELEM SCHOOL	HUNTSVILLE	TX	550
647 Jan 29 92	SCOTT JOHNSON ELEM SCHOOL	HUNTSVILLE	TX	700
648 Jan 30 92	PLEASANTON ELEM SCHOOL	PLEASANTON	TX	750
649 Jan 31 92	ROSE GARDEN ELEM SCHOOL	UNIVERSAL CITY	TX	460
650 Jan 31 92	NORTHVIEW ECC SCHOOL	UNIVERSAL CITY	TX	450
651 Feb 3 92	DENVER CITY ELEM SCHOOL	DENVER CITY	TX	1300
652 Feb 4 92	PLUM CREEK ELEM SCHOOL	LOCKHART	TX	600
653 Feb 5 92	FORESTRIDGE ELEM SCHOOL	DALLAS	TX	750
654 Feb 6 92	WINNSBORO ELEM SCHOOL	WINNSBORO	TX	550
655 Feb 7 92	BRAELINN ELEM SCHOOL	PEACHTREE CITY	GA	750
656 Feb 7 92	BIG CANOE HOMEOWNERS	BIG CANOE	GA	125
657 Feb 8 92	MASONIC LDGE 228 & RAINBOW DINNER	NORCROSS	GA	25
658 Feb 10 92	CAMP CREEK ELEM SCHOOL	LILBURN	GA	875
659 Feb 10 92	B. B. HARRIS ELEM SCHOOL	DULUTH	GA	950
660 Feb 11 92	HAMPTON ELEM SCHOOL	HAMPTON	GA	550
661 Feb 11 92	GWINNETT HOME SCHOOLERS	LILBURN	GA	450
662 Feb 11 92	CLARKSTON MASONIC LDGE 492	CLARKSTON	GA	100
663 Feb 12 92	ANNISTOWN ELEM SCHOOL	LITHONIA	GA	1000
664 Feb 13 92	MOUNTAIN PARK ELEM SCHOOL	LILBURN	GA	600
665 Feb 13 92	CEDAR HILL ELEM SCHOOL	LAWRENCEVILLE	GA	1650
666 Feb 14 92	T. G. RITCH ELEM SCHOOL	JESUP	GA	650
667 Feb 14 92	JESUP MIDDLE GRADE SCHOOL	JESUP	GA	700
668 Feb 17 92	COMO PICKTON ELEM SCHOOL	PICKTON	TX	300
669 Feb 18 92	OAKWOOD TERRACE ELEM SCHOOL	EULESS	TX	600
670 Feb 18 92	SOUTH EULESS ELEM SCHOOL	EULESS	TX	600

671 Feb 19 92	MIDWAY PARK ELEM SCHOOL	EULESS	TX	700
672 Feb 19 92	NORTH EULESS ELEM SCHOOL	EULESS	TX	550
673 Feb 20 92	WILSHIRE ELEM SCHOOL	EULESS	TX	600
674 Feb 20 92	LAKEWOOD ELEM SCHOOL	EULESS	TX	650
675 Feb 21 92	MEADOW CREEK ELEM SCHOOL	BEDFORD	TX	850
676 Feb 21 92	BELL MANOR ELEM SCHOOL	BEDFORD	TX	800
677 Feb 24 92	SHADY OAKS ELEM SCHOOL	HURST	TX	500
678 Feb 24 92	DONNA PARK ELEM SCHOOL	HURST	TX	575
679 Feb 25 92	BELLAIRE ELEM SCHOOL	HURST	TX	650
680 Feb 25 92	HARRISON LANE ELEM SCHOOL	BEDFORD	TX	550
681 Feb 26 92	HURST HILLS ELEM SCHOOL	HURST	TX	600
682 Feb 26 92	WEST HURST ELEM SCHOOL	HURST	TX	550
683 Feb 26 92	MASONIC HOME FOR AGED	ARLINGTON	TX	50
684 Feb 27 92	BEDFORD HEIGHTS ELEM SCHOOL	BEDFORD	TX	850
685 Feb 27 92	STONEGATE ELEM SCHOOL	BEDFORD	TX	550
686 Feb 28 92	SPRING GARDEN ELEM SCHOOL	BEDFORD	TX	900
687 Feb 28 92	SHADY BROOK ELEM SCHOOL	BEDFORD	TX	600
688 Mar 2 92	PLEASANT GROVE ELEM SCHOOL	TEXARKANA	TX	650
689 Mar 3 92	LINDEN KILDARE JR HIGH SCHOOL	KILDARE	TX	350
690 Mar 3 92	LINDEN KILDARE ELEM SCHOOL	KILDARE	TX	650
691 Mar 4 92	NEW BOSTON HIGH SCHOOL	NEW BOSTON	TX	300
692 Mar 5 92	PEWITT JR HIGH SCHOOL	OMAHA	TX	350
693 Mar 5 92	ATLANTA ELEM SCHOOL	ATLANTA	TX	500
694 Mar 6 92	NEW BOSTON JR HIGH SCHOOL	NEW BOSTON	TX	150
695 Mar 9 92	LAMAR MIDDLE SCHOOL	SAN MARCOS	TX	475
696 Mar 10 92	GOODNIGHT JR HIGH SCHOOL	SAN MARCOS	TX	1000
697 Mar 11 92	CROCKETT ELEM SCHOOL	SAN MARCOS	TX	850
698 Mar 11 92	BONHAM PRE-SCHOOL	SAN MARCOS	TX	300
699 Mar 11 92	DEZAVALA ELEM SCHOOL	SAN MARCOS	TX	850
700 Mar 12 92	BOWIE ELEM SCHOOL	SAN MARCOS	TX	750
701 Mar 13 92	TRAVIS ELEM SCHOOL	SAN MARCOS	TX	800
702 Mar 26 92	CARDEN ACADEMY	PARK CITY	UT	60
703 Mar 26 92	LUBBOCK ARTS FESTIVAL	LUBBOCK	TX	250
704 Mar 27 92	LUBBOCK ARTS FESTIVAL	LUBBOCK	TX	5000
705 Mar 28 92	LUBBOCK ARTS FESTIVAL	LUBBOCK	TX	3000
706 Mar 29 92	LUBBOCK ARTS FESTIVAL	LUBBOCK	TX	3000
707 Mar 30 92	AUSTIN ELEM SCHOOL	SLATON	TX	300
708 Mar 30 92	WEST WARD ELEM SCHOOL	SLATON	TX	600
709 Mar 30 92	KAPPA KAPPA GAMMA SORORITY	LUBBOCK	TX	100
710 Mar 31 92	ROPES, MEADOW & WELLMAN ELEM	MEADOW	TX	500
711 Mar 31 92	SEAGRAVES ELEM SCHOOL	SEAGRAVES	TX	450
712 Apr 1 92	FRENSHIP INTERMEDIATE SCHOOL	LUBBOCK	TX	800
713 Apr 1 92	REESE ELEM SCHOOL	LUBBOCK	TX	450
714 Apr 1 92	FIRST BAPTIST CHURCH	MEADOW	TX	50
715 Apr 2 92	SUDAN ELEM SCHOOL	SUDAN	TX	250
716 Apr 2 92	DILLMAN ELEM SCHOOL	MULESHOE	TX	400
717 Apr 2 92	DeSHAZO ELEM SCHOOL	MULESHOE	TX	400
718 Apr 3 92	LOCKNEY ELEM SCHOOL	LOCKNEY	TX	450

271

719 Apr 3 92	ROOSEVELT ELEM SCHOOL	LUBBOCK	TX	750
720 Apr 17 92	SPRING PLACE ELEM SCHOOL	SPRING PLACE	GA	1200
721 Apr 28 92	TNN LIVE TV SHOW	NASHVILLE	TN	1000
722 May 2 92	SNELLVILLE DAYS FEST. & PARA	SNELLVILLE	GA	20000
723 May 8 92	TRYON STREET ELEM SCHOOL	GREER	SC	550
724 May 9 92	GREER FAMILY FESTIVAL	GREER	SC	1000
725 May 14 92	DALTON H. S. HONORS BANQ	DALTON	GA	500
726 May 18 92	GREEN VALLEY ELEM SCHOOL	HOUSTON	TX	1000
727 May 24 92	CRISTY LANE THEATRE	BRANSON	MO	18
728 May 25 92	CRISTY LANE THEATRE	BRANSON	MO	17
729 May 27 92	CRISTY LANE THEATRE	BRANSON	MO	24
730 May 28 92	CRISTY LANE THEATRE	BRANSON	MO	34
731 May 15 92	CRISTY LANE THEATRE	BRANSON	MO	15
732 Jul 4 92	BOONE COUNTY CELEBRATION	HARRISON	AR	500
733 Jul 4 92	LYRIC THEATER	HARRISON	AR	85
734 Jul 18 92	LYRIC THEATER	HARRISON	AR	17
735 Jul 21 92	LYRIC THEATER	HARRISON	AR	7
736 Jul 22 92	LYRIC THEATER	HARRISON	AR	3
737 Jul 23 92	LYRIC THEATER	HARRISON	AR	13
738 Jul 24 92	LYRIC THEATER	HARRISON	AR	4
739 Jul 25 92	LYRIC THEATER	HARRISON	AR	28
740 Jul 28 92	LYRIC THEATER	HARRISON	AR	4
741 Jul 31 92	LYRIC THEATER	HARRISON	AR	10
742 Aug 1 92	LYRIC THEATER	HARRISON	AR	24
743 Aug 4 92	LYRIC THEATER B/D PARTY	HARRISON	AR	40
744 Aug 7 92	LYRIC THEATER	HARRISON	AR	6
745 Aug 8 92	LYRIC THEATER	HARRISON	AR	7
746 Aug 10 92	KIWANIS LUNCH MEETING	HARRISON	AR	50
747 Aug 13 92	LYRIC THEATER	HARRISON	AR	18
748 Aug 14 92	LYRIC THEATER	HARRISON	AR	6
749 Aug 15 92	LYRIC THEATER	HARRISON	AR	11
750 Aug 18 92	LYRIC THEATER	HARRISON	AR	11
751 Aug 19 92	LYRIC THEATER	HARRISON	AR	16
752 Aug 20 92	LYRIC THEATER	HARRISON	AR	16
753 Aug 21 92	LYRIC THEATER	HARRISON	AR	7
754 Aug 22 92	LYRIC THEATER	HARRISON	AR	9
755 Aug 25 92	LYRIC THEATER	HARRISON	AR	11
756 Aug 27 92	LYRIC THEATER	HARRISON	AR	5
757 Aug 28 92	LYRIC THEATER	HARRISON	AR	8
758 Aug 29 92	LYRIC THEATER	HARRISON	AR	21
759 Sep 1 92	LYRIC THEATER	HARRISON	AR	5
760 Sep 2 92	LYRIC THEATER	HARRISON	AR	9
761 Sep 4 92	LYRIC THEATER	HARRISON	AR	9
762 Sep 5 92	LYRIC THEATER	HARRISON	AR	7
763 Sep 8 92	LYRIC GRAND OPENING	HARRISON	AR	103
764 Sep 10 92	LYRIC THEATER	HARRISON	AR	6
765 Sep 11 92	LYRIC THEATER	HARRISON	AR	9
766 Sep 12 92	LYRIC WOODMEN OF WORLD	HARRISON	AR	103

767 Sep 16 92	LYRIC THEATER	HARRISON	AR	11
768 Sep 17 92	LYRIC THEATER	HARRISON	AR	17
769 Sep 18 92	A.A.R.P. MEETING	HARRISON	AR	20
770 Sep 18 92	LYRIC THEATER	HARRISON	AR	17
771 Sep 19 92	LYRIC THEATER	HARRISON	AR	23
772 Sep 22 92	LYRIC THEATER	HARRISON	AR	15
773 Sep 24 92	RODEO/FAIR PARADE	HARRISON	AR	5000
774 Sep 26 92	LYRIC THEATER	HARRISON	AR	10
775 Sep 29 92	LYRIC THEATER	HARRISON	AR	5
776 Sep 30 92	LYRIC THEATER	HARRISON	AR	7
777 Oct 1 92	LYRIC THEATER	HARRISON	AR	10
778 Oct 3 92	LYRIC THEATER	HARRISON	AR	8
779 Oct 7 92	CHURCH CONVENTION	ST. LOUIS	MO	50
780 Oct 9 92	LYRIC THEATER	HARRISON	AR	13
781 Oct 10 92	LYRIC THEATER	HARRISON	AR	13
782 Oct 13 92	PARISH DAY SCHOOL	DALLAS	TX	400
783 Oct 14 92	RED LICK ELEM SCHOOL	LEARY	TX	400
784 Oct 15 92	WINFIELD ISD SCHOOL	WINFIELD	TX	100
785 Oct 15 92	DOUGLAS INTERMEDIATE SCHL	SULPHUR SPRINGS	TX	330
786 Oct 16 92	DAINGERFIELD JR HIGH SCHOOL	DAINGERFIELD	TX	200
787 Oct 16 92	LIBERTY-EYLAU ELEM SCHOOL	TEXARKANA	TX	200
788 Oct 17 92	LYRIC THEATER	HARRISON	AR	19
789 Oct 22 92	HOME SCHOOLERS, LYRIC	HARRISON	AR	85
790 Oct 22 92	LYRIC THEATER	HARRISON	AR	7
791 Oct 23 92	LYRIC THEATER	HARRISON	AR	5
792 Oct 24 92	GIRL SCOUTS, LYRIC THEATER	HARRISON	AR	150
793 Oct 26 92	MURFREESBORO ELEM SCHOOL	MURFREESBORO	AR	350
794 Oct 28 92	LIONS CLUB LUNCHEON	HARRISON	AR	40
795 Nov 5 92	N.A.C.C.,STAY IN SCHL PROGRAM	HARRISON	AR	100
796 Nov 5 92	ROTARY CLUB LUNCHEON	HARRISON	AR	50
797 Nov 14 92	CIVIL WAR REENACTMENT	GREEN FOREST	AR	1000
798 Nov 16 92	PLEASANT HOPE ELEM SCHOOL	PLEASANT HOPE	MO	450
799 Nov 18 92	DORA SCHOOL	DORA	MO	300
800 Nov 19 92	RIVERVIEW BIBLE SCHL HONOR ST	HARRISON	AR	45
801 Dec 8 92	GREEN FOREST SCHOOL	GREEN FOREST	AR	700
802 Dec 15 92	ALPENA H. S. AT LYRIC THEATER	HARRISON	AR	55
803 Dec 30 92	HOWELL PL. RETIREMENT HOME	SANFORD	FL	80
804 Jan 13 93	MELALEUCA LAUNCH CONV.	TULSA	OK	2700
805 Jan 16 93	PHOTO OPS DOWNTOWN	WASHINGTON	DC	1000
806 Jan 17 93	CAPITOL MALL PLUS TV	WASHINGTON	DC	10000
807 Jan 18 93	CAPITOL MALL AREA	WASHINGTON	DC	20000
808 Jan 19 93	BUREAU OF ENGRAVING	WASHINGTON	DC	100
809 Jan 19 93	KENNEDY CTR SALUTE TO CHILDR	WASHINGTON	DC	10000
810 Jan 19 93	KENNEDY CTR SALUTE TO YOUTH	WASHINGTON	DC	10000
811 Jan 19 93	TOUR OF USA TODAY NEWSP	WASHINGTON	DC	50
812 Jan 20 93	UNION STATION	WASHINGTON	DC	1000
813 Jan 20 93	INAUGURAL PARADE RTE PHOTOS	WASHINGTON	DC	10000
814 Jan 20 93	CAP. MALL "48-HOURS" TV TAPING	WASHINGTON	DC	100

815 Jan 21 93	LINCOLN MEMORIAL	WASHINGTON	DC	50
816 Jan 22 93	BUREAU OF ENGRAVING	WASHINGTON	DC	250
817 Jan 22 93	LINCOLN MEMORIAL	WASHINGTON	DC	100
818 Jan 23 93	LYRIC THEATER SPECIAL SHOW	HARRISON	AR	25
819 Jan 25 93	WEST SIDE ELEM SCHOOL	HELENA	AR	500
820 Jan 25 93	WOODRUFF ELEM SCHOOL	HELENA	AR	400
821 Jan 26 93	JEFFERSON ELEM SCHOOL	HELENA	AR	300
822 Jan 26 93	HELENA CROSSING ELEM SCHL	HELENA	AR	175
823 Jan 27 93	J.F. WAHL ELEM SCHOOL	HELENA	AR	600
824 Jan 28 93	BEECH CREST ELEM SCHOOL	HELENA	AR	550
825 Jan 28 93	ELIZA MILLER J.H.SCHOOL	HELENA	AR	200
826 Jan 29 93	ELIZA MILLER J.H. SCHOOL	HELENA	AR	500
827 Feb 9 93	YALE ELEM SCHOOL	RICHARDSON	TX	850
828 Feb 10 93	BRENTFIELD ELEM SCHOOL	DALLAS	TX	750
829 Feb 12 93	UNION COUNTY ELEM SCHOOL	BLAIRSVILLE	GA	950
830 Feb 12 93	PEACHTREE MASONIC LDGE #732	ATLANTA	GA	60
831 Feb 14 93	70TH B'DAY PARTY-REV. WILLIS	GAINESVILLE	GA	25
832 Feb 15 93	JASPER ELEM SCHOOL	JASPER	GA	1000
833 Feb 16 93	HALL COUNTY HOME SCHOOLERS	GAINESVILLE	GA	225
834 Feb 17 93	MINERAL BLUFF ELEM SCHOOL	MINERAL BLUFF	GA	200
835 Feb 17 93	FULTON MASONIC LODGE #216	ATLANTA	GA	30
836 Feb 18 93	HUDDLESTON ELEM SCHOOL	PEACHTREE CITY	GA	650
837 Feb 19 93	ROSEMONT ELEM SCHOOL	LAGRANGE	GA	600
838 Feb 20 93	JASPER METH. CHURCH SPECIAL	JASPER	GA	100
839 Feb 22 93	EAST GREER ELEM SCHOOL	GREER	SC	300
840 Feb 23 93	SHRINER'S CHILDREN'S HOSPITAL	GREENVILLE	SC	50
841 Feb 24 93	MITCHELL ROAD ELEM SCHOOL	GREENVILLE	SC	670
842 Mar 2 93	BRUSHY CREEK ELEM SCHOOL	GREENVILLE	SC	750
843 Mar 3 93	LAKE FOREST ELEM SCHOOL	GREENVILLE	SC	400
844 Mar 9 93	KIRBY SCHOOL	KIRBY	AR	400
845 Mar 10 93	GLENWOOD ELEM SCHOOL	GLENWOOD	AR	200
846 Mar 10 93	GLENWOOD HIGH SCHOOL	GLENWOOD	AR	200
847 Mar 17 93	ROTARY CLUB LUNCH	JASPER	GA	25
848 Mar 25 93	BRADEN RIVER ELEM SCHOOL	BRADENTON	FL	750
849 Apr 8 93	SUMMIT MIDDLE SCHOOL	EDMUND	OK	950
850 Apr 13 93	DUNWOODY KIWANIS	DUNWOODY	GA	50
851 Apr 21 93	NORTHEAST ELEM SCHOOL	ARMA	KS	300
852 Apr 22 93	HADERLEIN ELEM SCHOOL	GIRARD	KS	550
853 Apr 22 93	MELALEUCA MEETING	PITTSBURG	KS	30
854 Apr 26 93	DELIGHT SCHOOLS	DELIGHT	AR	400
855 May 25 93	BERKELEY LAKE ELEM SCHOOL	DULUTH	GA	1200
856 May 27 93	ALAN LAUFMAN B/D PARTY	DALLAS	TX	5
857 May 31 93	MASONIC WIVES SUPPER	SMYRNA	GA	75
858 Jun 3 93	GOOD OLD DAYS SHOWS	FT. SCOTT	KS	80
859 Jun 4 93	GOOD OLD DAYS PARADE	FT. SCOTT	KS	5000
860 Jun 12 93	TASTE OF ATLANTA	ATLANTA	GA	2000
861 Aug 7 93	ROSE CREEK LIBRARY	WOODSTOCK	GA	25
862 Aug 7 93	WOODSTOCK LIBRARY	WOODSTOCK	GA	25

863 Sep 15 93	4TH ANN. ROTARY GOLF TOURN.	BENT TREE	GA	150
864 Sep 25 93	PIONEER DAYS CELEBRATION	FT. WORTH	TX	5000
865 Sep 26 93	PIONEER DAYS CELEBRATION	FT. WORTH	TX	3000
866 Nov 8 93	BIG SPRINGS ELEM SCHOOL	RICHARDSON	TX	700
867 Nov 9 93	GREENWOOD HILLS ELEM SCHL	RICHARDSON	TX	400
868 Nov 9 93	GREENWOOD HILLS ELEM SCHL PTA	RICHARDSON	TX	100
869 Nov 10 93	NORTHRICH ELEM SCHOOL	RICHARDSON	TX	450
870 Nov 10 93	PRESTONWOOD BAPTIST CHURCH	RICHARDSON	TX	100
871 Nov 11 93	CANYON CREEK ELEM SCHOOL	RICHARDSON	TX	300
872 Nov 11 93	CANYON CREEK ELEM SCHL PTA	RICHARDSON	TX	100
873 Nov 12 93	BOWIE ELEM SCHOOL	RICHARDSON	TX	600
874 Nov 15 93	LAKESIDE ELEM SCHOOL	IRVING	TX	25
875 Nov 16 93	NORTHLAKE ELEM SCHOOL	RICHARDSON	TX	550
876 Nov 17 93	TERRACE ELEM SCHOOL	RICHARDSON	TX	650
877 Nov 19 93	NANNIE BERRY ELEM SCHOOL	HENDERSONVILLE	TN	600
878 Nov 22 93	ROTARY CLUB LUNCHEON MTG	SANDY SPRINGS	GA	80
879 Jan 10 94	FAIRGLEN ELEM SCHOOL	COCOA	FL	1100
880 Jan 12 94	TALK OF THE TOWN TV SHOW	MELBOURNE	FL	10
881 Jan 12 94	MELALEUCA LAUNCH MEETING	ORLANDO	FL	2000
882 Jan 13 94	CHALLENGER 7 ELEM SCHOOL	PORT ST. JOHN	FL	1000
883 Jan 24 94	MILNER ELEM SCHOOL	HARTFORD	CT	500
884 Jan 27 94	LEDYARD CENTER SCHOOL	LEDYARD	CT	500
885 Jan 27 94	ST. JOSEPH CATHOLIC SCHOOL	BALTIC	CT	200
886 Jan 28 94	GALLUP HILL ELEM SCHOOL	LEDYARD	CT	450
887 Feb 1 94	DALTON J.H. SCHOOL	DALTON	GA	500
888 Feb 2 94	WESTWOOD ELEM SCHOOL	DALTON	GA	600
889 Feb 2 94	ROAN ELEM SCHOOL	DALTON	GA	500
890 Feb 3 94	FT. HILL ELEM SCHOOL	DALTON	GA	250
891 Feb 4 94	COMPTON ELEM SCHOOL	POWDER SPRGS	GA	1000
892 Feb 8 94	CLARKDALE ELEM SCHOOL	AUSTELL	GA	500
893 Feb 10 94	JASPER LIONS CLUB	JASPER	GA	60
894 Feb 11 94	ATHERTON PLACE FOR SENIORS	MARIETTA	GA	100
895 Feb 16 94	MUSTANG ELEM SCHOOL	MUSTANG	OK	775
896 Feb 17 94	MUSTANG VALLEY ELEM SCHOOL	MUSTANG	OK	700
897 Feb 18 94	MUSTANG TRAILS ELEM SCHOOL	MUSTANG	OK	900
898 Feb 21 94	STROUD ELEM SCHOOL	STROUD	OK	350
899 Feb 22 94	SKYVIEW ELEM SCHOOL	YUKON	OK	750
900 Feb 23 94	PARKLAND ELEM SCHOOL	YUKON	OK	600
901 Mar 10 94	PICKENS HIGH SCHOOL	JASPER	GA	50
902 Mar 21 94	GRACE CHRISTIAN ACADEMY	ELLIJAY	GA	35
903 Mar 27 94	FAIRGLEN ELEM BUS TOUR	WASHINGTON	DC	40
904 Mar 28 94	LINCOLN MEMORIAL, ETC.	WASHINGTON	DC	500
905 Mar 29 94	FORD'S THEATER	WASHINGTON	DC	500
906 Apr 07 94	SASAFRASS WRITING CLUB	JASPER	GA	50
907 May 02 94	APPALACHIAN HOME SCHOOLERS	JASPER	GA	125
908 May 20 94	BATTLE RE-ENACTMENT ENCAMPMENT	RESACA	GA	500
909 May 21 94	130TH ANNIVERSARY RE-ENACTMENT	RESACA	GA	5000
910 May 22 94	130TH ANNIVERSARY RE-ENACTMENT	RESACA	GA	5000

911 Jun 01 94	XYZ CLUB	ELLIJAY	GA	50
912 Jun 04 94	TASTE OF ATLANTA	ATLANTA	GA	1000
913 Jun 04 94	VALUJET PASSENGERS	IN THE AIR	VA	125
914 Jun 05 94	KICK OFF MEETING "STOP YOUTH VIOL	CHANTILLY	VA	20
915 Jun 16 94	MEET WITH SENATORS/CONGRESSMEN	WASHINGTON	DC	500
916 Jun 17 94	HONDA STATE RALLY	DALTON	GA	200
917 Jun 25 94	SUMMERFEST 94	PRINCETON	WV	500
918 Jun 26 94	SUMMERFEST 94	PRINCETON	WV	125
919 Jul 03 94	MOUNT RUSHMORE NATIONAL MEMORIAL	KEYSTONE	SD	5000
920 Jul 04 94	MOUNT RUSHMORE NATIONAL MEMORIAL	KEYSTONE	SD	10,000
921 Jul 06 94	NARFE LUNCHEON MEETING	MARIETTA	GA	65

Approx. total number of people seen since 1975...1,343,556

Chapter 18

Miscellaneous

THIS IS THE DESIGN ON THE NURSES' SHIRT:

The shirt is ash-color with the design (approx. 10" x 10") in red. Just send a check for $14.95 ($12.95 + $2 for S & H) Please specify size: M, L OR X-L to:

Sewell Enterprises
P.O. Box 13,
Jasper, GA 30143-0013

I WANT TO RECOMMEND SOME THINGS FOR YOU:

For those of you who are interested in Civil War reenactments, here is a great magazine. When you need to know the "who, what, where, when and how-to" this is what you need to subscribe to:

REENACTOR'S JOURNAL
P.O. BOX 1864,
VARNA, IL 61375
Subscription is $24 for one year.

For those of you who love to have fun saving money around the house, I came across a great little newsletter. If you send them a long S.A.S.E. and tell them ABE told you about them, they will send you a FREE sample. You'll love it! Honest!

THE TIGHTWAD GAZETTE
RR 1, BOX 3570
LEEDS, ME 04263-9710
Subscription is only $12 for one year.

For those of you wanting to add new life to your foods:
HATTIE'S SAUCE
Call 310-543-7326 and tell them ABE said to please send you a FREE sample of Hattie's Sauce.

Please do what you can to help these three youth oriented organizations. They are doing great work and need your financial help. If you are able to, please send them something with ABE's picture ($5) and tell them I asked you to do it. GOD will bless you for your help.

TO HELP STOP YOUTH VIOLENCE IN AMERICA:
National Stop Youth Violence in America
C/O-Mr. Jim Halley
P.O. Box 369
Centreville, VA 22020-0369

TO HELP FEED HUNGRY CHILDREN AROUND THE WORLD:
Feed the Children
P.O. Box 36,
Oklahoma City, OK 73101-0036

TO HELP STOP AIDS AMONG CHILDREN:
Pediatric AIDS Foundation
1311 Colorado Avenue
Santa Monica, CA 90404

I am going to do what I can to help these organizations. A portion of each book sold will be sent to them from THIS ABE. I want to thank you for whatever YOU can do to help them.

I ♥ ABE & THE USA

T-Shirt ....M, L, or X-L in red or blue trim. White
shirt with red and blue design of
U.S.-Shaped-Flag with Abe Silhouette
and "I (Heart) Abe & the USA" ....$12.00 _____

Picture ....8 x 10, Color, Abe with Flag, Autographed .2.00 * _____

Audio Cassette Tapes of Book.....Approx. 6 Hours............19.95 _____
(Recorded by the author)

Eagle...............Gold & Silver Plated in 3" Glass Ball.
Shake it and it "rains" gold flakes for
5 minutes ....29.95 _____

Key Chain ......3" Diameter with picture of Abe/Flag &
Slogan on back....."Soar with the Eagles..." 5.00 _____

Shovel.............Fireplace, Handmade of steel, Approx.
3' long, name "Abraham Lincoln"
welded in handle..25.00 _____

Hat..................Baseball-type in red, white or blue with
Abe's Silhouette &
"Abe Lincoln's America"............................10.00 _____

Wooden Abe ...Approx. 13", hand-painted, holding flag....12.00 _____

Clock ....Quartz Clock movement mounted on
wooden silhouette of Abe,
approx. 10" tall ....20.00 _____

Bookends........Wooden, approx. 10" tall of silhouette
of Abe. Set of two.......................................15.00 _____

Wallhanging ...Wooden, approx. 10" tall, silhouette of Abe.10.00 _____

Postcard..........Color picture of Abe & Flag..........................25 ¢ * _____
Set of 10 saves you 50¢...............................2.00 * _____
==

Order form continued...
(Please make a copy of these two pages
if you want to order anything.)

	Total	$ _____
(If shipped to you in Georgia) Add GA. State Tax		_____
	S & H	_____
	Grand Total	$ _____

(Send Order to Abe, P.O. Box 13, Jasper, GA 30143-0013)

==

Shipping and Handling: Please add $4.00 for the first item and $1.00 for each additional item ordered. Except for the items which have a (*) beside them. The total shipping and handling for them is only $2.00.
Thank you for your order.   HONEST!!!!!

==

Name: _____
Address: _____
City: _____ State: _____ Zip: _____

Chapter 19

And in Conclusion

Let me leave you with these thoughts... sometime in your future, you may be having some difficult times and wondering how you could possibly make it through another day. When that happens, I want you to look back to today when you saw someone dressed up like Abraham Lincoln and this is what I want you to stop and think about...

If a big, tall, ugly fellow like me could make it past all of that sadness...from my mom dying, my sister dying, my girlfriend dying, my father dying, two sons dying...all of those store failures...one right after the other...all those political failures...one right after the other...Marfan's disease on top of all of that.. without ever giving up...and going on to become President of this great country...the greatest country anywhere in the world...don't you ever give up in the pursuit of whatever it is you want to achieve with your lives. It can't possibly be as hard on you as it was on me! Be a dreamer...be a stargazer...be a rainbow chaser...and soar with the eagles. You can become and achieve anything you want with your lives. Just don't ever give up!

(And from the program I do for students) Now, students, let's go over the five main things I want you to remember from our little visit today...

1...Let's be sure we always tell the...TRUTH.

2...Every day, every chance we get, let's read lots of good...BOOKS.

3...Let's be sure when we get older, we always say "NO" to...DRUGS. And...

4...Let's be sure every day to give our teachers lots of...HUGS.

5...I will do what I can not to be involved in...VIOLENCE.

I want to leave you with a little poem I wrote just for you. It's called, "The Creator".

The Creator made a lot of things,
Some summers and a thousand springs.
The mornings and the afternoons,
The sky, the sea, the mist and moon.
The mountain winds and the new mown hay,
The little running brook and the oceans' spray.
And then there are some things you see
That HE made especially for me.
Red roses, yellow daffodils,
The sunlight on the purple hills,
Cobwebs pearled with morning dew,
A certain shining star...
And...YOU!!

I love you and thank you for coming. May GOD continue to bless you and your family. Keep reading lots of good books and I hope to see you again soon.

I hope you have enjoyed reading about my life and how ABE LINCOLN has become intertwined with my personal life. My hopes and prayers are that whoever you are and wherever you are, your life will be changed for the better.

I hope each day from now on when you get up in the morning and are standing in front of the mirror primping or shaving and getting ready to go out to face the world...you will say to yourself..."Mirror, mirror on the wall...I know I am the very best at what I do! I know I can be Number ONE! Today I will do something special for someone so that I, too, can help make this world a better place because 'I' was here."

I hope you will never give up in the search for your dreams and KNOW if you work at it hard enough, you can achieve anything you want to with your life.

Don't ever forget tomorrow will ALWAYS be a better day! GOD LOVES YOU AND "ABE" LOVES YOU TOO!!

GO TELL SOMEONE HOW MUCH YOU LOVE THEM TODAY!! ...AND HUG A TEACHER EVERYDAY!

IF WE HAVE MORE HUGGING...THERE WILL BE LESS MUGGING!

HAVE A GREAT DAY AND AN EVEN BETTER TOMORROW!!

BE A DREAMER, BE A STARGAZER, BE A RAINBOW CHASER AND KEEP SOARING WITH THE EAGLES!!

REMEMBER...YOU CAN'T SOAR WITH THE EAGLES IF YOU'RE STILL CLUCKING AROUND ON THE GROUND WITH THE CHICKENS!!!

If life ever starts to get you down and you think you need to get a "HIGH", please pick up your phone and call me at 706-692-3682 in JASPER, GEORGIA. You and I will get together and go climb one of my favorite mountains either here in North Georgia or up on the Blue Ridge Parkway in North Carolina. When we get up on that mountain, we will both be closer to GOD and that's one "HIGH" you can't ever get from anything artificial.

My plans for the near future include getting to the remainder of the 50 states. I also want to take a trip to Japan,

Australia, New Zealand and England and take my shows to people in those countries. I have three more books I want to work on. One will be a book of letters I have received from students all over the country. It will be entitled, "DEAR PRESIDENT LINCOLN". I also want to put together a coffee table size book of photographs I've taken in my travels around our country. Then I want to visit with my elderly friends and write a book about their lives.

Please take time to drop me a line and let me know what you thought about this book. I would love to hear from you to let me know what is happening in your life.

GOD BLESS YOU!